# YOGA
## Vacations

A Guide to International Yoga Retreats

Annalisa Cunningham

JOHN MUIR PUBLICATIONS
SANTA FE, NEW MEXICO

John Muir Publications, P.O. Box 613, Santa Fe, NM 87504

Copyright © 1999 by Annalisa Cunningham
Cover copyright © 1999 by John Muir Publications

Printed in the United States of America.
First edition. First printing September 1999.

Library of Congress Cataloging-in-Publication Data
Cunningham, Annalisa, 1957–
        Yoga vacations: a guide to international yoga retreats / by Annalisa Cunningham. — 1st ed.
        p.        cm.
        Includes index.
        ISBN 1-56261-474-6 (pbk.)
1. Yoga Directories. 2. Retreats—United States Directories. 3. Spiritual life Directories.
I. Title.
BL624.C85        1999
613.7'046'025—dc21
                99-24841
                        CIP

Editors: Laurel Gladden Gillespie, Jill Metzler, Lizann Flatt
Production: Janine Lehmann
Graphics Editor: Bunny Wong
Cover Design: Janine Lehmann
Typesetting: Laurel Avery
Printer: Publishers Press

Cover photos:
Large front cover: Rancho La Puerta, Tecate, Baja California, Mexico
Small front cover: Maya Tulum, Tulum, Quintana Roo, Mexico
Large back cover: Kripalu Center for Yoga and Health, Lenox, Massachusetts
Small back cover: Wilbur Hot Springs, Williams, California

Distributed to the book trade by
Publishers Group West
Berkeley, California

The information in this book is subject to change without notice. We strongly recommend that you call ahead to verify the information presented here before making final plans or reservations. The author and publisher make no representation that this book is absolutely accurate or complete. Errors and omissions, whether typographical, clerical, or otherwise, may sometimes occur herein. All destinations are included without charge to them.

# CONTENTS

Foreword iv
Acknowledgments v
Preface vi
Introducing Yoga Vacations viii
Guide Notes ix
What Is Yoga? xii

# FOREWORD

Sometimes it's not enough just to get away from it all. Often our vacations—with the rush of getting from place to place, the stress of leaving unfinished work behind—offer us little in the way of real relaxation and rejuvenation. We don't know how to turn off the noise in our heads, those voices that say, "You should check your e-mail. You have a mortgage payment due." How often do our vacations really leave us refreshed and ready to re-enter our everyday lives?

This book is for all of us who want something more from our vacations—and our lives. As millions of people begin to realize the healing power of yoga, specialized yoga vacations and yoga retreats have become more popular, promising to leave us with inner peace, physical health, and a greater sense of personal balance and well-being.

As the editor of *Yoga International* magazine, I have discovered that yoga has something to offer everybody, whether it be a way to reduce stress, to heal and grow stronger physically and emotionally, or to quiet the mind and become attuned to the things in life that are truly important. Those of us who practice yoga know how breath, posture, meditation, and diet can transform our way of thinking, feeling, and being. What better way to get more out of your vacation than to combine it with the nurturing practice of yoga? And what better way to launch into a healthier way of life than with a yoga vacation?

Annalisa Cunningham, who personally researched and selected the vacations listed in this book, has been offering yoga vacations herself for many years, and she knows what makes for a relaxing, healthy yoga vacation or retreat. Set in serene, beautiful locations all over the world—white sandy beaches, secluded green forests, high sweeping mountains—the vacations Annalisa describes in this book will help you find a new sense of yourself. You'll become immersed in a lifestyle that leaves you refreshed. And with free time to explore and play, these vacations are a lot of fun, too!

So read through the vacations and destinations listed here and listen to the part of yourself that needs a break from your ordinary vacations. These vacations could change the way you live your life.

Deborah Willoughby  
Editor  
*Yoga International*

# ACKNOWLEDGMENTS

The process of writing this book has been graced with the help of hundreds of people. I would like to thank everyone. Thank you to all the yoga teachers, retreat staff, and guests who willingly answered my endless questions and who provided the information I was seeking. What began as a research project developed into a community of wonderful new acquaintances and friends who were supportive and excited about the creation of this book. I especially want to thank those people who invited me to be a guest at their retreat. Traveling to various yoga vacations was by far the most rewarding part of my research.

Much of my research and writing was done on a computer. I'd like to thank Gil Mardilla, who came to my aid on several occasions when my computer skills were lacking. Gil's patience with my nontechnical mind helped my learning curve immensely. When my body ached from computer overload, I had two invaluable healers at my service. I'd like to thank Greg Williams for his wonderful back massages and Beejay Moore for her profound energy work that has helped shift my life on deeper levels.

I'd like to thank the entire staff at John Muir Publications. I especially want to acknowledge Jill Metzler, my editor, and Peggy Schaefer and Donna Galassi, who were always available to address my questions and concerns, giving insight and support.

I appreciate my students, colleagues, and administrators at the college, who accepted and encouraged the leave I took from teaching in order to travel for the book. The acknowledgment I received was heartwarming. As a yoga teacher and student I am continually grateful for the guidance and wealth of information given me by the yoga teachers with whom I have studied.

Lastly, I appreciate my family and friends, who grace my life with their love. In particular, I would like to thank my mother, Shirley Cunningham, who has gone out of her way to be there for me. From the beginning, she was supportive and excited about this project. When it came time for me to travel to the various yoga vacations, she took care of my animals. She has celebrated my progress all the way. This book is dedicated to her.

# PREFACE

I experienced my first yoga vacation in 1982, when I was 23 years old. An idealistic college student at the time, I was searching for natural ways to get high, and a friend suggested I take up yoga. I really had no idea what yoga was, or even what the word *yoga* meant, but it sounded interesting. I had gone to massage school and understood how stress and tension affect the body. My friend explained that yoga was another method of relieving stress and becoming more relaxed.

In those days yoga classes were not as popular as they are today. I couldn't find yoga in the yellow pages of my phone book. Most people I talked to were not even sure what yoga was. I finally discovered that there was a yoga community called Ananda situated in the foothills of the Sierra Nevada Mountains, a few hours from my home. Full of youthful curiosity and enthusiasm, I decided to go on a yoga vacation. I immediately called the people at Ananda and signed up for a monthlong stay.

That vacation changed my life. I soon found myself living in a small rustic cabin with no electricity, surrounded by manzanita bushes and wandering deer. Awakened each morning at 5:00 to the sound of a soft-ringing gong, I found my way to the nearest outhouse, shower house, and then the meditation hall, where people gathered for energization exercises, yoga postures, and meditation. These sessions were followed by a delicious breakfast (eaten in silence) and a morning filled with informative talks about yoga philosophy. Afternoons offered more yoga and meditation classes, interesting group discussions, long walks in nature, quiet time for personal reflection, and healthy vegetarian meals. In the evenings people gathered for personal sharing, chanting, and meditation. When I returned to my cabin each night for bed, I drifted off to sleep peacefully and soundly.

Within a few days I began to experience a peace and joy that I had never felt before in my entire life. Part of that, of course, was because I was on vacation. I didn't have to cook my own meals, answer phones, or drive in traffic. But I had been on vacation before and had never felt this good. What was unique and wonderful about this vacation was that the new level of peace I felt was a direct result of the yoga lifestyle I was living. This lifestyle taught me specific yoga practices and techniques for achieving greater health, harmony, and peace on a daily basis.

Before my stay at Ananda I didn't know how to use yoga breathing techniques for calming my emotions and energizing my body. I had never practiced the yoga postures that helped me gain greater flexibility, strength, and balance. Chanting and meditation were new activities for me that helped to quiet my mind, open my heart, and let me experience a feeling of inner peace. The benefits of a healthy vegetarian diet were also new to me, and I relished the tasteful recipes. Good digestion, sound sleep, energy and vitality, proper functioning of the internal organs, flexibility and muscle tone, happiness, and a centered, calm consciousness were some of the gifts I received from that first yoga vacation.

Now, almost 20 years later, I am still venturing on yoga vacations. These days I offer yoga vacations as well. I have been fortunate to make a career out of teaching, sharing, and learning about yoga.

In the past several years the popularity of yoga has increased tremendously. Yoga classes are offered in most health clubs, YMCAs, and even colleges. As a college yoga instructor I relish the opportunity to introduce yoga to students who are new to the practice. Many of my students are the age I was when I first discovered yoga. Sometimes, as I'm teaching in the classroom, I can't help thinking to myself: "I wish this class, which meets two hours a week, was a monthlong retreat." I would like my students to be able to experience the complete lifestyle of yoga the way I did. And of course they do have that option. Yoga retreats are offered throughout the world.

This book is a compilation of some of the best yoga vacations and retreats available internationally. Only those that include accommodations and meals are listed; thus the theme "vacation."

Various forms and styles of yoga are offered within these listings. My introductory chapter will give you a brief history and description of the types of yoga available. I encourage you to write or call each organization for more information about what its yoga philosophy and teaching entails.

In closing I will tell you that the Ananda Retreat Center where I stayed in 1982 is now called the Expanding Light, and it has grown to offer modern housing accommodations with full bathrooms and electricity. Many yoga centers still offer tent and camping options for those who are drawn to simple living. Personally, I'm glad I experienced the simplicity of rustic living while first learning yoga. I like to think of yoga vacations as retreats rather than resorts, where instead of being pampered, a yoga participant is fostered into a process of growth and transformation.

With this book I welcome you to the transformational process that yoga vacations offer. May your yoga vacation bring you much joy and peace.

# INTRODUCING YOGA VACATIONS

In today's world of stress and hurry, it is essential to take time out for relaxation and rejuvenation. Yoga retreats and vacations are ideal places for renewing our sense of wellness and wholeness.

The unique value of going on a yoga vacation is that yoga offers lifestyle skills for relieving stress, increasing health, and creating greater peace of mind. Health and peace are available to all of us when we place ourselves in a healing environment and are given the proper skills and knowledge for developing and maintaining these two precious gifts. Yoga retreats are designed specifically to teach people yoga approaches for attaining physical and spiritual rejuvenation. The practices and tools offered can be taken home and incorporated into one's daily life.

## A RETREAT AND VACATION COMBINED

There is a difference between a retreat and a vacation. A retreat is a period of withdrawal, often used for prayer, meditation, study, and instruction under a teacher or guide. It is a place of privacy and safety. Retreats are usually held in peaceful and secluded environments. They provide ideal settings for rest and rejuvenation.

Vacations, on the other hand, can be taken anywhere. They involve time spent away from our familiar routines, work, and home surroundings. Vacations that include heavy travel and activity can be fun, exciting, and sometimes exhausting. There have been times when I felt that I needed a retreat from my vacation.

This book introduces the concept of combining the two. Some of the places listed here are strictly retreats; places for quiet, in-depth yoga study. Others are held in vacation settings that allow free time for nearby shopping and sightseeing. Regardless of which setting or teacher and tradition you choose, your yoga vacation will not leave you exhausted. Yoga inspires healthy, balanced living. These vacation programs will recharge your energy and truly rejuvenate your body and mind.

# GUIDE NOTES

As you read through the book you will find a wide variety of yoga vacation and retreat opportunities. Listings are organized alphabetically by geographic destination. Some of the yoga teachers offer retreats in more than one location; in the index you will find a list of all the teachers included in this guide with page references to the vacations they offer. I recommend that you first turn to the color photos at the center of the guide. Here you will quickly get a feel for some of the wonderful retreats and yoga teachers listed. Not every listing includes a photo, so be sure to look through the entire book before deciding where you would like to go.

Once you have determined which vacation you are most drawn to, contact the retreat center or yoga teacher to ask for a current brochure. Check listed Web sites as well. Take time to ask any specific questions you may have about the yoga retreat you are considering. In addition to what you read in this guide you may want to find out more about the following information.

### Rates
As rates and costs are in constant fluctuation, please be aware that the prices quoted in this book may have changed. Be sure to ask what current rates are. Rate quotes don't always include taxes, services, gratuities, or all activities and travel expenses, so be sure to find out what these extra costs might be.

### Children or Nonparticipating Spouse
Some yoga vacations allow children or nonparticipating spouses to come at a reduced fee. While you are enjoying the yoga classes, your spouse may be reading a book, walking on the beach, or exploring the area. Ask about this possibility, as well as child care options and prices.

### Yoga and Health Considerations
If you have any health concerns or injuries, be sure to let yoga teachers know ahead of time. Make sure the yoga vacation you are choosing is appropriate for your specific condition. Suggested yoga experience levels are listed under "Student Criteria," and wheelchair access is listed under "Disability Access." Yoga can be beneficial for health challenges, so don't hesitate to ask questions.

### Diet
Most of the listings in this guide include meals with the vacation package,

although some do not. Read descriptions carefully. Many of the listings state that special diets can be accommodated. If you have special dietary needs, be sure to let the teacher know before you arrive. Many yoga vacations offer primarily vegetarian meals; if living without meat would be unpleasant for you, then be sure to ask if meat options are available. They may not be. Ask about coffee as well. I suggest going with an open attitude and enjoying the fresh, whole vegetarian meals that are often served at yoga retreats. You may find that you are quite satisfied and leave asking for recipes.

### Accommodations
Sleeping arrangements come in all shapes and sizes. Each listing gives a brief description of what you can expect. Ask for specific information, such as: number of people per room, bed size, closet and drawer space, convenience of bathrooms, number of showers available, and noise factors. If you snore or smoke, inform the person who is arranging the room assignments.

### Number of Participants Possible
This heading will let you know the maximum number of people that may be taking the yoga retreat with you. Some people sign up at the last minute, so teachers don't always know the exact number until just before the retreat begins. You might ask how many participants the teacher thinks will be there.

### What to Bring
Check out the suggestions for each vacation in this guide and ask the retreat teacher to send you a list if they have one. Be sure to ask about necessary passports and picture IDs when traveling out of the country.

### Weather
We all know that weather can be unpredictable, but it's great to have some kind of indication of temperature highs and lows when you're packing for a trip. Ask for guesstimated weather reports.

### Sample Daily Schedule
This section gives you a sample of what will be offered each day during the retreat. It lets you know approximately what time your day will begin and how full each day will be. Some people like to sleep in on their vacation and miss the morning class—ask if that is an option. Other people don't want to miss a thing. And then there are those who love their afternoon naps. Usually teachers are understanding of your needs. The word *sample* is used because schedules can change.

### Other Activities
All yoga vacations involve taking yoga classes. Often there are other activities

available in addition to the yoga that participants can enjoy during their free time. This heading gives you that kind of information. Be sure to ask what the costs are for additional activities such as snorkeling, bus tours, and boating. Ask if equipment can be rented or if you need to bring your own.

### Services

Healing and body work treatments such as massage are often available at yoga retreats for an additional fee. If you are considering this wonderful indulgence, find out what the fee is and the time allotted.

### Getting There

It's a good idea to check with yoga teachers about low-cost flights, airports, and road travel advice before you make travel plans. Some retreats provide maps and specific directions, which they will gladly send ahead of time. Find out if airport pickup is provided and if there will be someone to greet you when you arrive.

### Yoga Philosophy

This section gives you the philosophy of each teacher. Many teachers base their life and practice upon Patanjali's eight-fold path; see "What Is Yoga?" for a very brief introduction to the eight-fold path and the ideals it embraces. Those who observe Patanjali's eight-fold path have studied Patanjali's *Yoga Sutras* in depth.

# WHAT IS YOGA?

Evidence of yoga dates back thousands of years. It is an ancient science dedicated to the health of our bodies, minds, emotions, and spirits. This teaching of healthy living was developed in India thousands of years ago and is still valid today as a practical system for creating harmony and balance in our lives.

The word yoga comes from the Sanskrit root YUJ, which means to yoke or unify, join, harmonize, blend, integrate, unite. The traditional goal of yoga is to realize one's fullest human potential and to find union with a higher consciousness, God, truth, light, or whatever one chooses to call it. Although yoga does contain the idea of reaching a higher consciousness, yoga is not a religion. It is a discipline of techniques and practices for creating total harmony of body, mind, and spirit.

## PATANJALI'S EIGHT-FOLD PATH TOWARD ENLIGHTENMENT

One of the well-known ancient texts written on yoga philosophy and practice is Patanjali's *Yoga Sutras*. Patanjali, a great yoga exponent, mystic, and philosopher, contributed this first written record of yoga asanas, with some 840,000 positions. At the core of Patanjali's system is the "eight-fold path," which is also known as Ashtanga, or eight-limbed yoga. These eight limbs serve as guidelines and principles to living life with purpose and meaning.

### Yama and Niyama

The first two stages of Patanjali's eight-fold path are known as *yama* and *niyama*. Yama means control; niyama, noncontrol. These two stages constitute the don'ts and the dos on the spiritual path. They are like the Ten Commandments of yoga.

The five rules of yama are (1) *ahisma*, or nonviolence; (2) nonlying or truthfulness; (3) nonstealing; (4) continence or moderation in all things; and (5) nongreed.

Yamas are restraints, or ethical principles. They elicit a sense of integrity in conducting our deeds and actions in life for the highest good toward others and ourselves. It may be said that all five of the yamas unite in a single purpose: to prevent the yogi from misdirecting his or her energies so he or she may channel them toward constructive purposes and for the good of all humankind.

As in yama, there are also five rules of niyama. They are (1) purification and cleanliness; (2) contentment; (3) tapasy or austerity; (4) study of sacred scriptures and of oneself; and (5) devotion to the Supreme Lord—surrender to God.

Niyamas map out individual practices for self-discipline, introspection, and spiritual practice. Together the niyamas teach the yogi to take his or her energy and direct it positively toward self-awareness and oneness with God.

Both the yamas and niyamas can be understood on subtle levels of living as well as obvious ones. For instance, the yama ahisma, or nonviolence, refers not only to outward violence, but also to the harm we may do to one another, such as killing someone's enthusiasm or faith in something because of our own insensitivity or selfish motives. Also we must be conscious of noninjury toward our own selves. Every time we put ourselves down and think of ourselves in negative terms we are harming ourselves. An attitude of harmlessness and benevolence for all of life is what is meant by ahisma.

### *Asana*

The third stage on the eight-fold path is known as *asana*, which means posture. It is this stage that is often known as Hatha yoga. Originally Hatha yoga was developed and practiced to help prepare the body for sitting in meditation, giving the body the stamina in strength, flexibility, and balance needed for meditation practice.

### *Pranayama*

This is the fourth stage. The word *prana* means breath, energy, and life force. Through controlling the breath, the yogi is also controlling and directing his energy and life force. Pranayama exercises are practices and methods for channeling energy. These energies are usually directed toward the brain, which helps heighten one's awareness.

### *Pratyahara*

The fifth stage of Patanjali's journey is known as *pratyahara*, the interiorization of the mind. It is a withdrawing of the senses from their preoccupation with the external world so that one remains focused and centered on God.

### *Dharana*

Patanjali's sixth stage is known as *dharana*, or contemplation. In this stage the yogi lets go of his or her ego and becomes one with whatever he or she is meditating upon. It is a one-pointed concentration of the mind on a single object, a fixed inner awareness. This concentration is a prelude to meditation.

### *Dhayana*

The seventh stage is complete absorption of whatever thought or object one meditates upon. For instance, if a person meditates on joy and reaches the stage of *dhayana*, then that person begins to absorb the quality of joy into his or her own being.

## Samadhi

Finally, the last stage of Patanjali's eight-fold path is *samadhi*. It is oneness with all. It is a blissful identification with all of life, a feeling of divine union, and an interconnectedness with everything and everyone. It is a state of ecstasy.

## BRANCHES OF YOGA

Yoga is like a tree with various branches or paths to self discovery. Below is a brief description of the paths of yoga.

*Hatha yoga* is the branch of yoga that deals with the physical body, and it is the most popular in the United States. Hatha yoga combines stretching, breathing exercises, positive thinking, relaxation, meditation, and a healthy diet to create a practical method for improving one's health and for developing a foundation for deeper understanding. This path of physical improvement is offered in various forms and teaching styles that will be discussed in the next section.

*Bhakti yoga* is the way of love and devotion. Bhakti yoga appeals to people who are emotional by nature, and utilizes practices such as chanting, prayer, and the repetition of mantra (sacred sounds) for channeling devotion. Bhakti yoga teaches the ideal of seeing the divine in everyone and everything.

*Jnana yoga* is the way of attaining knowledge through intellectual, scholarly pursuits. This branch of yoga appeals to those who are intellectually inclined and requires in-depth study of the texts and scriptures of yoga traditions.

*Karma yoga* is the way of right action and selfless deeds done in daily life. This branch of yoga is the path of service. Those people who volunteer to help others in need without expecting anything in return are practicing karma yoga. Helping humanity, working in the world, and giving of oneself is the path of karma yoga.

*Mantra yoga* is the path of using sound vibrations, such as chanting, music, and prayer to help raise one's consciousness. In mantra yoga a short phrase is repeated, either audibly or silently, to focus and concentrate the mind. Traditionally the mantra would have a specific spiritual meaning and vibration. Different mantras are used for achieving specific states of consciousness.

*Raja yoga* is called the "royal yoga" and is the path of meditation, the goal of which is to attain an enlightened state of mind. This path incorporates Hatha yoga, which prepares the body for meditation. Raja yoga utilizes steady posture, breath regulation, concentration, and mind control practices for withdrawing from the senses in order to reach a true state of meditation.

*Tantra yoga* is the path of awakening the sexual and spiritual energy known as Kundalini energy, which lies dormant at the base of the spine. Practices are taught that allow this energy to circulate throughout the body, without release or dissipation. Tantra has been the most misunderstood yoga path among Americans. Sexual intercourse is not necessarily part of the practice; to the contrary, a celibate lifestyle is often recommended. Tantra practices tap into hidden reserves of energy, using ceremony and ritual as tools for honoring the sacredness of life.

## STYLES OF HATHA YOGA

The most common branch of yoga practiced in the United States today is Hatha yoga. *Ha* is the Sanskrit word for sun, and *tha* is the Sanskrit word for moon—suggesting the balance and integration of opposites united in a complete whole.

There are various styles of Hatha yoga practice that stem from the different yoga masters of India whose teachings had a strong influence in America. As yoga is passed from teacher to student, it evolves. Sometimes it can be confusing to sort out the diverse teaching viewpoints, techniques, and styles of practice.

I always tell my students to take yoga from as many teachers as possible until they find the style and teacher that they are drawn to. Choosing which style of yoga to practice is a personal choice. The vacation listings in this book all have information on which style of Hatha yoga is offered at each retreat and what each teaching philosophy consists of.

The following is a brief introduction to some of the more commonly practiced Hatha yoga systems available in the United States. This is only a partial list, intended to familiarize you with some of the description names you will find as you look through this guide.

***Iyengar yoga***: From the teachings of B. K. S. Iyengar, this method of teaching places strong emphasis on anatomical alignment and precision of the yoga asanas. Toward this accomplishment, a variety of props such as blocks, benches, blankets, bolsters, straps, and sandbags are used as supportive aids. The development of stamina, strength, flexibility, balance, and concentration are achieved as one becomes proficient in the practice. Instructors often give physical adjustment and direction, aiding the student further into correct alignment and understanding of the pose.

***Sivananda yoga***: From the teachings of Swami Sivananda, brought to the west by Swami Vishnu Devananda, this teaching system embraces a synthesis of yoga paths, combining Hatha yoga, bhakti yoga, raja yoga, and karma yoga. Hatha classes follow a routine of breathing exercises, sun salutations, a series of 12 classic yoga postures, and relaxation. Prayers and chanting begin and end each session. Swami Sivananda summarized yoga as "Serve, love, give, purify, meditate, realize." Swami Vishnu Devananda is one of the first yoga masters to coin the term "yoga vacation," calling it a disciplined adventure.

*Ashtanga Vinyasa yoga*: From the teachings of Pattabhi Jois, this method of teaching is sometimes referred to as Power yoga. An energetic and somewhat rigorous practice, this system works when the body is hot and sweaty from unceasing vinyasa movements. Vinyasa are flowing physical movements, similar to continuous sun salutations, which are performed between the asanas, or postures, linking them together. Emphasis is placed on strength, flexibility, and stamina. The practice encompasses six series of asanas that are mastered sequentially. The primary series consists of 75 postures.

*Viniyoga*: Developed by T. K. V. Desikachar, son of Krishnamacharya, this method of teaching emphasizes a one-on-one interaction between teacher and student. Asanas and pranayama practices are adapted to suit the needs of each individual student, and classes are often taught privately.

*Kundalini yoga*: Introduced by Yogi Bhajan, a Sikh from India, this practice is designed to awaken the Kundalini, or coiled energy, stored at the base of the spine. The use of several breathing techniques, postures, chanting, and meditation are used to awaken this innate energy and consciously direct it through the chakras, which are energy centers along the spine. This practice is dynamic and energizing.

*Integral yoga*: Developed by Swami Satchidananda, this methodology reflects the teachings of Swami Sivananda. Integral Hatha classes follow a set pattern and are 75 minutes in length. This format includes 45 minutes of asana, a deep relaxation, and a pranayama sequence and ends with meditation. Although challenging, these classes are also gentle and meditative. Ease in the body, peace of mind, and usefulness in life are the guiding principles of Integral yoga.

*Ananda yoga*: Developed by J. Donald Walters, also known as Swami Kryananda, this approach reflects the teachings of Paramahansa Yogananda, who was one of the first great yogis to come to the West. Postures are preparation for Kriya yoga, which involves the special use of breathing and meditation techniques. This style of yoga is gentle and deeply relaxing. Affirmations are used with the asanas, and each posture is viewed as a way to heighten or expand self-awareness.

*Kripalu yoga*: Developed by yogi Amrit Desai, this approach is directed toward inner development and insight. Postures taught in three stages are designed to promote an inner clearing process—a way of encountering and releasing physical, mental, and emotional blocks. Teachers encourage focused attention and discovery of strengths and weaknesses within. Inner clearing leads to inner freedom.

*Bikram yoga*: Created by Bikram Choudhury, the brother of Paramahansa Yogananda, this method teaches a series of 28 poses designed to give a complete workout. Perfect alignment is emphasized, and all the components of physical fitness (flexibility, weight reduction, muscular strengthening and endurance, and cardiovascular conditioning) are included. To facilitate elasticity, release of toxins, and prevention of injuries, classes are held in controlled-temperature rooms of 95 to 100 degrees Fahrenheit. This is a challenging routine and will enhance physical fitness.

*White Lotus yoga*: Ganga White and Tracey Rich of the White Lotus Foundation have developed a *vinyasa*, or flowing style practice, in which postures are synchronized with the breath and are linked together in flowing sequences. The pace and difficulty vary from class to class. Multiple variations are incorporated into the practice. Students are encouraged to use only what is appropriate for them.

*Integrative Yoga Therapy*: This approach to yoga, developed by Joseph La Page, bridges the ancient insights of yoga with the latest advances in mind-body health. It is a nonsectarian, nonhierarchical approach to yoga set within the framework of the human potential movement from a holistic perspective. Classes are offered in eight- to 10-week yoga and wellness programs in which each class has a specific theme and is adapted safely and effectively to the needs of specific health conditions, populations, and settings; or in one-on-one situations to meet the specific needs of the individual student. Affirmations are used, and detailed information on technique and alignment is given.

*Phoenix Rising Yoga Therapy*: This approach, developed by Michael Lee, combines yoga postures with elements of contemporary body/mind psychology to focus on your body's inner wisdom. Teachers provide one-on-one yoga therapy and assist students in holding postures while exploring emotions and beliefs that may have manifested themselves in chronic aches and pains. Nondirective dialogue techniques are used to explore the links between the sensations present in your body and the issues present in your life, in a safe and supportive environment.

*Anusara Yoga*: This system of Hatha yoga, developed by John Friend, integrates three key areas of practice: attitude, alignment, and action. Each pose is performed with an integrated awareness of all the different body parts; the practitioner is open to Grace and to awakening his or her own true nature. The central philosophy of this yoga is that each person is equally divine in every part—body, mind, and spirit. Individual creativity and self-investigation are supported and encouraged within the bounds of the basic priciples and philosphical precepts of Anusara Yoga.

## YOGA PROPS

Many yoga teachers work with yoga props that aid in the effectiveness of learning and practicing yoga postures or asanas. As you read through each listing in this book you will find under the heading "What to Bring" that some teachers ask you to bring yoga props to use while attending their retreat.

Some teachers and places provide props for you, and some teachers don't use props at all.

Below is a brief description of the yoga props that are commonly used. In the appendix you will find a resource list for purchasing yoga products. If you have any questions about the use of props, individual teachers will usually be helpful in telling you what they recommend.

*Yoga mats*: Sometimes referred to as "sticky" mats, these are made to be non-slippery on floors while providing a stable surface for yoga. Mats give a bit of cushioning and insulation from cool floors. They usually roll or fold easily for travel.

*Straps or belts*: Straps can be used for multiple purposes: they can help you extend your reach, open your shoulders and hips, maintain length and evenness in your arms or legs, and encourage you to move deeper overall into many yoga poses.

*Sand bags*: Used as gentle, soft weights, sandbags encourage the body to release beneath their weight, thereby increasing the depth of the stretch.

*Blankets*: One of the most versatile yoga props, blankets can be used for support in sitting poses, rolled into a bolster, folded into a shoulder stand or headstand pad, and used as a cover during relaxation and meditation.

*Blocks*: Another versatile prop, a block is helpful as a hand rest in standing poses such as the triangle. It can also be used under the sacrum, between the hands, and under the feet, giving the body lift and support.

*Bolsters*: The bolster supports and encourages your body to relax and stretch in areas that need it. Bolsters are primarily used in restorative poses.

*Eye bags*: We often hold tension in the muscles around the eyes and the brow. The gentle weight of an eye bag on these muscles helps them to relax, and the darkness provided by the eye bag lets the pupils and eye muscles relax.

*Meditation cushions*: Used for sitting meditation and pranayama practice, cushions give firm support and extra height to allow optimum length and alignment of the spine while sitting. This encourages the hips and legs to relax, thereby bringing lift and openness to the chest and lungs.

# *U.S. Yoga Vacations and Retreats*

# BRIAR PATCH INN
# SEDONA, ARIZONA

### *Yoga Retreat with Johanna (Maheshvari) Mosca*

## FEBRUARY, APRIL, JULY, OCTOBER AND DECEMBER
### FIVE-DAY RETREATS

Nestled in Oak Creek Canyon, three miles north of Sedona, along the lush banks of Oak Creek and at the base of the Red Rock Mountains, the Briar Patch Inn invites guests to experience nature on its nine quiet, creekside acres. The Briar Patch Inn has 17 cottages, furnished with Southwest charm and Native American arts, designed for comfort and rustic ambiance. Each season, yoga teacher Johanna (Maheshvari) Mosca offers five-day retreats during which participants experience yoga and hiking in the magnificent red rock beauty and spiritual energy of Sedona.

**Address**: Johanna (Maheshvari) Mosca
Sedona Spirit Yoga
P.O. Box 278
Sedona, AZ 86339
**Phone**: 520/282-9592
Briar Patch Inn toll free: 888/809-3030
**Fax**: 520/282-9592
**E-mail**: yogalife@sedona.net
**Web site**: www.sedona-web.com/yoga

**Airport Information**: Fly into Phoenix, Arizona. A shuttle ($60) is available for round-trip transportation between Phoenix and Sedona. Car rentals are advised, and Sedona Spirit Yoga will help participants get together to share car rental expenses.

**How to Get There**: The Briar Patch Inn is a 10-minute drive from the town of Sedona, up Oak Creek Canyon.

**Teacher Background**: Johanna (Maheshvari) Mosca, Ph.D., has been teaching yoga for more than 10 years. She is a certified Kripalu yoga teacher and a Phoenix Rising yoga therapist.

**Style of Yoga**: She offers gentle Hatha yoga, Kripalu yoga, and Phoenix Rising partner sessions. Sedona Spirit Yoga begins with Kripalu yoga of compassion and combines a variety of yoga styles, toning, and chakra balancing.

**Philosophy of Teacher**: "Yoga helps develop, strengthen, and integrate mind, body, and spirit. Through practicing the eight limbs of yoga in our daily lives we learn to release unwanted energies, receive divine grace, and follow inner guidance or knowing. Yoga cleanses and opens us to connect from the heart in harmony with all that is."

**Student Criteria**: Focus is on beginners with either no prior knowledge of yoga or just a few years' experience. All levels are welcome to participate.

**Disability Access**: Limited access; please call.

**What to Bring**: Comfortable yoga clothes, shorts and T-shirts, long-sleeved

Briar Patch Inn

shirts and pants, sweat clothes, a white outfit, one dressy outfit, a bathing suit, towel, sunscreen, hat, sunglasses, water bottle, hiking boots, and small backpack.

**Yoga Room Size and Description**: The light and airy Ponderosa House has a 20-foot cathedral ceiling, a stone wall with two fireplaces, wooden floors with movable area rugs, and a balcony that looks out on the red rocks. In warm weather, yoga is practiced on the large grass areas at the Briar Patch Inn. Yoga and meditation are also practiced on the red rocks during the hikes.

**Number of Participants Possible**: 15

**Accommodations**: Participants stay in cozy cottages with kitchens, fireplaces, and balconies. Each cottage has one or two large bedrooms with a king-size or queen-size bed, an alcove sleeping area, and one bathroom. Participants can also stay in the Ponderosa House, which has three private bedrooms, a dining area with a fireplace, a kitchen, and a bathroom.

**Meals**: A healthy buffet-style breakfast is served daily and includes a variety of fresh fruits, baked items, and quiche dishes. Vegetarian lunches of sandwiches, salads, and fruit are provided. Three vegetarian dinners are included during the week. A natural health food store and a variety of restaurants are within 10 minutes of the retreat. The Ponderosa House and cottages have full kitchen facilities.

**Fee**: $895 per person (double occupancy), $100 additional fee for single occupancy, $1,595 per couple (same bed). Retreat fee includes accommodations, three meals daily (except for two dinners), the yoga program, sweat lodge, activities, guided hiking tours, and transportation to all activity sites.

**Credit Cards**: Not accepted

**Sample Daily Schedule:**

| | |
|---|---|
| 7:30–9:30 a.m. | Yoga, pranayama, mediation, toning and chakra balancing |
| 9:30 | Breakfast |
| 10:30–3:00 p.m. | Hiking, meditation and standing postures in various red rock sites |
| 3:00–6:00 | Free time |
| 6:30–7:30 | Dinner |
| 7:30 | Evening activities |

Toward the end of the retreat there will be a sweat lodge ceremony, followed by dinner and sharing. The next day participants pair up for a guided introduction to Phoenix Rising yoga. On two afternoons an optional posture clinic is offered for those who wish assistance with asanas.

**Other Activities:** The area offers horseback riding, mountain biking, jeep tours, hot air balloon rides, helicopter rides, swimming in Oak Creek, fishing, golf, visits to art galleries and to an artists' colony in nearby Jerome, shopping in Sedona, and a possible side trip to the Grand Canyon. In addition, there is a private creek swimming hole at Briar Patch Inn.

**Services:** Open-air creekside massage and a variety of healing modalities are available, such as astrological and psychic readings.

**Guest Comment**: *"A yoga retreat in Sedona with Johanna is a unique experience. Johanna took care of all the details: accommodations, meals, classes, visits to ancient cultural sites, sweat lodge, etc. The yoga classes were amazing: she is a gifted teacher who makes students of all levels feel comfortable. Most memorable were Phoenix Rising sessions, the sweat lodge ceremony, and yoga among the red rocks. Come prepared to laugh, feel free, and be energized."*
Mark Raza—Washington, D.C.

**Summary**: This retreat offers the peace and exhilaration of doing yoga on the red rocks of Sedona, Arizona, with yoga teacher Johanna (Maheshvari) Mosca. The accommodations at Briar Patch Inn are spacious and peaceful, with spectacular views of the red rocks and the melodious sounds of Oak Creek. The Sedona Spirit Team staff join Johanna to offer a variety of healing modalities, including astrological readings, energy balancing, and a sweat lodge ceremony.

# COUNTRY CLUB ESTATES
# BODEGA BAY, CALIFORNIA

*Rest & Renewal Yoga Retreat with Tara Stiles*

## MARCH, AUGUST, AND OCTOBER
### Weekend Retreats

Yoga teacher Tara Stiles has been offering seasonal weekend retreats in the small town of Bodega Bay for 20 years. Her retreats provide a balance of private solitude and group interaction, with activities including yoga, tai chi, guided meditations, singing, shoulder massage, and partner yoga. Participants stay in a large, luxurious house one mile from the town of Bodega Bay in Country Club Estates. The house is just a short walk from the beach, with an ocean view and outside hot tub. A veranda surrounds the house, which faces the beach. The retreats are called "Rest & Renewal" because Tara and her staff design the weekend so that participants don't have to do a thing but rest, relax, and enjoy yoga at the beach.

**Address**: Tara Stiles
2526 27th St.
Sacramento, CA 95818
**Phone**: 916/454-5526

**Airport Information**: Fly into Sonoma County Airport or San Francisco International and rent a car to drive to Bodega Bay.

**How to Get There**: Bodega Bay is approximately one and one-half to two hours north of San Francisco on coastal Highway 1. It takes about 40 minutes to get there from the Sonoma County Airport. It is 20 minutes west of the town of Sebastopol.

**Teacher Background**: Tara Stiles began reading yoga philosophy and practicing Hatha yoga at the age of 15. A year later she learned Transcendental Meditation and has since studied many different approaches to physical and spiritual integration. She has been practicing yoga for more than 20 years.

**Style of Yoga**: Tara's classes blend classical and contemporary practices. She was originally trained in the Sivananda school of yoga and Vedanta Hindu philosophy and has since studied other styles of yoga, including the Iyengar method. She has developed her own unique, eclectic style of teaching, inspired by 20 years of regular personal practice, the principles and poses of the Iyengar method, and breath-release techniques.

**Philosophy of Teacher**: "Yoga is a means for exploring the somatic and spiritual realms, and for self-care in the context of physical, emotional, and spiritual health."

**Student Criteria**: Beginners and all levels of yoga experience are welcome.

**Disability Access**: No access

**What to Bring**: Comfortable casual clothes, windbreaker, sweatshirt, walking shoes, beach towel, sleeping bags, pillow, and personal toiletries. Also bring a kite if you would like to fly kites on the beach.

**Yoga Room Size and Description**: Yoga is practiced on the beach whenever weather permits. On colder days yoga is practiced in the house living room, which is spacious and carpeted.

**Number of Participants Possible**: 14

**Accommodations**: Participants sleep in rooms with two or three beds or on the living room floor in their sleeping bags. Four house bathrooms are shared. Some people enjoy sleeping on the outside deck to the tune of the ever-present fog horn out in the bay and the seals barking on Seal Island. Some adventurers choose to sleep on the beach.

**Meals**: Delicious vegetarian brunches and dinners are served daily, along with light morning snacks. Colorful, healthy meals are lovingly prepared.

**Fee**: $195 per person includes weekend lodging, vegetarian meals, and all classes with Tara.

**Credit Cards**: Not accepted

**Sample Daily Schedule**:

| | |
|---|---|
| 7:00 a.m. | Fruit, tea, and coffee |
| 8:00 | Morning yoga class |
| 9:30 | Break |
| 10:00 | Tai chi on the beach |
| 11:30 | Brunch |

Free, unstructured time for personal enjoyment.

| | |
|---|---|
| 6:00 p.m. | Dinner |
| 7:30 | Evening activity (singing, massage, dancing, drumming) |

On Sunday the group maintains silence until noon.

**Other Activities**: There are opportunities for short and long hikes, beach play (kite flying is a favorite), shopping in the quaint local shops of Bodega Bay, relaxing on the veranda, reading, and enjoying the house hot tub.

**Guest Comment**: *"I highly recommend Tara Stiles's ocean retreats because they are very affordable and can serve one's needs whether it is for a relaxing, introspective weekend, interaction with great people, or just to eat, sleep, and practice yoga."*
  Dora Furniss — Sacramento, California

**Summary**: This weekend ocean retreat offered by yoga teacher Tara Stiles includes group yoga, tai chi, and guided meditation sessions with unstructured relaxation time. Participants stay in a lovely private home near the beach with an outdoor hot tub and ocean views. Tara and her crew are caring and attentive to each individual's need. Participants enjoy great food, warm hospitality, ocean ambiance, yoga, and rest.

# DORAN BEACH
# BODEGA BAY, CALIFORNIA

*Mind, Body, and Spirit Yoga Retreat with Julia Tindall*

## JUNE
### FOUR DAYS, THREE NIGHTS

Bodega Bay is a quaint seaside fishing village along California's coastal Highway 1. It boasts some beautiful sandy beaches, the largest of which is Doran Beach, a mere five-minute drive from the site of this yoga retreat. The retreat is held in a large two-story home perched high up on the hillside overlooking the bay. It is part of a community of houses, most of which are used as holiday or retirement homes. Yoga teacher Julia Tindall uses this private coastal home to offer her annual healing yoga weekend designed for self-care and nurturing. The house has a large living room with a fireplace, comfortable sofas for relaxing, and a deck that has a magnificent view of the bay. The downstairs family room is used for yoga, with an adjoining patio and an outdoor hot tub located on a separate deck. Surrounded by typical coastal vegetation, guests often see wandering deer nearby.

**Address**: Julia Tindall
P.O. Box 601872
Sacramento, CA 95860
**Phone**: 916/486-4620
**E-mail**: yogajules@aol.com
**Web site**: www.globalff.org/Julia

**Airport Information**: Fly into Sonoma County Airport or San Francisco International and drive to Bodega Bay.

**How to Get There**: Bodega Bay is approximately one and one-half to two hours north of San Francisco on coastal Highway 1. It takes about 40 minutes to get there from the Sonoma County Airport. It is 20 minutes west of the town of Sebastopol.

**Teacher Background**: Julia Tindall is a certified Sivananda yoga teacher, massage therapist, and hypnotherapist. She is the creator of the video *Beginner's Yoga*

*with Julia*, which is based on what she refers to as Standing Wave Yoga.

**Style of Yoga**: Julia teaches Standing Wave Yoga, which is a gentle beginner practice based on the awareness of breath consciousness in the body. Movements are performed with softness. She incorporates partner yoga, breath work, and visualization. Julia's teaching combines Hatha yoga (physical stretching), pranayama, meditation, Bhakti yoga (chanting), Jnana yoga (the path of wisdom), and Karma yoga (selfless service).

**Philosophy of Teacher**: "Yoga is the consciousness we bring to our lives. It is a tool to help us improve the quality of our lives, to help us to grow and rise to the challenges that life presents with consciousness and awareness. The opportunity that yoga gives us is to bring the awareness learned during practice into everyday living so that eventually, for the yogi, nothing is outside of yoga."

**Student Criteria**: All levels of yoga experience are welcome.

**Disability Access**: No access

**What to Bring**: Comfortable clothes for yoga, yoga mat, linens or sleeping bag, towels, personal toiletries, bathing suit, hiking shoes, sweater or light jacket for cool evenings . . . and an open heart.

**Yoga Room Size and Description**: Yoga is practiced in a large basement room. The room is carpeted and features large sliding doors that open to nature.

**Number of Participants Possible**: 14

**Accommodations**: Three suites are available (double occupancy), each with its own bathroom. There is also indoor camping on carpeted floors anywhere in the house, with shared bathrooms. Private rooms are sometimes available.

**Meals**: Six homemade gourmet vegetarian meals are served, starting with dinner on Friday night. Dinners are sit-down, candle-lit with all participants at one large table. Special diets are accommodated.

**Fee**: $225 per person for a private room (one person, or double occupancy), or $185 per person for communal sleeping area. Includes weekend lodging, six vegetarian meals, and all classes with Julia.

**Credit Cards**: Not accepted

**Sample Daily Schedule**:

| | |
|---|---|
| 7:45 a.m. | Juice |
| 8:00–10:00 | Hatha yoga |
| 11:30 | Massage class |
| 12:30 p.m. | Visualization |
| 1:00 | Lunch |
| Free time | |
| 6:30 | Partner yoga |
| 7:30 | Dinner |
| 9:00 | Herbal facials, hot tub, evening stargazing |

**Other Activities**: The area provides wonderful hiking opportunities along the cliffs that separate the beaches. Rock pools offer a chance to see various forms of marine life. Guests enjoy being at the beach, hiking, bird-watching, golf, and soaking in the hot tub.

**Guest Comment**: *"I am a novice to yoga but was encouraged by Julia to attend at a level I would be comfortable with. I found the attitude of the other guests to be supportive and non-judgmental. I was encouraged to be myself, know myself, learn to regain trust in myself. Daily yoga and long walks awakened my body to a new awareness of energy."*
Cynthia Keller — Sacramento, California

**Summary**: This three-day weekend retreat is held at a luxurious private house in Bodega Bay, complete with ocean views and and outdoor hot tub. Yoga teacher Julia Tindall offers yoga, simple tai chi exercises, and massage instruction as well as group singing, meditation, and hiking. All activities are optional, and participants are invited to simply rest and relax if that is more appropriate for them.

# RAINBOW RANCH
# CALISTOGA, CALIFORNIA

*Yoga Retreat with Amy Cooper*

## MAY AND NOVEMBER
### WEEKEND RETREATS

Rainbow Ranch is a mountaintop retreat site located in the historical Mayacana Mountains on 80 acres of rolling hills. Formerly a Native American ceremonial site, the ranch enjoys an expansive view of five counties, lovely vineyards, and Mount St. Helena. Guests enjoy a 100,000-gallon swimming pool and a large in-ground hot-water spa, both located on top of a ridge offering gorgeous views of the surrounding mountains. Two ranch houses, three multi-unit bathhouse facilities, and five A-frame sleeping cabins provide overnight accommodations. The setting is expansive and peaceful, offering a natural environment for yoga, contemplation, and relaxation. Yoga teacher Amy Cooper has been offering her weekend yoga retreats at Rainbow Ranch for more than five years.

**Address**: Rainbow Ranch
3975 Mountain Home Rd.
Calistoga, CA 94515
**Phone**: 707/942-5127
**Fax**: 707/942-8887
**Web site**: www.rainbowranchretreat.com

**Address**: Amy Cooper
2149 Danberry Lane
San Rafael, CA 94903
**Phone**: 415/472-1330

**Airport Information**: Fly into Sonoma County Airport (in Santa Rosa) or into San Francisco International and drive two hours north. Rainbow Ranch is 25 minutes from the city of Santa Rosa. Airport transportation (bus) is available to Santa Rosa from San Francisco International.

**How to Get There**: Rainbow Ranch is located in the Napa-Sonoma Mountains, 10 minutes outside the town of Calistoga, California, 25 minutes from Santa Rosa.

**Teacher Background**: Amy Cooper has practiced yoga since 1981 and taught in the San Francisco Bay area for the last 12 years. She is certified in the Iyengar yoga method and also has experience with Ashtanga yoga, Buddhist meditation, and yoga therapy; she has more than 10 years of both practicing and receiving body work.

**Style of Yoga**: Iyengar Hatha yoga. Amy's teaching offers an integrated base of practice, emphasizing self-exploration in mindful movement, healthy postural alignment, and breath awareness.

**Philosophy of Teacher**: "Cultivating an awareness of the body, mind, and breath as a source of discovering strength, flexibility, and balance from the inside out."

**Student Criteria**: Some experience in yoga or other mindful movement experience is requested.

**Disability Access**: No access

**What to Bring**: Yoga mat; casual, comfortable clothes for yoga; walking shoes; swimsuit; towel; and personal toiletries. Props can be provided if notice of need is given in advance.

**Yoga Room Size and Description**: Yoga is practiced in a 1,000-square-foot room with lots of natural light. The floor is half hardwood and half carpeted.

**Number of Participants Possible**: 30

**Accommodations**: Guests sleep in two ranch houses, which provide 11 double-occupancy rooms, or in A-frame sleeping cabins that sleep four. The ranch house rooms offer two twin beds and lofts with exposed-beam ceilings and gorgeous views. The A-frames are small and very simple. Shared bathroom facilities are nearby.

**Meals**: Three gourmet vegetarian meals made from carefully selected organic produce and grains are provided daily. Breakfast before class is light. Lunch and dinner offer great variety.

**Fee**: $295 per person for the weekend includes accommodations at Rainbow Ranch, use of the pool and hot tub, daily vegetarian meals, and all yoga classes with Amy.

**Credit Cards**: Not accepted

**Sample Daily Schedule:**
| | |
|---|---|
| 7:30–8:30 a.m. | Light Breakfast |
| 9:30–11:30 | Yoga class |
| Noon–1:00 p.m. | Lunch |
| 1:00–4:00 | Free time |
| 4:30–6:00 | Yoga class |
| 6:00–7:00 p.m. | Dinner |

Evenings are open for personal time, massage, use of hot water spa, and quiet reflection. One night is set aside for an optional group circle.

**Other Activities**: The property offers lots of hiking trails, a spring-fed lake for fishing and swimming, a 100,000-gallon swimming pool, and a large in-ground hot-water spa. The town of Calistoga, five miles away, is popular for its restorative hot mineral water, mud baths, glider and balloon rides, natural geyser, and a selection of fine restaurants.

**Services**: Massage and herbal facial steams are available by appointment.

**Guest Comment:** *"From the Rainbow Ranch ridge, the surrounding hills, and the endless sky, I found the first step to pulling me back into myself. The real joy, though, is the warmth and intimacy of the yoga studio, where Amy's careful, loving instruction creates the deep quiet and freedom that I seek in my yoga practice. From the meteor showers over the hot tub at night to the heat of the wood stove on a chilly morning, I am fed by the quiet healing of these sacred grounds."*
Ellie Dwight—San Francisco, California

**Summary**: This mountaintop retreat center sits on the rolling hills of a volcanic ridge and has a 360-degree view of five counties. It is surrounded by higher mountains in a healing symmetry. Facilities include two ranch houses, a large L-shaped swimming pool, and a hot-water spa. Yoga teacher Amy Cooper offers weekend retreats in this tranquil setting, where guests enjoy yoga instruction, gourmet vegetarian meals, and beautiful rainbow sunsets.

# RAILROAD PARK
# DUNSMUIR, CALIFORNIA

*Mount Shasta Camping Adventure with Julia Tindall*

## AUGUST
### FIVE DAYS, FOUR NIGHTS

Railroad Park is a beautiful campsite situated amid a peaceful pine forest next to a rushing mountain stream. Looking up one sees the towering peaks of Castle Crags State Park. Elevation is at 4,000 feet, so the air is fresh and clean and the sky is bluer than blue. Every year yoga teacher Julia Tindall offers an outdoor living yoga experience and adventure at this Shasta mountain environment. The trip includes daily yoga, hearty breakfasts, group hikes, meditation in nature, and relaxing in the healing water of Stewart Mineral Springs. Also included is a visit to the famous St. Germain "I Am" pageant, a play about the story of Jesus's life up to the ascension, performed on stage with Mount Shasta in the background. Participants return to the campground each night for storytelling and singing around the campfire.

**Address**: Julia Tindall
P.O. Box 601872
Sacramento, CA 95860
**Phone**: 916/486-4620
**E-mail**: yogajules@aol.com
**Web site**: www.globalff.org/Julia

**Airport Information**: Mount Shasta is 45 minutes north of Redding and four hours north of Sacramento. Fly into Sacramento or Redding. Renting a car is necessary.

**How to Get There**: The campsite is located at Railroad Park, about three miles south of Dunsmuir and 15 minutes south of the town of Shasta, underneath Castle Crags State Park.

**Teacher Background**: Julia Tindall is a certified Sivananda yoga teacher, massage therapist, and hypnotherapist. She is the creator of the video *Beginner's Yoga with Julia*, which is based on what she refers to as Standing Wave Yoga.

**Style of Yoga**: Julia teaches Standing Wave Yoga, which is a gentle beginner practice based on the awareness of breath consciousness in the body. Movements are performed with softness. She incorporates partner yoga, breath work, and visualization. Julia's teaching combines Hatha yoga (physical stretching), pranayama, meditation, Bhakti yoga (chanting), Jnana yoga (the path of wisdom), and Karma yoga (selfless service).

**Philosophy of Teacher**: "Yoga is the consciousness we bring to our lives. It is a tool to help us improve the quality of our lives, to help us to grow and rise to the challenges that life presents with consciousness and awareness. The opportunity that yoga gives us is to bring the awareness learned during practice into everyday living so that eventually, for the yogi, nothing is outside of yoga."

**Student Criteria**: Everyone is welcome. Participants should enjoy camping and hiking.

**Disability Access**: No access

**What to Bring**: Sleeping bag, sleeping pad, flashlight, hiking shoes, swimsuit, day pack, water bottle, plastic tea mug, towel, personal toiletries, sunscreen, sun hat, and insect repellent. Optional items include a tent, folding chair, lantern, camp stove, and camera. Plates and utensils are provided.

**Yoga Room Size and Description**: Yoga is practiced in a large patch of soft grass in the shade under pine trees and the blue sky.

**Number of Participants Possible**: 50

**Accommodations**: Participants stay in a privately run campsite that is clean and friendly. The group camps together under the trees. There are two communal bathrooms, one for women and one for men. There is also a hotel next to the campsite in an old railcar, so participants can rent a "caboose" at their own expense if they don't want to camp.

**Meals**: All breakfasts, lunches, and two vegetarian dinners are included. Meals are prepared camp-style, with cereals, eggs, fruit, and toast for breakfasts; picnic sandwiches and snacks for lunches; and campfire-cooked vegetarian dinners.

**Fee**: $195 per person includes four nights' camping, most meals, a mineral bath at Stewart Mineral Springs, guided hikes, and daily yoga classes with Julia.

**Credit Cards**: Not accepted

**Sample Daily Schedule**:

| | |
|---|---|
| 8:00 a.m. | Morning yoga |
| 10:00 | Breakfast |
| 11:00 | Daily excursions: Hike Mount Shasta, take a mineral bath at Stewart Mineral Springs, swim in the river, browse the Shasta shops, visit Castle Crags State Park, picnic, and enjoy meditation sessions in nature |
| 6:00 p.m. | Dinner around the campfire or at local restaurants |
| 8:30 | Campfire and singing |

**Other Activities**: The area offers lots of hiking, swimming, visiting Stewart Hot Springs for the hot tub and sweat lodge, shopping in Shasta, and many secluded spots for meditation in the mountain environment.

**Guest Comment**: *"My yoga experience under the magic spell of Mount Shasta with Julia is one of my most memorable journeys. She showed me asanas that I had not done before. They were matched to my intermediate level of yoga and were a perfect warm-up for the hiking that followed. The outdoor camping setting made for a relaxing and refreshing atmosphere, with the beautiful scenery allowing me to stretch myself in many ways under Julia's expert guidance."*
Doug Scott—Sacramento, California

**Summary**: This camping weekend with yoga teacher Julia Tindall includes picnics in nature, mountain hiking, soaking in mineral baths, attendance of the "I Am" festival in Shasta, evening singing around the campfire, and daily yoga.

# HEARTWOOD INSTITUTE
# GARBERVILLE, CALIFORNIA

*Hatha Iyengar Yoga Retreat with Gayna Uransky*

## JUNE
### SEVEN-DAY INTENSIVE

## SEPTEMBER
### WEEKEND RETREAT

Heartwood Institute of Healing Arts, located in a pristine mountain setting at 2,000 feet, provides guests with a gorgeous 180-degree view of surrounding mountains. The campus is set on 240 acres containing rolling meadows and forests of Douglas fir, oak, buckeye, madrone, manzanita, and California bay laurel. Lots of wildlife shares the land, including deer, feral pigs, silver and red foxes, bobtail cats, raccoons, red-tailed hawks, wild turkeys, owls, and redheaded woodpeckers. The narrow, winding roads providing access to Heartwood prepare newcomers for the remote, retreatlike mountain setting as they twist and climb. It is advisable to arrive during daylight hours, both to enjoy the beauty of the land, and to avoid driving in the dark on unfamiliar mountain roads.

Heartwood originated 20 years ago as a massage school and has now expanded to include many other retreats and avenues of study. The community center, which houses the programs, is a log-cabin lodge that also serves as a dining room, where meals are presented buffet style, and as a gathering place between classes. Outside the lodge is a spacious deck, where meals are taken in nice weather. Guests are nurtured with a healing community environment, fresh organic food, an outdoor hot tub, a wood-fired sauna, a large swimming pool, and the beauty of the land.

**Address**: Heartwood Institute
220 Harmony Lane
Garberville, CA 95542
**Phone**: 707/923-5005 (Heartwood)
707/923-9363 (Gayna)
**Fax**: 707/925-5010
**E-mail**: woodsky@humboldt.net,
gaynauransky@hotmail.com
**Web site**: www.humboldt.net/~woodsky

**Airport Information**: From San Francisco International rent a car and drive five hours north. Or fly into Arcata, California, rent a car, and drive two to three hours south. Some-

times airport pickup can be arranged in Arcata for a fee.

**How to Get There**: Garberville is 200 miles north of San Francisco. From Garberville, Heartwood is only 20 miles, but it takes 45 minutes to drive there because of the curvy mountain roads.

**Teacher Background**: Gayna Uransky, M.Ed., certified Iyengar yoga instructor, is the resident yoga teacher at Heartwood, where she teaches daily and offers one weeklong intensive and one weekend retreat each year. Gayna has been teaching yoga since 1971. She studied with B. K. S. Iyengar and his daughter Gita in Pune, India. She also offers retreats in Mexico.

**Style of Yoga:** Hatha Iyengar yoga.

**Philosophy of Teacher:** "I encourage students to explore challenges that they are capable of. Yoga allows for continued expansion and growth."

**Student Criteria:** Intermediate level

**Disability Access:** No access

**What to Bring:** All props are provided.

**Yoga Room Size and Description:** Heartwood has a large, carpeted, well-equipped yoga studio with high ceilings and views of the surrounding mountains to give students a spacious, expansive ambiance.

**Number of Participants Possible:** 15–20

**Accommodations:** Rustic dorm-style rooms are small and simple, with double- or single-bed options. Many rooms have bunk beds, which makes this feel like going to summer camp. Bathrooms are shared. Each room has its own separate entrance. Camping is also available, with campsites tucked among the trees.

**Meals:** Vegetarian meals are made with fresh organic food. Much of the fresh, seasonal produce is harvested daily from vegetable gardens on Heartwood's land. A brick oven is used for making bread from freshly ground organic whole grain flour—it smells heavenly and tastes delicious. Alternatives to foods such as wheat, dairy, and eggs are available.

**Fee:** Total cost for seven-day retreat: $831 for a private room, $713 per person for two sharing a room, $635 for camping or classroom sleep space. Total cost for two-day retreat: $237 for private room, $204 per person for two sharing a room,

$181 for camping or classroom sleep space.

**Credit Cards:** Visa and Mastercard

**Sample Daily Schedule:**

| 7:30–8:00 a.m. | Pranayama |
| 8:00–8:30 | Meditation |
| 8:30–10:30 | Asanas |
| 10:30 | Fruit snack |
| Noon–2:00 p.m. | Lunch |
| 4:30–6:00 | Inversions (yoga asanas) |
| 6:00 | Dinner |

**Other Activities:** Endless hiking, nature walks, hot tub, sauna, swimming pool, quiet reading, resting, enjoying the company of other yoga participants. There is a meditation temple on the grounds providing sanctuary for those who desire it.

**Services:** Massage is readily available. (Heartwood is a massage school, after all.) Massage options include Swedish, deep tissue, polarity, and shiatsu.

**Guest Comment:** *"I have attended a number of Gayna's summer yoga intensives at Heartwood and have always left feeling renewed in body, mind, and spirit. Gayna is highly skilled, very knowledgeable, and able to teach all levels of ability with individual attention and a lot of love. She pushes me to do more than I thought I could, but I always feel completely accepted and respected for who I am and whatever I am comfortable doing in her class."*
Margaret Sjogren—Ashland, Oregon

**Summary:** Gayna Uransky's Hatha Iyengar Yoga Retreats at Heartwood Institute offer a vehicle for self-discovery in the quiet and beauty of California's North Coast Mountains. An environment for total immersion in learning and healing, the retreat setting offers nurturing organic food, simple accommodations, and a beautiful yoga room for classes. Gayna encourages people to work at—and sometimes beyond—their self-imposed limitations.

# SIVANANDA ASHRAM YOGA FARM
# GRASS VALLEY, CALIFORNIA

## YEAR-ROUND

Located on 80 secluded acres of rolling hills and meadows in the gold country of the Sierra Nevada foothills, the Sivananda Ashram Yoga Farm is a year-round spiritual retreat where students live according to the traditional yogic teachings of Sivananda. Founded in 1971 by Swami Vishu Devananda, author of *The Complete Illustrated Book of Yoga*, the Ashram Yoga Farm is one of more than 30 Sivananda Yoga Centers and Ashrams around the world. The organization promotes universal peace through personal spiritual practice.

My first visit to the Sivananda Ashram Yoga Farm was on a rainy winter day. Driving through country back roads to get there, I did indeed feel that I was on farm land. The countryside is quite lovely, with a variety of fruit trees and nice views. Two goats, an elderly dog, and a few prowling cats share the land with the ashram residents. A simple farmhouse serves as an all-purpose lodge, dining hall, and practice and meeting facility. In the spring and summer, classes are held on an outdoor deck shaded by a grove of oak trees. In the winter, activities are held indoors in the wood-stove-heated farmhouse.

**Address**: Sivananda Yoga Ashram Farm
14651 Ballantree Lane
Grass Valley, CA 95949
**Phone**: 530/272-9322,
800/469-YOGA
**Fax**: 530/477-6054
**E-mail**: yogafarm@sivananda.org
**Web site**: www.sivananda.org

**Airport Information**: Fly into Sacramento Metro. Airport pickup is available at an extra charge.

**How to Get There**: Sivananda is two and one-half hours from San Francisco, one and one-half hours from Sacramento. Buses go to Grass Valley and Auburn, the closest towns.

**Teacher Background**: Classes are taught by ashram staff on a rotating basis. All staff teachers have been trained in the Sivananda yogic teachings and philosophy.

**Style of Yoga**: Classical yoga, which includes a synthesis of Raja (which includes Hatha), Jnana, Karma, and Bhakti yoga. There is a strong emphasis on breathing. Each class includes 12 basic postures and their variations to give a comprehensive class that is both relaxing and meditative. Devotional practices such as silent meditation, chanting, prayers, and Sanskrit verses are used daily to help cultivate the teachings.

**Philosophy of Teachers**: "Vedanta philosophy, exploring the nature of self and truth. Five basic principles of health: proper exercise, proper breathing, proper relaxation, proper diet, positive thinking, and meditation."

**Student Criteria**: A sincere desire to learn; all levels welcome.

**Disability Access**: Generally, yes. Please call for details.

**What to Bring**: Modest, comfortable clothing. Yoga mat and pillow if possible.

**Yoga Room Size and Description**: Outside deck for asana class is 50' x 20'. In wet or cold weather the meditation room is used—30' x 20'.

**Number of Participants Possible**: 30 people for indoor yoga programs and 40 people for outdoor yoga when weather permits. There are 40 beds available and unlimited tent and camping space.

**Accommodations**: The choice is between cabins and rooms indoors. The indoor rooms are simple and pleasant, part of a 100-year-old farmhouse. Choose from three- to four-person dorms, double-occupancy rooms, or limited single rooms. Bathrooms and showers are shared and are separate from the rooms. The brand-new double-occupancy cabins are set on the hillside overlooking the pond. There are also two Native American tee-pees on site. Guests who are camping need to bring their own tents and sleeping bags.

**Meals**: Two buffet-style vegetarian meals are served according to yogic dietary principles. No meat, fish, fowl, eggs, garlic, onions, or caffeinated beverages are served. The meals are mostly vegan, but some dishes are prepared with yogurt or milk.

**Fee**: Friday and Saturday, tent space is $30, dorms are $40, double rooms are $50, and private rooms are $90. Sunday through Thursday, prices are $5 less; $10 less for private rooms. Kids under 12 are half price. Rates include accommodations, meals, classes, and programs.

**Credit Cards**: Visa and Mastercard; personal checks accepted with ID.

**Sample Daily Schedule**:

| | |
|---|---|
| 5:30 a.m. | Wake-up bell |
| 6:00 | Morning satsang |
| 8:00 | Asana-Pranayama class |
| 10:00 | Brunch |
| 11:00 | Karma yoga |
| Noon | Free time |
| 2:00 p.m. | Special workshops |
| 4:00 | Asanas and Pranayama |
| 6:00 | Dinner |
| 8:00 | Evening satsang |

Satsang includes chanting, meditation, readings, discussion. Attendance at classes and meditations is mandatory.

**Other Activities**: Year-round hiking, summer swimming in pond, visiting nearby historical gold-rush towns, and the Yuba River. A cedar sauna is open year-round.

**Guest Comment**: *"I like the peaceful, supportive environment and the philosophy of nonviolence in thought as well as deed. The world seems so violent today; it's nice to be away from that. Being here has helped me get closer to my spiritual self. At first I thought getting up so early would be a problem, but now I look forward to it. I love starting my day in spiritual practice and meditation. The seeds of discipline have been planted for when I return home. I'd like to continue meditation and eating this wonderful vegetarian diet."*
Pamela Hellens—Auckland, New Zealand

**Summary**: The 80-acre farm gives an opportunity for serious study and experience of Sivananda's yogic teachings. Guests are asked to participate in all scheduled classes and to contribute time to communal activities. Emphasis is on personal discipline in the practices, which results in finding inner silence and peace. You may arrive on any day and stay as long as you wish. The environment is simple, rustic, and clean. A variety of retreat programs and trainings is available, including work-study programs.

SEE PHOTOS, PAGE 143.

# SEA RANCH
# GUALALA, CALIFORNIA

*Coastal Yoga Retreat with Annalisa Cunningham*

## JULY AND OCTOBER
### FOUR DAYS, THREE NIGHTS

The Sea Ranch vision, first conceived in the early 1960s, was of people joining the natural environment with minimal impact. Overgrazed lands were left to rest and natural processes allowed to take their course. Indigenous grasses, shrubs, and trees were planted, and the entire ranch was designated a wildlife and game refuge. Today an abundance of deer, birds, and other wildlife inhabit the property. Whales can be seen migrating off the coast, and in the spring, the meadows are brilliant with wildflowers. Award- winning homes with natural-wood exteriors and low-profile roofs blend with the land in forest, meadow, and oceanfront settings. Many of the Sea Ranch homes are available for vacation rental, and yoga teacher Annalisa Cunningham has found the setting to be a wonderful place for practicing yoga, hiking, and playing at the beach.

**Address**: Annalisa Cunningham
P.O. Box 3363
Chico, CA 95927
**Phone**: 530/343-9944
**E-mail**: RioAnalisa@aol.com

**Airport Information**: Sea Ranch is three hours north of San Francisco. Fly into San Francisco International and rent a car or take a private plane to an air strip on the Sea Ranch or one above Gualala (pronounced "Wa-la-la" and meaning "where the waters meet") at Ocean Ridge, where there is a 2,600-foot paved landing strip.

**How to Get There**: The Sea Ranch is 30 miles north of the small town of Jenner on Highway 1, just below the small town of Gualala.

**Teacher Background**: Annalisa Cunningham, M.A. Counseling, has been offering yoga classes and retreats since

1985. She has certification in the Ananda Yoga Teacher Training and White Lotus Teacher Training and as an Integrative Yoga therapist.

**Style of Yoga**: Gentle Hatha yoga practiced in an atmosphere of acceptance and calmness. Annalisa combines yoga postures, breathing techniques, meditation, massage, and healing visualizations to invite participants to open their hearts as well as their bodies.

**Philosophy of Teacher**: "It takes willingness, patience, and acceptance to practice yoga. Our bodies have their own rates of opening and surrender. Our inner wisdom will guide us as we pay attention. Accepting where we are now while patiently continuing to practice brings healing to the body, mind, and spirit. "

**Student Criteria**: All are welcome.

**Disability Access**: Limited access; please call.

**What to Bring**: Yoga mat and blanket, warm comfortable clothes, beach towel, swimsuit, personal items, a good pair of walking shoes, and a journal or writing paper.

**Yoga Room Size and Description**: If weather permits, yoga is practiced on a protected outside wood deck overlooking the meadow and ocean. If it is foggy, yoga is practiced inside, in a large carpeted living area with large ocean-view windows and cozy wood-stove heat.

**Number of Participants Possible**: 10

**Accommodations**: Participants stay in two vacation houses that are adjacent to each other on the same property. The main house is large, with three bedrooms, two bathrooms, and a loft. The smaller house has two bedrooms, one bathroom, and a loft. Guests select from double-bed, single-bed, and foam-mattress options. Each house has beautiful decking and a private hot tub, and the two houses are joined by a plant-filled atrium. Windows, views, and light abound in both houses.

**Meals**: Two whole-food vegetarian meals are served each day, including a late-morning brunch after yoga and dinner. Early risers help themselves to fruit, bagels, toast, and tea. Special diets can be accommodated.

**Fee**: $295 per person includes three nights', four days' accommodations, catered whole-food vegetarian meals, daily yoga classes, guided hikes, and full use of Sea Ranch facilities: pool, sauna, tennis courts, golf, and beach access.

Discounts are given for those who sleep in lofts.

**Sample Daily Schedule**:

| | |
|---|---|
| 8:00–10:00 a.m. | Morning yoga |
| 10:30 | Brunch |
| Noon | Optional group walks, beach exploration, river kayaking |
| 4:30–6:00 p.m. | Afternoon yoga |
| 6:00–6:30 | Hot tub, sauna |
| 6:30 | Dinner |
| 8:00 | Healing imagery, visualization, ritual, and meditation |

**Other Activities**: Full use of swimming pool, two hot tubs, sauna, tennis courts, and hiking trails. Paths give access to forests, rivers, and beaches. The town of Gualala is nearby and offers local art, gift shopping, and kayak-rental services for exploring the Gualala River. Horseback riding and whale watching are activities enjoyed at Gualala Point Regional Park.

**Guest Comment**: *"The retreat was wonderful! I felt nurtured by the healthy meals, the atmosphere, the beach, and Annalisa's gentle yoga practice. She had a special way of focusing on every participant, giving us each individual yoga instruction. For those beautiful few days I felt a part of a small, loving community, yet I also had the freedom and time to be by myself to relax, reflect, or retreat."*
Patti Wickes—Paradise, California

**Summary**: Majestic redwoods, sunny open hillsides, dramatic vistas, fresh ocean air, and sandy beaches make Sea Ranch a beautiful place to rest and revitalize your energy. Yoga teacher Annalisa Cunningham offers four-day yoga retreats at this wild and lovely north-coast location.

# HARBIN HOT SPRINGS
# MIDDLETOWN, CALIFORNIA

## *Seasonal Yoga Retreats*

Harbin Hot Springs Retreat Center is situated on 1,160 private acres of woodland, with hiking trails, gurgling streams and waterfalls, and hot mineral baths to soak away tension. The facilities include a warm mineral pool, hot pool, cold plunge tub, swimming pool, and sauna, all surrounded by redwood decking for sunbathing (clothing optional). The pools are fed directly with chlorine-free spring water that bubbles up from the earth. The water that flows from the showers and sinks on the property is also chlorine free. Deer and other wildlife roam freely on the land, which is surrounded by many more acres of undeveloped wilderness.

Harbin Hot Springs hosts a variety of workshops and training sessions, including seasonal yoga retreats (please check calendar below). The general ambiance is simple, rustic, and natural rather than fancy or elegant.

**Address**: Harbin Hot Springs
P.O. Box 782
Middletown, CA 95461
**Phone**: 800/622-2477
**Web site**: www.harbin.org

**Airport Information**: Fly into San Francisco International and rent a car. Harbin Hot Springs is two and one-half hours north of San Francisco.

**How to Get There**: Harbin Hot Springs is located in Middletown, California, above the town of Calistoga and California's wine country.

**Disability Access**: No access

**What to Bring**: Towel, linens, flashlight, sandals, and footwear appropriate for rocky terrain; a sleeping bag and pad if camping; rain gear during the winter.

**Yoga Room Size and Description**: Teachers usually rent a private facility for practicing yoga. Four separate workshop facilities are available. Facility rooms are carpeted and have windows.

**Accommodations**: Outdoor camping on the redwood decks or at sites along the creekside (some wooden platforms) require that you bring a pad and sleeping bag. Some yoga groups allow participants to sleep in the rented yoga room facility. For additional costs, private and shared rooms are available through Harbin Hot Springs. Basic rooms and dorms use shared bathrooms; dorms are not furnished with towels or bedding. Some rooms have private baths.

**Meals**: Yoga teachers often provide catered meals as part of the retreat. Harbin Hot Springs has a vegetarian restaurant, café, and health-food store on the property. There is also a guest kitchen available for guests who want to prepare their own meals (vegetarian only).

**Other Activities**: There are wonderful hiking trails all around the property.

Soaking in the hot mineral pools, the sauna, and the refreshing swimming pool is enjoyable and relaxing. Harbin has its own movie theater open to guests.

**Services**: There is a wide variety of massage treatment available, including Swedish, deep tissue, shiatsu, rebalancing, acupressure, and Harbin's own Watsu (water massage). At times there are people offering psychic readings, tarot card readings, and similar services.

**Summary**: Harbin Hot Springs is operated and maintained by a New Age community of more than 150 residents and volunteers. Weekend or week-long workshops are held throughout the year and encompass a variety of subjects, including yoga. Body acceptance is a key component at Harbin, and a clothing-optional policy is a tradition for the pools, sauna, and trails.

# CALENDAR OF YOGA RETREATS AT HARBIN HOT SPRINGS:

## FEBRUARY
### WEEKEND RETREAT
*Heal Mind, Body & Spirit Yoga Retreat with Julia Tindall*

**Yoga Teacher**: Julia Tindall
**Address**: P.O. Box 601872
Sacramento, CA 95860
**Phone**: 916/486-4620
**E-mail**: yogajules@aol.com
**Web site**: www.globalff.org/Julia

**Teacher Background**: Julia Tindall is a certified Sivananda yoga teacher, massage therapist, and hypnotherapist. She is the creator of the video *Beginner's Yoga with Julia*, which is based on what she refers to as Standing Wave Yoga.

**Style of Yoga**: Julia's teaching combines Hatha yoga (physical stretching), pranayama, meditation, Bhakti yoga (chanting), Jnana yoga (the path of wisdom), and Karma yoga (selfless service). Her workshop at Harbin includes the "Five Rites of Rejuvenation" and "The Way of the Hot Tub."

**Philosophy of Teacher**: "Yoga is the consciousness we bring to our lives. It is a tool to help us improve the quality of our lives, to help us to grow and rise to the challenges that life presents with consciousness and awareness. The opportunity that yoga gives us is to bring the awareness learned during practice into everyday living so that eventually, for the yogi, nothing is outside of yoga."

**Student Criteria**: All levels of experience are welcome.

**What to Bring**: Yoga mat, sleeping bag for indoor/outdoor camping, towel, hiking shoes, flashlight, and an open heart.

**Number of Participants Possible**: 14

**Meals**: Six home-cooked meals are provided, starting with dinner on Friday night. Special diets can be accommodated. Dinners are sit-down and candlelit, and everyone eats at the same table.

**Fee**: $225 per person for the weekend includes camping or indoor group lodging (sharing floor space), six vegetarian meals, and all yoga classes with Julia.

**Credit Cards**: Not accepted

**Sample Daily Schedule**:
| | |
|---|---|
| 7:45 a.m. | Fruit juice and snack |
| 8:00 | Asana practice |
| 10:00 | Breakfast |

| | |
|---|---|
| 11:30 | Jnana yoga: yoga of wisdom |
| 12:30 p.m. | Visualization, Pranayama |
| 1:00 | Lunch |
| Free time | |
| 6:00 | Five Rites of Rejuvenation and Partner Yoga |
| 7:30 | Dinner |

**Guest Comment:** *"Being a happy veteran of a number of Julia Tindall's Harbin yoga retreats, I enthusiastically recommend these wonderful weekend experiences for anyone who enjoys expert yoga instruction; blissful surroundings; physical and spiritual rejuvenation; delicious, healthful dining; the company of enlightened people; meeting new friends; and just having fun. During these pampered weekends all stress just melts away! Julia is a uniquely gifted guide to the world of yoga whom I wholeheartedly recommend."*
Michael Doughton—Sacramento, California

# SEPTEMBER
## Weeklong Retreat
*Women's Yoga Retreat with Angela Farmer*

**Address:** Attention: Simran Skie
14621 Tomki Road
Redwood Valley, CA 95470
**Phone:** 707/485-5926

**Teacher Background:** Angela Farmer studied for many years with B. K. S. Iyengar in India, becoming quite accomplished in the Iyengar method of teaching. She then moved away from that system to create a more internal and meditative approach to yoga. She has influenced many leading teachers in the West today with her unique and supportive "inner body" work in yoga.

**Style of Yoga:** Angela teaches from the deep internal flow of energy she calls the "inner body" rather than from the muscles. Instead of focusing on external alignment, she guides students to internal awareness and movement. Asanas are "maps" or tools to help explore how energy moves inside. Her practice is explorative and empowering, leading to each individual's own development and practice.

**Philosophy of Teacher:** "To guide students toward the abundant richness that the internal world provides."

**Student Criteria:** This is a women's retreat. All levels are welcome.

**What to Bring:** A yoga mat and blanket, towel, sleeping bag, hiking shoes, and flashlight.

**Number of Participants Possible:** 40

**Meals:** Beautifully prepared organic meals are provided as part of the retreat.

**Fee:** $1,275 per person for the week includes camping, full use of Harbin Hot Springs, organic meals, and two yoga classes daily with Angela.

**Credit Cards:** Not accepted

**Sample Daily Schedule:**

| | |
|---|---|
| Mornings | Three-hour asana and movement class |
| Afternoons | Free for hot springs enjoyment |
| Evenings | One-and-one-half-hour breathing and sitting (meditation) class |

**Guest Comment:** *"It's a hot summer day at Harbin. In the poolside yoga studio, overhead fans hum faintly as Angela invites a room full of women to tune into and follow their deepest sensate intuition. 'The male side of each of us sees a goal and has to go for it,' Angela explains. 'Here we're trying to awaken the female side, which can let go of form and enter into chaos. Because it's out of chaos and darkness that the possibility for life emerges.' Process becomes more important than poses; asanas happen almost incidentally, as a by-product of an internal voyage."*
Simran Skie—Redwood Valley, California

# THE EXPANDING LIGHT AT ANANDA
# NEVADA CITY, CALIFORNIA

## YEAR-ROUND

Driving through the rolling foothills of Northern California's Sierra Nevada Mountains, you will pass by the Yuba River as you head to the Expanding Light. This year-round retreat center is nestled amid oak and pine forests, separated by broad, grassy meadows. With 750 acres of land, wherever you look there is beauty.

For 30 years the Expanding Light has been the retreat center of Ananda Village, a spiritual community where 350 residents make the teachings of yoga the basis of their daily lives. Ananda was founded in 1968 by Swami Kriyananda (J. Donald Walters), a direct disciple of Paramahansa Yogananda, author of *Autobiography of a Yogi*. The retreat center utilizes the teachings of Yogananda to inspire participants to have a deep, personal experience of their own higher essence through yoga and meditation.

**Address**: The Expanding Light
14618 Tyler Foote Road
Nevada City, CA 95959
**Phone**: 800/346-5350,
530/478-7518
**Fax**: 530/478-7519
**E-mail**: info@expandinglight.org
**Web site**: www.expandinglight.org

**Airport Information**: Fly into Sacramento or Reno. Foothills Flyer shuttle service (800/464-0808) shuttles guests between Ananda and Sacramento airport/train station/bus station.

**How to Get There**: The Expanding Light is 20 minutes above Nevada City; three hours from San Francisco; one and one-half hours from Sacramento.

**Teacher Background**: Staff members take turns leading daily energization, yoga postures, and meditation sessions and assist in teaching the various courses offered there.

**Style of Yoga**: Ananda yoga integrates the practices of yoga postures, breathing exercises (pranayama), energy-control techniques, affirmation, and meditation. All yoga teachers at the Expanding Light have been inspired by the teachings of Yogananda and Kriananda.

**Philosophy of Teachers**: "Yoga is a way of life. One's yoga practices should support one's daily life, and vice versa. Yoga should be practiced at—and should benefit—all levels of our being: body, mind, and soul. Ananda teachers strive to help each student, no matter what level of experience or flexibility, to find his or her own comfort level with the postures. We focus on adapting the posture to the individual in order to derive the greatest benefits from yoga practice."

**Student Criteria**: Just an open heart and mind, and a sincere desire and willingness to explore yourself.

**Disability Access**: Wheelchair ramps and grip bars available; however, outdoor transit is via gravel paths.

**What to Bring**: Comfortable, modest clothing in layers. Good walking shoes for outings. If you have one, bring an asana blanket or yoga mat.

**Yoga Room Size and Description**: Yoga is taught in a 1,600-square-foot hexagonal room with windows facing the meadow.

**Number of Participants Possible**: 35 maximum for yoga posture programs. Guest capacity is 60.

**Accommodations**: Harmony House offers deluxe rooms with private baths, private entrances, and air-conditioning. Serenity House offers inn-style lodging with hall bathrooms and a shared lounge. Friendship House is a cozy bungalow with four rooms and a shared bathroom. Cabins have one big room and nearby bathhouses. Campers can bring their own tents. Campsites are level and shaded. RVs are welcome, although there are no hookups on the premises.

**Meals**: Three meals per day are prepared by Ananda chefs. Cuisine is lacto-ovo vegetarian with dairy-free options. Breakfasts and dinners are light; the main meal is lunch. The food includes appetizing, fresh salads, breads, and tasty warm dishes.

**Fee**: $89 per person per night includes meals, accommodations, and classes in a shared standard room; $113 per night for a private room. Deluxe rooms are $112 per night if shared, and $157 per night if private. Bring your own tent or RV for $68 per night.

**Credit Cards**: Visa and Mastercard

**Sample Daily Schedule**:

| | |
|---|---|
| 6:30 a.m. | Morning spiritual practices (energization exercises, yoga postures, and meditation) |
| 8:30 | Breakfast in silence |
| 10:00 | Class, group activity |
| noon | Meditation |
| 12:30 p.m. | Lunch |
| 2:00 | Class, group activity |
| 4:30 | Afternoon spiritual practices (energization exercises, yoga postures, chanting and meditation) |
| 6:30 | Dinner |
| 7:30 | Evening event |

**Other Activities**: Year-round hiking, nature walks, swimming in the nearby Yuba River. The expansive vista of Sunset Meadow is just a 10-minute walk from the retreat.

**Services**: The Center for Radiant Health, part of Ananda, offers massage, Ayurveda, energy therapy, Polarity, Reiki, herbology, and counseling.

**Guest Comment**: *"I liked the emphasis on safety and the encouragement to use variations of the postures according to your physical ability. I also liked the emphasis on your own personal experience, yoga represented as a spiritual expression, encouraging students to be aware of breath and energy and guiding them to spiritual upliftment."*
Cynthia Kimball—Angwin, California

**Summary**: The Expanding Light offers a beautiful setting and supportive environment for experiencing a retreat in a yoga-based community. The staff shows a genuine care and concern for participants. The food is wonderful. The programs, based on the teachings of Paramhansa Yogananda, apply to all aspects of life, from health to relationships, from career to spiritual development. Program options offer workshops and retreats, teacher trainings, holiday retreats, personal retreat (for stays of any length) and work-study programs.

SEE PHOTOS, PAGE 144.

# MONTECITO RETREAT
# SANTA BARBARA, CALIFORNIA

*Yoga and Reflection Retreat with Diana Lang*

## APRIL AND AUGUST
### WEEKEND RETREATS

This private facility sits on 27 acres in the hills overlooking the Pacific Ocean near Santa Barbara. The retreat property is quite lovely, with oak trees, orange trees, and a flowing creek that runs along the grounds near the rooms, allowing guests to fall asleep while listening to the water's song. The retreat has two meditation chapels, sculpture gardens, ponds, an Olympic-sized swimming pool, a tennis court, ping pong tables, and wonderful hiking opportunities. Exploring the grounds brings unexpected surprises, such as a garden planted with a peace sign design of flowers and big four-by-four-foot boulders with hidden inscribed Japanese carvings. Yoga teacher Diana Lang uses this peaceful, beautiful environment to hold her annual yoga weekend retreats. Just driving to this retreat setting is relaxing—the road takes you along the ocean, up winding roads, and into the hills, surrounding you with acres of green rolling meadows, oak tree forests, and gorgeous views.

**Address**: Diana Lang
5046 Marmol Drive
Woodland Hills, CA 91364
**Phone**: 818/888-7319
**Fax**: 818/702-6502
**E-mail**: Lifeworks@aol.com

**Airport Information**: Fly into Santa Barbara, or fly into LAX, which is one hour away.

**How to Get There**: The retreat is in Montecito, just south of Santa Barbara.

**Teacher Background**: Diana Lang has been teaching yoga and meditation training since 1980 and has been doing spiritual counseling for the past 10 years.

**Style of Yoga**: Diana's yoga training was originally in the Iyengar style of yoga, but over the years she has studied many other forms and teaches a blended and gentle Hatha yoga.

**Philosophy of Teacher**: "I like to create an atmosphere of meaning, movement, and playfulness. My goal as a teacher is to help the students find their own voices, their own personal connections, and to help them trust this knowing absolutely."

**Student Criteria**: All levels are welcome and represented in the retreats.

**Disability Access**: Yes

**What to Bring**: Comfortable clothes for yoga, swimsuit, walking shoes, and an open heart and mind to take another step on the road to health, love, and awareness.

**Yoga Room Size and Description**:
Yoga is practiced in a beautiful, stone room overlooking the meadow above the sea. This carpeted room has glass French doors on three sides that look out to expansive green meadows and a large fireplace on the fourth side.

**Number of Participants Possible**: 22

**Accommodations**: Rooms are set up for one, two, or three people, each with its own bathroom and shower. Guests sleep in single beds. The rooms are simple and pleasant and have no phones or televisions. The retreat center is quite large, with approximately 60 rooms available. Views from the rooms look out to California oak trees, which are abundant on the property.

**Meals**: Three buffet-style meals are served daily, with vegetarian and vegan options.

**Fee**: $300 per person for triple occupancy, $390 per person for double occupancy, and $500 per person for single occupancy. Includes accommodations, three meals daily, and all classes with Diana.

**Credit Cards**: Not accepted

**Sample Daily Schedule**:

| | |
|---|---|
| 7:30 a.m. | Morning meditation |
| 8:00 | Breakfast |
| 10:00–11:30 | Yoga class |
| noon | Lunch |
| 3:00–5:30 p.m. | Restorative yoga |
| 5:30 | Dinner |
| 7:30 | Special entertainment/ guest speaker |

**Other Activities**: There is a swimming pool on the grounds, as well as tennis courts, ping pong tables, and great places for hiking in the surrounding hills. A little gift shop on the premises sells journals and books for quiet writing, reflection, and reading.

**Services**: Massage is available by appointment.

**Guest Comment**: *"Attending Diana Lang's yoga retreat is an exquisite opportunity for coming to know one's self in an environment that is supportive, nurturing, and healing. Diana has a special gift: a way of supporting others while at the same time allowing them to draw upon their own inner strengths, enabling growth to occur. Her retreats have evolved from more of an emphasis on physical yoga to encompassing the internal healings of not only body, but mind and spirit as well. As she has evolved, Diana has willingly chosen to share what she has learned with others. This is her greatest gift. I am forever changed for the better for having experienced the teachings of Diana's retreats under her wisdom, intuition, caring, and loving guidance."*
Adrian Krauss — Encino, California

**Summary**: This retreat center is filled with beauty and peace. At one time a convent, the sanctuary is now a gathering place for spiritual conferences and groups. Yoga teacher Diana Lang uses this facility for the weekend yoga retreats she offers several times a year. Beginning students are welcome, and participation in classes is optional.

# WHITE LOTUS FOUNDATION RETREAT CENTER SANTA BARBARA, CALIFORNIA

## YEAR-ROUND

The White Lotus Foundation is dedicated to the development of the total human being through the practice of yoga. The mountain retreat center rests in a steep canyon on 40 acres near San Marcos Pass. This land was once sacred to the Chumash Indians, who called it Taklusmon, which means "the gathering place." The central building of this retreat sits at the top of the canyon and overlooks the city of Santa Barbara, the ocean, and the Channel Islands. A large yoga room, kitchen and dining area, library, bathroom, and loft are housed in this main facility. Most guests sleep in yurts that are situated along the steep canyon property. The natural beauty of this canyon terrain offers plenty of secluded places for meditation and exploration.

**Address**: White Lotus Foundation
2500 San Marcos Pass
Santa Barbara, CA 93105
**Phone**: 805/964-1944
**Fax**: 805/964-9617
**E-mail**: info@whitelotus.org
**Web site**: www.whitelotus.org

**Airport Information**: Santa Barbara Airport is 15 minutes from White Lotus. Yellow Cab and Rose Cab offer special low rates from Santa Barbara.

**How to Get There**: On Highway 154 at San Marcos Pass, 10 minutes from Santa Barbara; 5.8 miles from Highway 101 coming from the north.

**Teacher Background**: Ganga White, president of the White Lotus Foundation, has been a yoga instructor for more than 30 years. He has taught internationally, trained hundreds of yoga teachers, and studied and lived in India. He founded yoga centers in major U.S. cities and for five years served as vice president of the International Sivananda Yoga Vedanta Society. He studied personally with many great teachers, including J. Krishnamurti, B. K. S. Iyengar, and K. Pattabhi Jois.

Tracey Rich, associate director, has been studying and teaching nationally since 1978. Her background includes yoga training, dance, health, and philosophy. She leads seminars regularly at the Esalen Institutes.

**Style of Yoga**: Ganga and Tracey offer a synthesis of Hatha yoga forms, with emphasis on Vinyasa yoga and Jnana yoga. They have developed what is called "the flow series," which incorporates Ujjayi breath yoga with vinyasas (linking the poses together in a flow) to give participants an exhilarating and well-balanced yoga routine.

**Philosophy of Teachers**: "We are here to offer inspirational and practical tools for health, well being, and insight. Everything we do at White Lotus is meant to empower the individual, not to make him or her conform to dogma. We aim to awaken the fire of yoga within each student, to offer the vision of yoga with the art of living."

**Student Criteria**: All levels welcome

**Disability Access**: Limited access. Retreat is on steep, rugged terrain.

**What to Bring**: Comfortable casual clothing, towel, shoes for canyon terrain, flashlight, day pack, and sunscreen.

**Yoga Room Size and Description**: The yoga room is 20' x 40', has hardwood floors, and is surrounded by the mountain garden and ocean views.

**Number of Participants Possible**: 30

**Accommodations**: A few small, private cabins are available, although most guests sleep in yurts, which house up to four people on futon beds. Port-o-let bathrooms are nearby, as well as a beautiful showerhouse. Campsites are available to those who prefer to bring their own tent or to sleep outside along the spring-fed creek or bay laurel forest. Some people choose to sleep in the loft in the main building.

**Meals**: All meals are gourmet vegetarian and mostly vegan. Retreats include a light breakfast (tea, fruit, and cereal) before morning yoga class and a plentiful brunch afterward. Dinner follows the late-afternoon yoga class. Special diets can be accommodated.

**Fee**: Weekends run from $350 to $400 and are all-inclusive. Personal retreats, available Mondays, Tuesdays, and Wednesdays, include lodging and use of facilities for a cost of $40 per day per person or $70 per day per couple.

**Credit Cards**: Visa, Mastercard, and Discover

**Sample Daily Schedule**:

| | |
|---|---|
| 7:30 a.m. | Morning meditation |
| 7:30–8:30 | Light morning breakfast |
| 8:30 | Asana practice |
| 11:30 | Brunch |
| 12:30–3:30 p.m. | Free time |
| 3:30 | Asana and pranayama practice |
| 6:30 | Dinner |
| 8:00 | Evening program (discussions, yoga philosophy, music, dancing, meditation) |

**Other Activities**: Hiking, swimming in the creek, meditation next to a small waterfall, chanting in the kiva, outings to nearby Chumash Medicine Caves, Red Rock pools, and Santa Barbara beaches.

**Services**: Body work is available, including Thai massage, deep tissue, shiatsu, and Swedish massage.

**Guest Comment**: *"The White Lotus Center is a retreat I love to visit. It is also a place that stays with me, a still point deep within me that I can go to wherever I happen to be geographically. Ancient Native American rock drawings, wildlife, cultivated and indigenous trees, and wonderful food combine with Ganga and Tracey's inspired teaching to create an integrated, enlightening experience for each guest."*
Susan Fleming—Santa Monica, California

**Summary**: White Lotus Mountain Retreat Center offers a variety of weekend and weeklong programs, personal retreats, teacher trainings, and workshops. Most programs include daily yoga classes, hikes, outings, music, dance, ceremonies, dialogue, discussion, and inquiry. Organic, gourmet vegetarian meals are served at workshops and trainings. The beauty and ruggedness of the canyon terrain adds to the experience of White Lotus.

# ZACA LAKE RETREAT
# SANTA BARBARA, CALIFORNIA

*Embracing the New Millennium:*
*New Year's Eve Yoga Retreat with Max Strom*

## DECEMBER AND JANUARY
### Six Days, Five Nights

Zaca Lake Retreat is a private retreat center that is utilized for yoga retreats, meditation, and other programs offered by individual groups and teachers. It is a secluded,
pristine, natural lake and 320-acre wilderness preserve six miles up a private road that
soars through green forests and past five shallow creeks. The emerald lake is surrounded by wild, wooded mountains teeming with wildlife. The retreat center is rustic,
and a dining room hangs over the water's edge. This quiet, peaceful setting is an ideal
place for entering the new millennium. Yoga teacher Max Strom offers this special New
Year's yoga retreat, which includes inner work from various spiritual traditions and a
full day of silence.

**Address**: Max Strom
P.O. Box 1114
Topanga, CA 90290
**Phone**: 310/712-1221

**Airport Information:** Fly into Santa
Barbara. There is also a national airport
just outside Santa Barbara in a town
called Goleta.

**How to Get There**: Zaca Lake Retreat
is only a one-hour drive from Santa Barbara in the foothills above the Santa Inez
Valley.

**Teacher Background:** Max Strom
has studied with many of the world's
renowned teachers, including K. Pattabhi
Jois (Ashtanga yoga), Gabriella Giubi-
laro (Iyengar yoga), and Master Hong
Lu (Chi Gong). He has been teaching
yoga for over six years.

**Style of Yoga:** Max offers rigorous and
flowing classes that purify and realign
the body while cultivating a feeling of
deep inner peace. Pranayama and Chi
Gong are incorporated into his system.

**Philosophy of Teacher:** "It is nearly
impossible to have a spiritual life while
the mind is in chaos with stress and
noise and our bodies are weak and sick-
ly. The aim of yoga is to calm the mind
and bring vigor to the body so that we
may begin to truly feel our heart of
hearts and hear the small voice within
that is meant to guide our destiny. Yoga
was designed to revolutionize our lives;
anything less is simply exercise."

**Student Criteria:** The classes are suitable for advanced, intermediate, and
beginners with some experience. This
retreat is not advisable for first-time
students.

**Disability Access:** No access

**What to Bring**: A mat and towels for yoga practice, sunscreen, hiking shoes, flashlight, and toiletries. It could rain; temperatures vary from warm to cool.

**Yoga Room Size and Description**: Yoga is practiced in the main lodge, which has hardwood floors. The room has a large stone fireplace and windows that overlook the lake.

**Number of Participants Possible**: 35

**Accommodations**: Charming lakefront log cabins with porches, hickory lounge chairs, and stone fireplaces (firewood is provided). Each cabin has a bathroom with a custom-built tiled two-person Jacuzzi.

**Meals**: A light breakfast of tea and fruit is available in the mornings. Vegetarian (primarily vegan) lunches and dinners are prepared by a gourmet chef brought in specially for this retreat. Special diets are accommodated if possible.

**Fee**: $975 per person (double occupancy cabin), $825 per person (four people per cabin), and $675 (six people per cabin). Includes accommodations, all meals, yoga, and special events with Max. The cabins that sleep six do not have a Jacuzzi. A single-occupancy cabin is available for an additional fee.

**Credit Cards**: Not accepted

**Sample Daily Schedule**:

| | |
|---|---|
| 7:30 a.m. | Fruit and tea |
| 9:00–11:00 | Yoga |
| 11:30–12:30 | Lunch |
| 12:30–4:30 p.m. | Free time |
| 4:30–6:00 | Yoga |
| 6:30–7:30 | Dinner |
| 9:00–10:00 | Meditation |

**Other Activities**: Fabulous wilderness hiking and polar-bear swimming for those so inclined.

**Services**: Body work and massage are available.

**Guest Comment**: *"The lake is magical. There are carp, catfish, ducks, swans, lilies and lotus blossoms, pine and oak trees, mysterious fog, wildflowers, and hyperactive bluejays. The cabins have fireplaces and Jacuzzis. I don't know how to describe how beautiful the energy is up there. And then there's Max. His teaching attracts a wide variety and a great group of people. Max has a way of using the 'less is more' approach: he'll come over and fine tune with 'more energy in your feet,' or 'breathe deeper,' and I go into another realm. I have experienced magic in Max's classes and true miracles at Zaca Lake."*
Michael Now—Santa Montica, California

**Summary**: This five-day retreat is centered on the once-in-a-lifetime New Year's event—heralding in the new millennium. Together the group will set its intention to help create a world based on love and not fear. Purification, strength, and clarity will be the focus of classes taught by yoga teacher Max Strom throughout the week. Acres of wilderness, daily yoga, inner spiritual work, and a day of silence make this retreat a powerful and positive environment for embracing the new millennium.

# THE ANGELA CENTER
# SANTA ROSA, CALIFORNIA

*Explorations in Stillness with Richard C. Miller*

## SEPTEMBER
### THREE TO FIVE DAYS

The Angela Center is a nonprofit learning and retreat center sponsored by the Ursuline Sisters, a Roman Catholic community of religious women. Once a convent, the center sits on approximately 10 acres on a lovely hillside and is bordered by 100 acres of farm fields and pastures. The beautiful acreage offers a variety of natural vistas, gardens, and peaceful spaces for meditation and introspection. The staff at the Angela Center fosters a caring, nonintrusive environment for adults involved in the spiritual journey, promoting conscious commitment to self, our human family, and our planet. To help maintain a private environment, there are no phones or paging systems. (A pay phone is available for necessary calls.) Yoga teacher Richard Miller offers his annual retreat at this quiet setting as an exercise in awakening self-understanding through the disciplines of self-inquiry, meditation, and yoga.

**Address**: Richard Miller
900 5th Ave., Suite 203
San Rafael, CA 94901
**Phone**: 415/456-3909
**E-mail**: milleryoga@aol.com
**Web site**: www.milleryoga.com

**Airport Information**: Fly into San Francisco International or Oakland. Another option is to fly to the Sonoma County airport, which is nearby.

**How to Get There**: From San Francisco or Oakland, take the airport bus to Santa Rosa and then a taxi to the Angela Center. The Angela Center is readily accessible from Highway 101.

**Teacher Background**: Richard Miller has a Ph.D. in clinical psychology and has been teaching meditation through the disciplines of yoga since 1974. He has spent years integrating nondualistic

approaches to self-understanding. Two of the most influential teachers he has studied with are Jean Klein (teacher of nondualism) and T. K. V. Desikachar.

**Style of Yoga**: Nonduality—the emphasis on meditative awareness. Richard's classes aim at awakening students to self-understanding by utilizing the disciplines of self-inquiry, meditation, and yoga. His style is geared toward those who seek inquiry and self-exploration.

**Philosophy of Teacher**: "Yoga means to me to bring forth an investigation of what we take ourselves to be, through body, mind, and senses, to come to what we really are—presence."

**Student Criteria**: Interest and curiosity. All levels are welcome.

**Disability Access**: Full access

**What to Bring**: Yoga mat and meditation cushion are helpful but not necessary. Comfortable clothes, walking shoes, and personal toiletries.

**Yoga Room Size and Description**: Yoga is practiced in a carpeted 40' x 100' hall. The hall has a wonderful fireplace and windows that look out on the garden.

**Number of Participants Possible**: 40

**Accommodations**: The Angela Center is a two-story building that accommodates 24 to 48 overnight guests. Each of the 24 guest rooms has two single beds and a wash basin (single or double occupancy). The rooms are simple and surround a lovely courtyard. Guests share hall bathrooms.

**Meals**: Three vegetarian meals are prepared by a gourmet chef, who brings in a variety of theme dishes from different countries, such as Italy, India, and Mexico. Special diets are accommodated.

**Fee**: $350 per person for three days of the retreat, $450 per person for four days, and $550 per person for all five days. Includes accommodations, meals, and classes.

**Credit Cards**: Not accepted

**Sample Daily Schedule**:

| | |
|---|---|
| 7:00–8:00 a.m. | Morning meditation |
| 8:00–9:00 | Breakfast |
| 10:00–noon | Yoga asanas |
| noon | Lunch, free time |
| 4:00–6:00 p.m. | Afternoon program— |
| | pranayama, yoganidra, mudra, or discussion |
| 6:00–7:00 | Dinner |
| 7:30–9:00 | Evening dialogue |
| 9:15–10:00 | Evening meditation |

**Other Activities**: At the Angela Center there is plenty of land for hiking and enjoying solitude. Nearby attractions in the area include the Luther Burbank Gardens in Santa Rosa (a 15-minute drive), the mud baths and warm mineral springs in Calistoga (a 30-minute drive), Armstrong Woods State Park in Gurneville (a 30-minute drive), and the ocean and beaches at Bodega Bay (a 45-minute drive).

**Guest Comment**: *"A Retreat with Richard Miller was for me an experience of expansion and deepening surrender into individual and group presence. The knowledge and wisdom that he imparts through meditation and yoga embody the essence of unity that I easily integrated into daily practice. The Angela Center in beautiful Sonoma county was the perfect container in its simplicity, stillness, and nourishing (great food) environment. An experience not to miss!"*
Gaye Abbott— Santa Rosa, California

**Summary**: "Explorations in Stillness" offered by Richard Miller at the Angela Center in Santa Rosa is a retreat opportunity for investigating who and what we are. Yoga and meditation are utilized as methods for self-inquiry and self-exploration. Participants are guided toward exploring their own ground of being and moment-to-moment awareness of self, other, and environment.

# WESTERBEKE RANCH
# SONOMA, CALIFORNIA

*Autumn Yoga Retreat with Elise Miller and Judith Lasater*

## NOVEMBER
### WEEKEND RETREAT

Located in the heart of the wine country near Sonoma, California, Westerbeke Ranch sits on 100 acres of unspoiled beauty that was originally a Native American healing ground. Now the ranch is used as a conference center for a variety of groups, and Elise Miller and Judith Lasater offer their Autumn Yoga Retreat here every year in November. Facilities include three large conference rooms, comfortable redwood cabins, sun decks, Jacuzzis, and a large swimming pool. A Mexican-tile dining room is enhanced with colorful ethnic art, a marvelous hand-built stone fireplace, rough-hewn beams, and rustic charm. The ranch is surrounded by open space and country roads for hiking, jogging, and horseback riding from the nearby stable.

**Address**: Westerbeke Ranch
Conference Center
2300 Grove
Sonoma, CA 95476
**Phone**: 707/996-7546
**Fax**: 707/996-7081

**Address**: Judith Lasater
156 Madrone
San Francisco, CA 94127
**Phone**: 415/759-7430
**Fax**: 415/759-0847

**Address**: Elise Miller
P.O. Box 60746
Palo Alto, CA 94306
**Phone**: 650/493-1254
**Fax**: 650/857-0925

**Airport Information**: Fly into San Francisco International.

**How to Get There**: The Westerbeke Ranch is 50 miles north of San Francisco and five miles west of the town of Sonoma. Thirty miles east are the sloping vineyards of the Napa Valley and the Calistoga mineral spas.

**Teacher Background**: Elise Miller, M.A. in Therapeutic Recreation, is a certified senior Iyengar teacher who is a longtime student of B. K. S. Iyengar. She has studied with the Iyengars in India numerous times. Elise has corrected her own scoliosis with yoga and has been specializing in the use of yoga for back problems for more than 20 years.

Judith Lasater, Ph.D., P.T., has taught yoga since 1970. One of the founders of *Yoga Journal* magazine, Judith gives workshops internationally and holds a Ph.D. in East-West Psychology. She is recognized as an authority of asana, therapeutics, and integrating the *Yoga Sutras* into daily life.

**Style of Yoga**: Iyengar

**Philosophy of Teachers**: "Our goal is to

provide the teaching of yoga in a safe environment with precise instruction and the ability to handle special needs."

**Student Criteria**: A willingness to play and to learn.

**Disability Access**: Limited access

**What to Bring**: A yoga mat and two blankets. Bring a belt and block, as well, if needed.

**Yoga Room Size and Description**: Three meeting rooms are available at Westerbeke, and Judith and Elise utilize all three. Casa Nueva is the most spacious and has hardwood floors, a fireplace, a stereo system, and sliding doors that open to view the gardens and pool. The room holds up to 80 people. Casa Vista, nestled on the hillside above the pool area, is a carpeted room accommodating up to 60 people. The chapel, a converted wine-storage tank, is now a circular meeting room used for yoga, meditation, and quiet space for up to 30 people.

**Number of Participants Possible**: 50

**Accommodations**: Guests sleep in rustic redwood cabins that sleep two to five people per room and have shared baths. Cabins vary in size and foorplan, but all have a cozy atmosphere and windows.

**Meals**: Vegetarian California cuisine. Everything is prepared with a special emphasis on herbs and natural flavors. Breads and desserts are baked at the ranch. Fresh vegetables, fish, and cheese come from nearby farms. Guests eat in a Mexican-tile dining room that seats 50 at polished redwood tables or in an open-air garden patio that is nice on sunny afternoons.

**Fee**: $350 per person if paid in full at registration, or pay a $100 deposit and then the $270 balance.

**Credit Cards**: Not accepted

**Sample Daily Schedule**:

| | |
|---|---|
| 7:00–7:30 a.m. | Meditation |
| 7:30–10:30 | Light breakfast |
| 8:00–10:00 | Intermediate yoga class |
| 10:15–12:15 | Beginning yoga class |
| 12:30–1:30 p.m. | Lunch |
| 1:30–3:15 | Free time |
| 3:15–4:45 | Intermediate yoga class |
| 4:45–6:15 | Beginning yoga class |
| 6:30–7:30 | Dinner |

Retreat begins at 4:00 p.m. Friday and ends after lunch on Sunday.

**Other Activities**: Westerbeke Ranch offers beautiful areas for walking, sitting, reflecting, sketching, reading, and writing. Guests are invited to use the pool, hot tub, sauna, and racquetball court. Nearby Glen Ellen is the former home of writer Jack London. The historic Sonoma plaza, a short five minutes away, features many charming shops and restaurants. The area is surrounded by dozens of historic wineries.

**Services**: Massage is available.

**Guest Comment**: *"Wonderful food, homey atmosphere, great fires on chilly evenings. This is truly a peaceful place to do yoga and wind down from the hectic pace of everyday life."*
Diana Peats—Burlingame, California

**Summary**: Originally a Native American healing ground, the 100-acre home of Westerbeke Ranch is filled with the spirit of California heritage. Redwood cabins, a Mexican-tile dining room, a garden patio, and a selection of intimate and spacious meeting rooms make this setting a wonderful place to experience the autumn yoga retreat taught by senior Iyengar teachers Judith Lasater and Elise Miller. During the weekend, participants have the ranch to themselves to enjoy quiet walks under ancient oaks, soaking in the Jacuzzi, and restoring their energy through yoga.

# MOUNT MADONNA CENTER
# WATSONVILLE, CALIFORNIA

## YEAR-ROUND

Mount Madonna Center for the Creative Arts and Sciences is a community dedicated to the daily living of spiritual ideals through the practice of yoga. Located on 355 mountaintop acres of redwood forest and grassland overlooking Monterey Bay, the center offers a supportive atmosphere for relaxation, reflection, and a wide variety of learning experiences.

Inspired by the teachings and example of Baba Hari Dass, a yoga master from India, the Center supports residents, members, and guests in the spiritual disciplines of yoga, selfless service, and the pursuit of personal growth. Baba Hari Dass and his staff teach classic Ashtanga (eight-limbed) yoga. Mount Madonna Center offers several four-day Ashtanga retreats a year, and for those who would like to experience an extended period of living in a yoga community, there is a six-week resident program available. In addition to its own yoga retreats and trainings, the center hosts a variety of personal-growth workshops and yoga seminars with internationally renowned teachers. Call for a catalog.

**Address**: Mount Madonna Center
445 Summit Road
Watsonville, CA 95076
**Phone**: 408/847-0406
**Fax**: 408/847-2683
**E-mail**: programs@mountmadonna.org
**Web site**: www.mountmadonna.org

**Airport Information**: One and one-quarter hours from San Jose Airport and two hours from San Francisco International (more if traffic is heavy).

**How to Get There**: One hour north of Monterey, 45 minutes south of Santa Cruz on Highway 1, the Center is situated in the Santa Cruz Mountains between Gilroy and Watsonville.

**Teacher Background**: Various staff members of Mount Madonna take turns leading yoga postures and meditation sessions and assist in teaching the vari-ous courses offered. For background information on visiting teachers please call for a brochure.

**Style of Yoga**: The Mount Madonna staff offers Ashtanga (eight-limbed) yoga including methods of body/mind purification, asana, pranayama, *mudra* (energy raising techniques), and meditation. Visiting teachers offer other styles.

**Philosophy of Teachers**: "Programs offered are designed to nurture the creative arts and the health sciences within the context of personal and spiritual growth. The foundations of yoga and selfless service are the foundations of our lives. We try to live what is taught."

**Student Criteria**: All are welcome.

**Disability Access**: Complete wheelchair access

Mount Madonna Center

*Mount Madonna Center overlooking Monterey Bay*

**What to Bring**: Towels, a flashlight, warm clothing for cool nights, an alarm clock, sturdy shoes, toiletries, and a swimsuit for swimming or hot tub. Please do not bring pets, alcohol, drugs, or food. Please do not wear scented body products, as these can cause severe toxic reactions in some people.

**Yoga Room Size and Description**: There are three rooms used for yoga. The largest is 52' x 52'. The others are 28' x 40' and 28' x 32'. All have great views of the hills overlooking Monterey Bay.

**Number of Participants Possible**: Up to 200 for yoga programs. Guest capacity up to 500 people.

**Accommodations**: Indoor rooms are available for single, double, triple, or dormitory (four to seven people per room) occupancy. Some rooms have private baths; others share baths down the hall. Campgrounds are located in

secluded redwood groves and have running water. Tents are provided by the center.

**Meals**: Strictly vegetarian, highly nutritious meals are provided daily, including breakfast, lunch, snack, and dinner. Meals are served cafeteria style and include nondairy choices. The garden on the property supplies some of the fresh food that is served each day.

**Fee**: $29 for your own tent or van, $36 for one of the center's tents, $47 for dormitory or triple occupancy, $60 for double occupancy, $78 for single occupancy, and $92 for single occupancy with bath. Additional program fees vary depending on the length and content of program. Tuition fee for the four-day Ashtanga yoga retreats taught by the Mount Madonna staff and Baba Hari Dass is $75.

**Credit Cards**: Not accepted

**Sample Daily Schedule**: Varies widely with each program.

**Other Activities**: The center facilities include hiking trails; volleyball, tennis, and basketball courts; a large gymnasium; a small lake for swimming; and a hot tub. The beach and ocean are a half-hour drive away.

**Services**: Ayurvedic herbal steam treatments and oil massage are available.

**Guest Comment**: *"I arrived at Mount Madonna worn out and dispirited from my life in New York and an ongoing medical problem in my family. What I experienced was a place of great healing where I was able to nurture my mind, my body, and my spirit. Mount Madonna's location on top of a mountain felt wonderfully sequestered. The staff and residents were always friendly, helpful, and caring. The vegetarian food was superb. Yoga is a wonderful way to begin each day, and ours was gentle enough even for beginners. I left feeling empowered, with the heart restored to my art and my work in sacred and healing spaces."*
Karen Lukas — New York, New York

**Summary**: Mount Madonna Center provides a peaceful environment for individuals and groups from five to 500 people to rest and recharge their energy. With 355 mountaintop acres of redwood forest, grassy meadows, and beautiful views at 2,000 feet, the setting is expansive. The Center is inspired by Baba Hari Dass and is sponsored by the Hanuman Fellowship, a group whose talents and interests are unified by the common practice of yoga. The retreat center is open year-round and sponsors a wide variety of personal growth and yoga workshops.

# STEWART MINERAL SPRINGS RETREAT
# WEED, CALIFORNIA

*Yoga Retreat with Johanna (Maheshvari) Mosca*

## AUGUST AND SEPTEMBER
### FIVE DAYS EACH MONTH

The Stewart Mineral Springs is a 40-acre rural creekside mountain retreat widely known for its therapeutic mineral baths. It was founded in 1875 by Henry Stewart, who was brought to the grounds when he was on the verge of death. Stewart regained his health and attributed his recovery to the miraculous healing qualities of the mineral water and the incredibly beautiful environment.

Located just 15 miles from Mount Shasta, the wooded site includes an A-frame house, five private cabins, six apartment units, four dormitories, three authentic Native American–style teepees, a number of campsites, and a Native American sweat lodge. The main attraction is the bathhouse, which offers 13 individual bathing rooms where the mineral water is piped into old-fashioned tubs for guests to relax in while listening to soothing music. There is also a large wood-heated sauna and a meditation room. The property is landscaped with ponds, gazebos, bridges, and pools. Yoga teacher Johanna (Maheshvari) Mosca of Sedona Spirit Yoga leads five-day yoga retreats in this healing environment during the time of the full moon in August and September.

**Address**: Johanna (Maheshvari) Mosca
Sedona Spirit Yoga
P.O. Box 278
Sedona, AZ 86339
**Phone**: 520/282-9592
**Fax**: 520/282-9592
**E-mail**: yogalife@sedona.net

**Airport Information**: The closest airport is Redding. The nearest major airports are in Sacramento, San Francisco, and Reno. The Greyhound bus stops in the town of Mount Shasta, where tour leaders will meet participants.

**How to Get There**: Weed is in Northern California, north of Redding.

**Teacher Background**: Johanna (Maheshvari) Mosca, Ph.D., has been teaching yoga for more than 10 years. She is a certified Kripalu yoga teacher and a Phoenix Rising yoga therapist.

**Style of Yoga**: Gentle Hatha yoga, Kripalu yoga, and Phoenix Rising yoga partner sessions. Sedona Spirit yoga begins with Kripalu yoga of compassion and combines a variety of yoga styles, toning, and chakra balancing.

**Philosophy of Teacher**: "Yoga helps develop, strengthen, and integrate mind, body, and spirit. Through practicing the eight limbs of yoga in our daily lives, we learn to release unwanted energies, receive divine grace, and follow inner guidance or knowing. Yoga cleanses and opens us to connect from the heart in harmony with all that is."

**Student Criteria**: This retreat is for beginners. You must be able to do easy hiking.

**Disability Access**: Stewart Springs Resort is disability accessible, although there is no access for the hiking part of the program.

**What to Bring**: Comfortable yoga clothes, shorts and T-shirts, long-sleeved shirts and pants, sweat clothes, light jacket, one dressy outfit, swimsuit, towel, bathrobe, sunscreen, hat, sunglasses, hiking boots, small hiking backpack, and water bottle.

**Yoga Room Size and Description**: Yoga is practiced in a 16' x 24' carpeted lower-level room of the A-frame house. Outdoor yoga is practiced on two 14' x 30' decks that overlook the creek.

**Number of Participants Possible**: 15

**Accommodations**: Yoga participants stay in an A-frame house and in two cabins on the property. The three-floor A-frame has five bedrooms: two with two twin beds, two with one full bed, and one with a king-sized bed. Guests share three bathrooms. The cabins are nearby, and each has two twin beds or two full beds, a bathroom, and a kitchen.

**Meals**: Three daily vegetarian meals are included. Lunches will include sandwiches and salads—picnic style—to be carried on hikes.

**Fee**: $895 per person (double occupancy); $100 additional fee for single occupancy; $1,595 per couple (same bed). This includes lodging, three meals daily, yoga classes, sweat lodge, mineral baths, and guided hiking tours.

**Credit Cards**: Not accepted

**Sample Daily Schedule**:

| | |
|---|---|
| 7:30–9:30 a.m. | Yoga, pranayama and chakra balancing |
| 9:30–10:30 | Breakfast |
| 10:30–3:30 p.m. | Guided hiking and meditation tours to Mount Shasta |
| 3:30–6:30 | Free time for mineral baths, optional posture clinics for refining postures |
| 6:30–7:30 | Dinner |
| Evening | Welcome orientation, Eight Limbs of Yoga workshop, a Native American sweat lodge, fire circle, and final celebration |

**Other Activities**: The area offers hiking, swimming, fishing, boating, mountain biking, mountain climbing on Mount Shasta, and shopping in Shasta City. Stewart Springs has mineral baths, a sauna, and decks for sunbathing.

**Services**: Private massage, energy balancing, and Phoenix Rising therapy sessions are available.

**Guest Comment**: *"It was renewing for me to be at the Stewart Mineral Springs, sharing the peace of yoga, the healing mineral baths, and the ethereal energy of Mount Shasta. My yoga with Johanna was a sacred spiritual practice. I treated my body as a temple and felt my heart open to overflowing."*
     Diana Spirit Hawk—Laguna Beach, California

**Summary**: This retreat, offered by yoga teacher Johanna (Maheshvari) Mosca, is a gathering of those who wish to explore yoga, enjoy healing mineral baths, and hike and meditate in the natural beauty and spiritual energy of Mount Shasta during the full moon. Included is a Native American sweat lodge ceremony, evening fire circle gatherings with drumming, an interactive workshop on the eight limbs of yoga, and guided hiking tours of Mount Shasta.

# WILBUR HOT SPRINGS
# WILLIAMS, CALIFORNIA

*Spring Renewal Hatha Yoga Retreat with Annalisa Cunningham*

## MAY
### FIVE DAYS, FOUR NIGHTS

For centuries, the powerful hot mineral waters of Wilbur Hot Springs have drawn people to seek out its healing properties. Sheltered by a bathhouse, the water is channeled into three long baths with temperatures ranging from a gentle 98 degrees Fahrenheit to a challenging 112 degrees. There is also a cool mineral-water swimming pool outdoors next to a hot mineral sitting pool and a dry sauna.

Every year yoga instructor Annalisa Cunningham brings people to the springs for her annual Spring Renewal Hatha Yoga Retreat. Guests stay in a three-story historic hotel that is sheltered in a 240-acre private valley within a 15,000-acre nature preserve. The property offers panoramic ridge views, peaceful valleys, high meadows, and rare remnants of century-old mining operations.

**Address**: Wilbur Hot Springs
Wilbur Springs, CA 95987-9709
**Phone**: 530/473-2306
**Web site**: www.wilbursprings.com

**Yoga Teacher**: Annalisa Cunningham
**Address**: P.O. Box 3363
Chico, CA 95927
**Phone**: 530/343-9944
**E-mail**: RioAnalisa@aol.com

**Airport Information**: Wilbur Hot Springs is one and one-half hours north of the Sacramento Airport and two and one-half hours northeast of San Francisco.

**How to Get There**: In the Coastal Range foothills of Colusa County, the hotel is 22 miles west of Williams and 22 miles east of Clearlake.

**Teacher Background**: Annalisa Cunningham, M.A. Counseling, has been offering yoga classes and retreats since 1985. She is certified in Ananda Yoga Teacher Training and White Lotus Teacher Training and as an Integrative Yoga Therapist.

**Style of Yoga**: Gentle Hatha yoga. Annalisa combines yoga postures, breath awareness, visualization, and meditation practice with an emphasis on mind/body healing.

**Philosophy of Teacher**: "It takes willingness, patience, and acceptance to practice yoga. Our bodies have their own rates of opening and surrender. Our inner wisdom will guide us as we pay attention. Accepting where we are now while patiently continuing to practice brings healing to the body, mind, and spirit."

**Student Criteria**: All are welcome.

**Disability Access**: No access

**What to Bring**: Yoga mat and blanket, a robe, slip-on/off shoes for use in hot springs, towels, sunscreen, toiletries, casual clothes, walking or hiking shoes, and a journal for writing.

**Yoga Room Size and Description**: Yoga is practiced on a large, covered wooden deck up a trail on the side of a hill overlooking the valley. The deck has two levels: 15' x 20' and 20' x 30'.

**Number of Participants Possible**: 16. Spouses and friends are welcome at the hotel, provided space is available.

**Accommodations**: The hotel offers a choice of 21 private guest rooms. All rooms have their own special touches and Victorian flavor. None of the rooms has a television or phone. There is also a comfortable 11-bed bunk room for those on a more modest budget. The toilets are located, European style, in nearby rooms throughout the hotel. Private showers are found outside, adjacent to the bathhouse. There are a few campsites.

**Meals**: The retreat includes a catered vegetarian dinner each evening. You prepare your other meals. Wilbur has a large professional kitchen, well equipped with cookware, utensils, and dishes.

**Fee**: $395 per person includes private room (double occupancy) for four nights, four catered vegetarian dinners, daily yoga classes, guided hikes, and full use of the facility, including the hot springs, pool, and sauna. Pay $365 per person if you want to sleep in the bunk room, $295 per person if you want to camp.

**Credit Cards**: Not accepted

**Sample Daily Schedule**:

| | |
|---|---|
| 8:00–10:00 a.m. | Yoga practices |
| 11:00 | Brunch |
| 1:30 p.m. | Optional group walks, wildflower hike in Bear Valley exploring the nature preserve |
| 4:00 | Soak in the hot springs |
| 5:00–6:30 | Yoga practices |
| 7:00 | Dinner |
| 9:00 | Evening meditation |

The retreat is held Monday through Friday, a quiet time at Wilbur Hot Springs.

**Other Activities**: Expansive decks surround the pool, sauna, and hot springs area, giving lots of space for basking in the sun, sitting in the shade, and enjoying the beauty outdoors. Inside the hotel there is a large library for reading, writing, and snoozing. The great room provides billiards, a piano, guitars, and a few bamboo flutes for guests to share and enjoy. The area is excellent for walking, hiking, jogging, and mountain biking. Stargazing on a clear night while sitting in a hot mineral pool is an awesome experience.

**Services**: Professional massage and body work is available.

**Guest Comment**: *"Wilbur Hot Springs is a wonderful environment. The wilderness area that surrounds the retreat provides a relaxing atmosphere for walking, sunning, meditation, and yoga. The experience of doing yoga and soaking in the soothing waters enhanced my ability to relax and practice my breathing and meditation. Annalisa's retreat gave me time to enjoy both the peaceful solitude of the setting and the company of others."*
Patricia Smiley—Chico, California

**Summary**: Combining yoga practice with soaking in the mineral waters, daily walks, wildflower hikes, reflective writing exercises, and stargazing at night make this yoga retreat a quiet, healing, renewal time. Springtime brings a wide variety of wildflowers, while birdwatching is excellent and wildlife thrive year-round.

SEE PHOTO, BACK COVER.

# TRINITY AND KLAMATH RIVERS
# WILLOW CREEK, CALIFORNIA

*Yoga and White Water Canoe Trip with Mary Pafford and Dezh Pagen*

## JULY
### ONE WEEK

This trip offers seven days of canoeing on the beautiful Trinity and Klamath rivers in Northern California, camping in secluded coves along the way, and practicing yoga each morning and evening while relaxing by the river. The group canoes for three to six hours each day, guided by canoe instructor Dezh Pagen. Dezh paddles between the canoes in his kayak, informing people of what is ahead, suggesting ways to navigate the rapids or rocks, and checking on those who need more guidance. Canoes glide with the current most of the time, but occasionally the group must maneuver through rapids. Although participants do wear lifejackets, it is essential to be a competent swimmer. In the late afternoon the group sets up camp in a sandy cove, where participants unwind with a yoga session before dinner. As night falls participants circle around a campfire to tell stories, sing, and eventually drift off to sleep with the sound of the river flowing gently by.

**Address**: Mary Pafford
c/o Canoe Yoga
511 Fitch St.
Healdsburg, CA 95448
**Phone**: 707/433-5432; talk to Susan
**E-mail**: slb95448@aol.com

**Airport Information**: Eureka, which is small, has the nearest airport. Some people fly from San Franciso to Eureka.

**How to Get There**: The trip begins in Willow Creek, which is one hour east of Arcata, one and one-half hours northeast of Eureka, and six hours north of San Franciso.

**Teacher Background**: Mary Pafford has studied with many senior Iyengar teachers worldwide and with the Iyengar family in India. Upon completing the teacher training program at the Iyengar Institute

in San Francisco in 1985, she began to teach classes and workshops in California, Hawaii, and other parts of the United States and in Europe. Her practices have been influenced by the work of Angela Farmer and her own Vipassana meditation practice, out of which and into which her asana practice flows.

Dezh Pagen is the director and chief instructor of Laughing Heart Adventures Trinity Outdoor Center. Dezh has a B.A. in Outdoor Recreation, an M.A. in Environmental Education, and more than 16 years experience in leading groups on outdoor adventures. He is a white-water-rafting guide, certified canoe instructor, EMT-1, and farmer.

**Style of Yoga**: Mary's teaching draws on many influences, including her work with Angela Farmer, her interest in body-mind centering and other body work disciplines, and commitment to her Vipassana meditation practice.

**Philosophy of Teacher**: "In my work I strive, through the profound and the playful, to unearth the inner guru."

**Student Criteria**: Some yoga experience is helpful, and some canoe experience is helpful, although neither is essential. Participants must be competent swimmers. This trip is not appropriate if you have serious back problems.

**Disability Access**: No access

**What to Bring**: Sleeping bag, tent, camping gear, and rain gear.

**Yoga Room Size and Description**: Yoga is done on sandy beaches in the open air next to the river.

**Number of Participants Possible**: The group size is limited to 11 or 12 participants and four or five staff.

**Accommodations**: Beautiful tenting campsites next to the river.

**Meals**: A staff chef plans and prepares three tasty, simple vegetarian meals each day. Trip members are expected to help with the food preparation and cleanup. Bring your own munchies and snacks.

**Fee**: $700–$750 per person includes seven-day canoe trip, two yoga sessions per day, three vegetarian meals per day, and lots of information and guidance about the rivers.

**Sample Daily Schedule**:

| | |
|---|---|
| 7:00 a.m. | Morning yoga (vigorous, for waking up) |
| 8:30 | Breakfast |
| 9:30 | Break camp, canoe |
| noon | Lunch, canoe |
| 4:00 p.m. | Set up camp |
| 4:30 | Afternoon yoga (gentle, relaxing) |
| 6:00 | Dinner |
| 8:00 | Campfire stories |

**Other Activities**: While you're canoeing, the scenery is exquisite and gives opportunities for seeing lots of wildlife, such as eagles, herons, ospreys, and bears at close range. You may want to bring a camera. Once on shore most participants just want to relax in the sun or shade, while others enjoy exploring hiking opportunities and swimming in the pristine waters. Plan on all the usual activities involved in camping outdoors: loading and unloading the boats and camping equipment, setting up camp, preparing food, and cleaning up.

**Services**: Professional massage is available (without massage table, but with great hands) by arrangement.

**Guest Comment**: *"I've done this trip twice, and each time was very different. The adventure is multifaceted; the river is a challenge. Yoga in the sand is wonderful, and the groups are great. I would highly recommend this to anyone who is interested—the combination of canoeing and yoga sounds unusual, but it is a terrific adventure vacation. The Trinity is a beautiful river. Dezh is an excellent guide, Mary's yoga is very special, and the food is exceptional. A fabulous combo!"*
Susan Bierwirth—Healdsburg, California

**Summary**: This is a vacation that combines the tranquility of the river, the excitement of white-water canoeing, and the joys of practicing yoga in the open air. Participants spend seven days canoeing in the pristine waters of the Trinity and Klamath rivers, gliding past old-growth forests and canyons, camping in sandy coves, practicing yoga twice a day, and enjoying warm campfires and clear, starry skies at night.

# HOT SULPHUR SPRINGS RESORT
# HOT SULPHUR SPRINGS, COLORADO

*Weekend Yoga Retreat with Victoria Strohmeyer*

## MAY, SEPTEMBER, AND OCTOBER
### WEEKEND RETREAT

Hot Sulphur Springs is Colorado's oldest spa, established 130 years ago, and was discovered hundreds of years before that by local Native Americans. The Ute Indians considered these waters to be sacred and referred to them as "Big Medicine." In 1996 the local Ute Indians were invited to the rededication of the spa as a healing facility after new owner Charles Nash gave the resort a one-million-dollar renovation.

The entrance to the resort is through a winding, beautifully landscaped road that crosses the Colorado River. The resort is nestled at the foot of a hill, with 10 hot pools, private hot baths, and a summer swimming pool. Nature provides more than 200,000 gallons of fresh, hot spring water daily for the baths—and keeps them at temperatures of 104 to 112 degrees Fahrenheit. The elevation is 7,600 feet, and no chemicals or recirculation are used in the pools. Utilizing the relaxing, rejuvenating qualities of the waters, yoga teacher Victoria Strohmeyer brings people to the springs for her annual Hatha yoga retreat.

**Address**: Victoria Strohmeyer
P.O. Box 775524
Steamboat Springs, CO 80477
**Phone**: 970/879-2990
**Fax**: 970/870-0586
**E-mail**: Victoria@cmn.net
**Web site**: www.ytoc.org/strohmeyer

**Airport Information**: Fly into Denver International Airport and take a shuttle to Hot Sulphur Springs. (Local shuttle service is Home James, 800/451-4844). Cars may be rented at the airport.

**How to Get There**: Hot Sulphur Springs is approximately a three-hour drive northwest of Denver via I-70 to Highway 40.

**Teacher Background**: Victoria Strohmeyer has been leading retreats for more than six years and has 17 years of expe-

rience in the corporate world as a health-care executive. She teaches what she has had to learn for herself . . . to slow down and live life more simply and fully. Her training is in Kripalu, Phoenix Rising, and Bikram yoga, and she studied at the Himalayan Institute.

**Style of Yoga**: Kripalu Hatha yoga, with an emphasis on breathing practice (pranayama). Vigorous yoga posture series in the style of Bikram Choudury will also be taught, depending on the level of the students at the retreat. Partner yoga and colistening practices will also be included as part of yoga practice.

**Philosophy of Teacher**: "All the answers lie within you . . . often all we need is the time and space to access the deep well of inner knowing."

**Student Criteria:** An intention to access one's own inner voice and a willingness to open one's heart. Experienced and new students are equally welcome.

**Disability Access:** Hot Sulphur Springs does have handicap access to the lodge and the pools, but it does not have access to the sleeping rooms. Please call for accommodation suggestions.

**What to Bring:** Water bottle, swimsuit, large beach towel, layered clothing (it can be cool in all seasons in the mountains), personal items, meditation cushion or bench, shawl or blanket, and yoga mat. Some extra mats, blankets, and cushions are available if you don't have these.

**Yoga Room Size and Description:** Yoga is practiced in a large carpeted conference room that is adjacent to the solarium hot pool. The room is private and affords a quiet place for yoga and meditation. There is also a large outdoor deck, where yoga is practiced in nice weather. The view from the deck is of the river, mountains, and lush evergreen forest.

**Number of Participants Possible:** 20

**Accommodations:** There are 17 rooms at Hot Sulphur Springs. The decor is western/modern with double beds, queen beds, or two twin beds in each room. Windows show views of the Colorado River or the mountains. There are no televisions or telephones in the rooms. No smoking is allowed on the premises. Other hotels within walking distance can accommodate overflow.

**Meals:** Three vegetarian meals are served daily. Many of the meals are eaten in silence. Special diets can be accommodated with advanced notice. Some diets may require additional charge.

**Fee:** Cost ranges from $300 to $400 per person depending upon choice of room.

This includes weekend lodging, meals, and yoga classes.

**Credit Cards:** Not accepted

**Sample Daily Schedule:**

| | |
|---|---|
| 7:30 a.m. | Breakfast |
| 8:15 | Yoga, breathing, and meditation |
| 9:15 | Walk |
| 10:15 | Yoga and meditation |
| 11:00 | Walk |
| noon | Lunch |
| 2:00 p.m. | Partner yoga stretches and meditation |
| 5:00 | Dinner |
| 6:00 | Interactive talk, colistening |
| 8:00 | Meditation |

**Other Activities:** Hot Sulphur Springs has 10 hot pools, private hot baths, and a summer swimming pool. Hiking is available directly from the resort on 90 acres of hilly, wooded terrain. The Colorado River runs through the property, as does the Amtrak railroad. The small town of Hot Sulphur Springs (200 residents year-round) has a few shops and restaurants, all within walking distance of the resort.

**Services:** The resort offers massages, facials, and body wraps.

**Guest Comment:** *"The combination of yoga and soaking in the beautiful pools—in such a peaceful setting—is very healing."*
Josi Olson—Fraser, Colorado

**Summary:** This weekend yoga retreat offered by teacher Victoria Strohmeyer combines yoga with the healing, soothing qualities of hot sulphur baths. The resort is situated on 90 acres of mountain property bordering the Colorado River. The ambiance is quiet and calm and supports Victoria's encouragement for participants to slow down, feel deeply, and discover the miracle of breath, movement, and spirit.

# BELLYACHE MOUNTAIN RANCH
# OAK CREEK, COLORADO

*Yoga and Meditation Retreat with Victoria Strohmeyer*

## JANUARY, MARCH, AND AUGUST
### ONE WEEKEND EACH MONTH

The Bellyache Mountain and Resort is the oldest, highest working ranch in the state of Colorado. Drivers pass by many working ranches, rolling hills, and groves of aspens and pines en route to Bellyache Ranch. The county dirt road dead-ends at the entrance of the ranch; it then requires a four-wheel-drive vehicle in the summer and a snowmobile in the winter to arrive at the cabin itself, which is approximately two miles through aspen groves, national forest property, wooded glens, and high mountain meadows.

The Bellyache cabin is rustic but well maintained and comfortable. It has a wrap-around porch and a large hot tub that overlooks the meadow, stream, and small ponds. Because the resort used to be a hunting lodge, there are many trophy animals (stuffed animals), such as a pheasant, a ram, a coyote, and an elk hanging in the main lodge.

**Address**: Victoria Strohmeyer
P.O. Box 775524
Steamboat Springs, CO 80477
**Phone**: 970/879-2990
**Fax**: 970/870-0586
**E-mail**: Victoria@cmn.net
**Web site**: www.ytoc.org/strohmeyer

**Airport Information**: The nearest airport is the Yampa Valley Regional Airport in Hayden. It is a 30-minute drive from Steamboat Springs. Taxi service is available from Alpine Taxi ($38 round trip) 800/343-7733. You may also fly into Denver International Airport and take a shuttle to Steamboat Springs ($104 round trip with Alpine Taxi).

**How to Get There**: The Bellyache Ranch is about 45 minutes south of Steamboat Springs, near the town of Yampa.

**Teacher Background**: Victoria Strohmeyer has been leading retreats for more

than six years and has 17 years of experience in the corporate world as a health-care executive. She teaches what she has had to learn for herself . . . to slow down and live life more simply and fully. Her training is in Kripalu, Phoenix Rising, and Bikram yoga, and she studied at the Himalayan Institute.

**Style of Yoga**: Kripalu Hatha yoga with an emphasis on breathing. The focus is on mindfulness in body, mind, and spirit and on "being" instead of "doing," so all yoga, meditation, and pranayama will be slow, internally focused, and mindful. Partner yoga and colistening practices are included as part of the yoga practice. This is not a posture clinic.

**Philosophy of Teacher**: "All the answers lie within you . . . often all we need is the time and space to access the deep well of inner knowing."

**Student Criteria**: Experienced and new students are equally welcomed. An intention to access one's own inner voice and a willingness to open one's heart are good to have.

**Disability Access**: No access

**What to Bring**: Meditation cushion or bench and meditation shawl or small blanket, yoga mat (Victoria has some extra cushions and mats), sleeping bag, water bottle, layered clothing (it can drop to below freezing in all seasons in the mountains).

**Yoga Room Size and Description**: Yoga is practiced in the living room/ kitchen area of the retreat cabin. This area is approximately 600 square feet. Double glass doors from the living room open onto a deck surrounded by aspen and fir trees. A large meadow and small stream are also visible from the living room.

**Number of Participants Possible**: Six in the winter; more in the summer with camping.

**Accommodations**: There are two large bedrooms at the retreat, with a total of three double beds, three single beds, and one full bath. There is also an outdoor shower with hot water on the deck. This is a rustic, high mountain experience, and the accommodations require that you share rooms with others.

**Meals**: The meals are vegetarian, and most special diets can be accommodated with advanced notice (although some may require additional charges). Many of the meals are eaten in silence, and instruction will be given on conscious eating.

**Fee**: $300 per person includes meals, weekend lodging, and transportation to the Bellyache Mountain Ranch from Steamboat Springs.

**Credit Cards**: Visa and Mastercard

**Sample Daily Schedule**:

| | |
|---|---|
| 7:30 a.m. | Breakfast |
| 8:15 | Yoga, breathing, meditation |
| 9:15 | Walk |
| 10:15 | Yoga, meditation |
| 11:00 | Walk |
| noon | Lunch |
| 2:00 p.m. | Partner yoga stretches, meditation |
| 5:00 | Dinner |
| 6:00 | Interactive talk, colistening |
| 8:00 | Meditation |

**Other Activities**: There are dozens of hiking trails on the ranch that connect to the Flattops Wilderness trail system. There is a stocked trout lake within walking distance, and daily or weekly fishing licenses can be prearranged. The large hot tub on the deck of the cabin is operational year-round. You can ski and snowshoe in the winter.

**Guest Comment**: *"I went to Victoria's yoga retreat at Bellyache Ranch with a cluttered mind and left clear, refreshed, peaceful, mindful—and I found myself."*
Audrey Kole—Steamboat Springs, Colorado

**Summary**: Yoga teacher Victoria Strohmeyer offers weekend yoga and meditation retreats in this invigorating setting at the edge of a wilderness that extends for miles and miles. The Belly-ache Ranch Resort cabin is on the border of the Flattops National Wilderness area and offers spectacular scenery. High mountain meadows are filled with wildflowers in the spring, summer, and fall. A wide variety of wildlife abounds, including great horned owls, bald eagles, and many species of hawks. Participants support each other through compassionate listening and spend much time in sitting meditation interspersed with yoga, stretching, and walks.

# SHOSHONI YOGA RETREAT
# ROLLINSVILLE, COLORADO

## YEAR-ROUND

Named after nearby Shoshoni Mountain, Shoshoni Yoga Retreat was founded by Sri Shambhavananda, who believes that when people are allowed to rest and recharge in a nurturing environment, they naturally discover the beauty and love within themselves. The retreat sits on 210 acres of lush aspen groves, tall ponderosa pines, hidden valleys, and spring-fed streams. Bright prayer flags and large Buddhas painted on rock walls adorn the valley. Visitors are welcomed to log cabins nestled in the forest by the smell of sweet pine. Originally a children's summer camp, the property now has six rustic duplex guest cabins, a lodge, a meditation building, a shrine, and a temple. A large variety of wildflowers, including lavender, columbine, and Indian paintbrush blossom abundantly in spring and summer. Deer and elk are sometimes seen.

**Address:** Shoshoni Yoga Retreat
P.O. Box 410
Rollinsville, CO 80474
**Phone:** 303/642-0116
**Fax:** 303/642-0116
**E-mail:** kailasa@shoshoni.org
**Web site:** www.shoshoni.org

**Airport Information:** Denver International Airport. The retreat is a two-hour drive from there. There is a commercial ground shuttle from Denver to Boulder. Shoshoni staff will pick you up in Boulder for a fee.

**How to Get There:** Forty miles from Denver, high in the Colorado Rockies; 23 miles west of Boulder on Route 119, between Nederland and Rollinsville. Shoshoni is 35 minutes from downtown Boulder.

**Teacher Background:** Various trained staff members of Shoshoni Yoga Retreat take turns leading the yoga classes and assist in teaching various courses.

**Style of Yoga:** Classic Hatha yoga, with an emphasis on breath awareness and meditation. Classes are geared toward beginners, although those with more yoga experience can also be accommodated.

**Philosophy of Teachers:** "Shoshoni is a resident ashram (hermitage of yogis) and spiritual retreat. Our primary purpose is to assist people in the understanding and experience of their true nature, which is known in yoga as *sat-chit-ananda* (being-consciousness and bliss)."

**Student Criteria:** Everyone is welcome.

**Disability Access:** No access

**What to Bring:** Warm clothing, even in the summer months. Evenings can be chilly. Loose, comfortable clothes for yoga, swimsuit, sunscreen, and hiking boots. Also bring slippers or socks, as shoes are removed before entering all buildings. Yoga mats, pillows, and blankets are provided.

**Yoga Room Size and Description**: Two rooms are used for yoga. Both are carpeted and easily accommodate 15 people per class.

**Number of Participants Possible**: 25

**Accommodations**: Guests sleep in small, rustic cabins that offer the basics, plus some extras, such as all-natural toiletries. Sacred pictures of deities such as Ganesha, the Healing Buddha, and the Buddha of Compassion adorn the walls of each cabin, which are white, bare plywood, or pine. Each cabin has two to four beds, carpeting, and a bathroom with a shower. There is also a men's and women's dorm, which house four or more people. Campsites are available for those who bring tents.

**Meals**: Low-fat, nondairy vegetarian meals are provided. Many of the recipes are featured in the Shoshoni cookbook. Food is made with organically grown ingredients as often as possible. Ayurvedic meals are featured as well.

**Fee**: Prices include three vegetarian meals per day, daily yoga, meditation classes, and overnight accommodations. A private cabin with private bath is $125 per person per night; a double cabin with private bath is $75 per person per night; the dorm (men's or women's, four or more) is $60 per person per night. A retreat cabin (rustic) with a bathhouse nearby is $55 per person per night; and tent camping (bring your own tent) is $45 per person per night. Special programs are individually priced (call for a catalog).

**Credit Cards**: Visa and Mastercard

**Sample Daily Schedule**:

| 5:30–7:00 a.m. | Guru Gita and Arati (devotional ceremony) |
| 7:00–7:30 | Meditation |
| 7:30 | Breakfast |
| 10:00–10:30 | Pranayama |
| 10:30–11:50 | Hatha yoga |
| 11:50–noon | Chanting |
| noon | Lunch |
| 1:00 p.m. | Free time |
| 4:45–5:45 | Hatha yoga |
| 6:00–7:00 | Meditation |
| 7:00 | Dinner |
| 8:00–8:30 | Deep relaxation |

**Other Activities**: Wonderful hiking trails: a 45-minute hike through the aspen and pine forests leads to a view of the Continental Divide. A nearby lake hosts a few canoes and is inviting to those who like to swim in the summer. Eldora ski resort is 20 minutes away.

**Services**: Massage, aromatherapy facials, herbal body scrubs, and private yoga classes are available at an extra fee.

**Guest Comment**: *"Shoshoni is a place for true and deep soul nourishment. My whole being felt fed after spending three weeks at Shoshoni. So much is offered: yoga, scrumptious food, meditations, fresh, beautiful mountain environment—and added to this is the unique and special gift of the energy of genuine love carried and lived by the community members."*

Sanjiv Bhatnagar—
Durham, North Carolina

**Summary**: Shoshoni is a resident ashram and spiritual reteat center in a valley surrounded by national forest and mountain peaks. This peaceful sanctuary offers pristine mountain air, pure spring water, wonderful food, and the abundance of nature. The resident yogis open their home to visitors, giving them personal experience of the yoga lifestyle. They practice chanting and meditation daily and feel that the *shakti* (meditative energy) that permeates their environment is healing and cleansing and restores people who visit Shoshoni.

# CONQUINA BEACH VILLAS
# SANIBEL ISLAND, FLORIDA

*Iyengar Yoga with Bobbie Goldin*

## APRIL AND MAY
### ONE WEEK

With smooth white sand and amazing shells of all sizes and shapes, Sanibel Island, off the west coast of Florida, is one of North America's finest shelling beaches. Safe, friendly, and easily accessible from Fort Meyers, this 12-mile-long island offers a casual, laid-back Gulf of Mexico setting, with clear blue skies and daytime temperatures in the 80s. The fresh sea air from the Gulf of Mexico is warm and calming. With 20-plus miles of paved bike paths and more than 5,000 acres of wildlife refuge lands and waterways, Sanibel Island offers an ideal natural environment for practicing yoga.

Since the early 1980s Bobbie Goldin and the Yoga Institute of Miami have been bringing folks together to share yoga and a weeklong vacation on this beautiful island. Participants stay in charming condos on the beach. Sanibel is known for its variety of restaurants of all types and prices. Strict zoning ordinances and firm dedication to preserving nature keep buildings on the island less than three stories high, and shopping areas are tucked away among pines, palms, and tropical flowers.

**Address:** The Yoga Institute of Miami c/o Bobbie Goldin
9350 So. Dadeland Blvd., Suite 207
Miami, FL 33156
**Phone:** 305/670-0558
**Fax:** 305/661-9943
**E-mail:** BOBBiji@HotMail.com
**Web site:** www.Hutton.net/~Roy/yoga

**Airport Information:** Fly into Fort Myers.

**How to Get There:** Have Sanibel Taxi take you to Conquina Beach Villas, on Nerita Street and Middles Gulf Drive.

**Teacher Background:** Bobbie Goldin has studied with B. K. S. Iyengar in India and is certified by him. She is the director of the Yoga Institute of Miami and has been teaching there since 1971.

She is strongly influenced by Ramanand Patel, Felicity Green, John Schumacher, Gabriella Guilaro, and Judith Lasater.

**Style of Yoga:** Iyengar method of Hatha yoga. Bobbie is known for her ability to individualize in her classes so that everyone's needs are met and each feels personally touched.

**Philosophy of Teacher:** "We do yoga to quiet the mind and soothe the heart. When we are physically and mentally strong, elastic and stable, the quality of life is high, and then each day is a gift."

**Student Criteria:** Previous experience is not required. All levels will be encouraged to stimulate minds and bodies by expanding known boundaries and letting go from the inside.

*Yoga instructor Bobbie Goldin*

**Disability Access**: Yes

**What to Bring**: Please bring a yoga mat and a sturdy belt, along with an open mind and a sense of humor. Mats and belts are available for purchase.

**Yoga Room Size and Description**: Classes are held in the large, inviting community room of a local church, which is within walking, biking, or driving distance (two miles) from the beach housing. The space is light and airy, with ceiling fans and air-conditioning if needed.

**Number of Participants Possible**: 35

**Accommodations**: Participants stay in two-bedroom, two-bath condos right on the beach. Each unit is completely furnished with air-conditioning, TV, phone, full linens, a complete kitchen, and a washer and dryer. There are three to four people per apartment unless otherwise requested. The apartments are two miles from the yoga room.

**Meals**: Meals are of your own choice and at your own expense. There is a variety of restaurants of all types and prices on the island. Many feature excellent local seafood. There are also food markets and a well-stocked health-food store if you prefer to cook in the condo kitchen.

**Fee**: $710 per person for yoga and housing. $610 per person for yoga with no housing. $285 extra fee for a private bedroom or for housing for nonparticipating friends, if space allows.

**Credit Cards**: Not accepted

**Sample Daily Schedule**:
8:30–11:00 a.m.   Yoga session
5:00–6:30 p.m.   Yoga session
On some evenings the group meets for a Crystal Bowl Meditation and for instruction in massage and in Chi Gong.

**Other Activities**: Between classes there is time for bicycling (rent a bike) and all kinds of beach and water sports, such as windsurfing, sailing, fishing, kayaking, and swimming in the gulf. There is also a freshwater swimming pool at the condo as well as a tennis court. A golf course is within walking distance. Evenings commence with a spectacular sunset over the Gulf of Mexico and might include local community theater, comedy club, or a movie.

**Guest Comment:** *"Bobbie's gentle spirit, love of yoga, and dedication to her students are reflected in her high-quality, well-planned classes, taught with experience, sensitivity, and good humor. Thanks to Bobbi's attention to all details the gift of this magic week leaves you somehow touched . . . restored, renewed, and anxious to return the following spring for another retreat."*

Jane Bastian Barrett —
Holly Springs, North Carolina

**Summary:** Every year, yoga teacher Bobbie Goldin brings people to Sanibel Island for her weeklong Iyengar yoga vacation. This small, quiet island in the Gulf of Mexico offers an environmentally conscious resort area for practicing yoga. The island has bike trails everywhere and two wildlife and bird sanctuaries. The beach is one of the finest shelling beaches in North America.

# KALANI OCEANSIDE RETREAT
# HILO, HAWAII

*Seasonal Yoga Retreats*

## YEAR-ROUND

Kalani Oceanside Retreat comprises 113 coastal acres of botanical forest within Hawaii's largest conservation area. Situated on "the big island" of Hawaii, this retreat center is on the southeast shore of the island, which is rural, breezy, and sunny. Twenty acres are dedicated to landscaped lawns and retreat/conference facilities. On-site amenities include an Olympic-size swimming pool, two Jacuzzis, and a sauna. Among nearby attractions are a black-sand beach, tidepools, thermal springs, natural steam vents, Volcanoes National Park, botanical gardens, and hiking to waterfalls.

Throughout the year a variety of yoga teachers and vacation opportunities are available at Kalani Oceanside Retreat (see schedule below). Kalani accommodates groups of up to 100 people in three large lodges, seven cottage units, and a three-acre camping area. Often more than one group is using the retreat facility at a time. The sea cliffs of the Kalani coastal area provide for close-up views of turtles, dolphins, and migrating whales.

**Address**: Kalani Oceanside Retreat
RR 2 Box 4500
Pahoa Beach Rd.
Hilo, HI 96778
**Phone**: 800/800-6886 or 808/965-7828
**E-mail**: kalani@kalani.com
**Web site**: www.kalani.com

**Airport Information**: Fly to Honolulu, then fly to Hilo with Aloha or Hawaiian Air.

**How to Get There**: Kalani is 45 minutes from Hilo Airport, on the southeast shore of "the big island" of Hawaii.

**Disability Access**: Limited access; please call.

**What to Bring**: Flashlight, mosquito repellent, bathing suit, beach towel, snorkeling equipment, comfortable clothes, rain poncho, and a jacket for evenings.

Many of these items are available at the gift shop.

**Yoga Room Size and Description**: The room most often used for yoga and dance has a 2,500-square-foot suspended wood floor. There are also two other rooms available for group use. Two of the yoga rooms have wonderful views of the ocean.

**Accommodations**: There are three main lodges on the property. Each lodge features eight rooms, with shared and private baths. Also, eight private cottages for two, with private baths, are available. All rooms are simple, rustic, and comfortable and have adequate closet space and fans. There is also a three-bedroom, two-bath guest house available. Housekeeping services are included. For those who prefer to camp, there is a three-acre camping area with hot showers and restroom facilities.

**Meals**: The three meals daily are wholesome vegetarian (with fresh fish and chicken options), featuring local Hawaiian fruits and organic produce. Meals are served on the open-air dining lanai.

**Other Activities**: The black-sand beach, which is frequented by dolphins, is a 10- to 15-minute walk and is well worth seeing. There are tidepools with calm water for swimming and snorkeling and other ocean activities available, including kayaking, diving, surfing, and fishing. Nature exploration includes on-site native plants and orchards and nearby botanical gardens, Volcanoes National Park, waterfalls, warm springs, natural steam vents, and the world's newest beach at Kalapana. Amenities at the retreat center include a 25-meter three-lane Olympic pool, two hot tubs, and a sauna.

**Services**: Massage therapists offer various techniques of body work and Watsu (water shiatsu while floating in a warm spring).

**Summary**: Kalani Oceanside Retreat is located on 113 spacious acres along the sunny and secluded Puna Coast of the big island of Hawaii. Bordered by tropical forest and rugged lava coastline and near Kilauea, the most active volcano in the world, Kalani is the only coastal lodging facility within Hawaii's largest conservation area. The retreat center provides comfortable lodging, wonderful meals, large grass lawns, an Olympic-size pool, a sauna, and Jacuzzis. Guests can drive to nearby rain forests, snorkeling, and waterfalls.

# CALENDAR OF YOGA RETREATS AT KALANI OCEANSIDE RETREAT:

## JANUARY
## TWO WEEKS

**Yoga Teacher**: Manouso Manos
**Address**: Iyila Hawaii
c/o Leslie
8233 W. Third St.
Los Angeles, CA 90048
**Phone**: 213/653-0357

**Teacher Background**: Manouso Manos is a highly experienced senior certified Iyengar yoga instructor. Following more than 17 trips to Pune, India, and more than 26 years of practice, Manouso is a strong exponent of B. K. S. Iyengar's teachings.

**Style of Yoga**: Iyengar yoga.

**Philosophy of Teacher**: "Yoga has long been mankind's quest for reality and understanding."

**Student Criteria**: The first of the two weeks offered is designed for beginning and intermediate students. At least six months to one year of Iyengar yoga experience is recommended for beginners. The second week is designed for intermediate and advanced students.

**Number of Participants Possible**: 40

**Fee**: $1,300 per person for one week or $2,400 per person for both weeks includes accommodations at Kalani Oceanside Retreat Center, three meals a day, and all yoga classes with Manouso.

**Credit Cards**: Not accepted

**Sample Daily Schedule**:

| | |
|---|---|
| 7:00–8:00 a.m. | Pranayama |
| 9:00–noon | Yoga asanas |
| 12:30 p.m. | Lunch |
| Free time | |
| 4:30–6:00 | Yoga class |
| 6:30 | Dinner |

One evening each week will be devoted to questions and discussion.

**Guest Comment:** *"A week of yoga with Manouso Manos at Kalani Oceanside Retreat is an intense, transformational experience in a completely restorative environment."*
Leslie Peters — Los Angeles, California

～

# FEBRUARY
## ONE OR TWO WEEKS

**Yoga Teacher:** Lynne Minton
**Address:** P.O. Box 190121
Anchorage, AK 99519
**Phone:** 907/248-1965
**Fax:** 907/248-1776
**E-mail:** minton@alaska.net

**Teacher Background:** Lynne Minton has been a student of yoga since 1975. Lynne attended the summer quarter at the Iyengar Yoga Institute in San Francisco in 1980, has traveled to India three times to attend intensives with the Iyengars, and has frequented the Feathered Pipe Ranch and various other locations to continue studies with the best teachers of the method. She was certified by Iyengar in 1984. Lynne founded "Yoga, the Inner Dance" in 1982 and has taught yoga full-time ever since.

**Style of Yoga:** Iyengar yoga.

**Philosophy of Teacher:** "Embrace and embody the ethics and principles of yoga (the yamas and niyamas) while incorporating the discipline of practice (asana, pranayama, and dhayana) into daily life. We support each other in yoga by taking the practice, but not ourselves, seriously, so that the light and joy of yoga will not be lost on us but will shine through with increasing intensity as the veils become thin."

**Student Criteria:** Week one is for beginning-level students and week two is for intermediate-level students.

**What to Bring:** Yoga mat, belt, foam block, and foam shoulder stand pads or three firm blankets.

**Number of Participants Possible:** 40

**Fee:** $795 per person per week includes seven nights at Kalani Oceanside Resort, three meals daily, two yogas classes daily with Lynne, and evening programs.

**Credit Cards:** Not accepted

**Sample Daily Schedule:**

| | |
|---|---|
| 7:00–7:30 a.m. | Meditation (optional) |
| 7:30–8:30 | Breakfast |
| 9:15–11:45 | Asana class |
| noon–1:00 p.m. | Lunch |
| 1:00–4:30 | Free time (pool, beach, hot springs, massage, ect.) |
| 4:30–6:00 | Asana and pranayama |
| 6:00–7:00 | Dinner |
| 7:30 | Evening program. May include discussion, Hawaiian cultural events, or music |

**Guest Comment:** *"Hearing the birds, feeling the warm ocean breezes, master quality yoga instruction, and a fun-loving heart-warming atmosphere. It just doesn't get any better than yoga in paradise with Lynne."*
Rona Mason — Anchorage, Alaska

～

# APRIL
## ONE WEEK

**Yoga Teacher:** Amy Cooper
**Address:** Amy Cooper
2149 Danberry Ln.
San Rafael, CA 94903
**Phone:** 415/472-1330

**Teacher Background:** Amy Cooper has practiced yoga since 1981 and has taught in the San Francisco Bay area for the past 12 years. She is certified in the Iyengar yoga method and also has experience with Ashtanga yoga, Buddhist meditation, and yoga therapy; for more than 10 years she has been practicing as well as receiving body work. Amy is the instructor of asana for the Integrative Yoga Therapy Training Program.

**Style of Yoga**: Iyengar Hatha yoga. Amy's teaching offers an integrated base of practice, emphasizing self-exploration in mindful movement, healthy postural alignment, and breath awareness.

**Philosophy of Teacher**: "Cultivating an awareness of the body, mind, and breath as a source of discovering strength, flexibility, and balance from the inside out."

**Student Criteria**: Some experience in yoga or other mindful movement experience is requested.

**Number of Participants Possible**: 40

**Fee**: $775 per person for double occupancy or $725 per person for triple occupancy includes six nights accommodations at Kalani Oceanside Resort, three vegetarian meals daily, and two to four hours of yoga daily with Amy. Nonparticipating spouse or child over 12, $525; children from 3–12, $325.

**Credit Cards**: Not accepted

**Sample Daily Schedule**:
| | |
|---|---|
| 7:00–8:00 a.m. | Light breakfast |
| 9:30–11:30 | Yoga class |
| noon–1:00 p.m. | Lunch |
| 1:00–4:30 | Free time or island excursion |
| 4:30–6:00 | Yoga class |
| 6:00–7:00 | Dinner |

Evening time is open for rest, massage, optional hula, Hawaiian mythology, or other group activity.

**Guest Comment**: *"Amy's retreat provides a safe, nurturing, nonjudgmental atmosphere in which to expand your yoga practice. The setting in the wild and dynamic big island environment in and of itself is a treat. The combination of Amy's 18 years of experience practicing yoga, her gentle guidance, and the community created among the retreat attendees offers the perfect opportunity for new openings in oneself. I have attended two of Amy's Big Island retreats and am always amazed at the new strength that I have found in my body."*

Ann Salsbury—
San Francisco, California

# APRIL/MAY
## ONE WEEK

**Yoga Teacher**: Barbara Kaplan
**Address**: 1331 Linda Vista Dr.
El Cerrito, CA 94530
**Phone**: 510/232-9955

**Yoga Teacher**: Mark Horner
**Address**: 475 Chalda Way
Morago, CA 94556
**Phone**: 925/927-7279
**E-mail**: markyoga@best.com

**Teacher Background**: Barbara Kaplan has practiced yoga and meditation since 1978. She teaches ongoing classes at the Yoga Room in Berkeley and at her private studio in Oakland. Barbara studied with the Iyengars in India in 1992, and she is also a certified Phoenix Rising yoga therapist. Barbara enjoys leading partner yoga workshops and educating students in depth about the chakras.

Mark Horner is the codirector of the Yoga and Movement Center in Walnut Creek, California, where he teaches weekly yoga classes. Mark has been practicing yoga and meditation for more than 15 years. He has trained in both the Iyengar and Ashtanga Vinyasa styles of yoga. His background includes eight years experience as a certified rolfer and consultant. Mark is especially interested in exploring and sharing with others the purifying effects of yoga, which help to awaken our inherent ease, well-being, happiness and freedom.

**Style of Yoga**: Eclectic—Iyengar, Ashtanga Vinyasa, and partner yoga.

**Philosophy of Teachers**: "We strive to create a gentle, supportive yoga environment with clear guidance, humor, and passion."

**Student Criteria**: All levels are welcome.

**Number of Participants Possible**: 40

**Fee**: $1,025 single occupancy in lodge with shared bath; $875 double occupancy in lodge with shared bath, $950 double occupancy in private cottage; $730 camping. Includes room, meals, and classes.

**Credit Cards**: Not accepted

**Sample Daily Schedule**:

| | |
|---|---|
| 7:00–9:00 a.m. | Yoga Class |
| Breakfast | |
| Free time | (beach, snorkeling, waterfall, etc.) |
| 5:00–7:00 p.m. | Yoga class |
| Dinner | |
| 8:45 | Meditation |

**Guest Comment**: *"The yoga retreat with Barbara Kaplin and Mark Horner at Kalani Hanua was a scrumptuous feast for body and soul. From the warm and friendly service and accommodations to the delicious food so creatively prepared, to the wondrous sights and smells of the tropical island, and most of all to the wonderful yoga instruction given to us by Barbara and Mark, the depth of their understanding and love for yoga was imparted to us in a way that was safe, challenging, and inspiring. It resulted in a memorable week that truly transformed our bodies and nourished our souls."*

Marlene Tobias—Albany, California

# DRAGONFLY RANCH
# HONAUNAU, HAWAII

### *Yoga Retreat with Joyce Anue and Cheri Clampett*

## OCTOBER
### ONE WEEK

Near the ocean on a lightly traveled road, Dragonfly Ranch is just two miles above Honaunau Bay on the sunny Kona coast of the "big island" of Hawaii. This peaceful country estate is ideal for nature lovers. Nestled in a lush tropical setting, the main house is built under the canopy of a giant monkeypod tree and is a community space for all to enjoy. There are both indoor and outdoor dining areas, a large sun deck, and treetop-covered lanais with gorgeous views. Three additional suites offer unique guest quarters with private entrances. All facilities include secluded outdoor showers for bathing in the sunshine or under the stars. The area is famous for an abundance of playful dolphins, friendly turtles, and the finest snorkeling in all of Hawaii.

**Address**: Dragonfly Ranch
c/o Barbara Moore
P.O. Box 675
Honaunau, HI 96726
**Phone**: 800/487-2159 or 808/328-9570
**Fax**: 808/328-9570
**E-mail**: dfly@dragonflyranch.com

**Address**: Joyce Anue and
Cheri Clampett
24010 Summit Rd.
Los Gatos, CA 95033
**Phone**: 408/353-6264
**Fax**: 408/353-6476
**E-mail**: joyceanue@aol.com

**Airport Information**: Dragonfly Ranch is 45 minutes from the Kona airport.

**How to Get There**: Dragonfly Ranch is located in south Kona, directly above the Pu'uhonua O Honaunau National Historic Park.

**Teacher Background**: Joyce Anue is an Iyengar-based eclectic teacher. Her background as a physical therapist has given her a detailed understanding of body mechanics and movement. She has been teaching yoga since 1983 and studied with the Iyengars in India in 1984. Joyce specializes in yoga for back pain.

Cheri Clampett has been teaching and studying yoga for more than 10 years. She has studied with various teachers and received her yoga teacher training certification from the White Lotus Foundation and from Integrative Yoga Therapy. Cheri teaches a flowing yoga class with an emphasis on structure and the healing aspects of yoga.

**Style of Yoga**: Vinyasa-style and Iyengar-based yoga. Teachers allow freedom to explore internal awareness in asanas.

**Philosophy of Teachers**: "What we seek we already are. There's nowhere to look but inside." — Joyce

"I attempt to live my life and teach from a place of acceptance, self-exploration, and love."—Cheri

**Student Criteria**: All levels welcome.

**Disability Access**: No access

**What to Bring**: Yoga mat and strap, one firm blanket, writing tablet, comfortable clothes, sunscreen, beach towel, swimsuit, and walking shoes.

**Yoga Room Size and Description**: Yoga is practiced in an outdoor lanai overlooking the ocean (28' x 30').

**Number of Participants Possible**: 15

**Accommodations**: The main house has two bedrooms separated by a shared full bath with tub. The Dolphin Room has a queen-size bed and a single-framed futon. The Pele Room has a king-size bed. There are also three unique suites on the property, each with a private entrance, indoor bathroom, and outdoor shower.

**Meals**: Three meals are served daily. Special diets can be accommodated.

**Fee**: $1,500 per person includes all meals, lodging (dorm style, limited number of singles or doubles), all classes with Joyce and Cheri, transportation to and from airport, and one individual yoga therapy session per person.

**Credit Cards**: Not accepted

**Sample Daily Schedule**:

| | |
|---|---|
| 6:45 a.m. | Meditation or pranayama |
| 7:15–8:45 | Morning asana class |
| 9:00 | Breakfast |
| 10:00–11:30 | Group class exploring creativity (journal writing, movement work, psychodrama, partner yoga, yogassage) |
| 12:30 p.m. | Lunch |
| 1:00–5:30 | Planned island adventure (snorkeling, swimming with dolphins, or kayaking) |
| 6:00 | Dinner |
| 7:30–9:00 | Evening Program (yoga philosophy, dance, and hula class) |

**Other Activites**: Dragonfly Ranch is very near the Pu'uhonua O Honaunau National Historic Park, 10 minutes from Kealakeklua Bay Underwater Sea Life Preserve, and 15 minutes from Ho'okena Beach Park, a lovely sandy cove. These areas are famous for an abundance of playful dophins and the finest snorkeling in all of Hawaii. The Dragonfly provides towels and rents snorkel gear.

**Services**: The ancient Hawaiian rejuvenation treatment Lomi Lomi will be available by appointment.

**Guest Comment**: *"My stay at Dragonfly Ranch was very sweet. The warm days and cool nights of Kona were perfect for enjoying the open-air ambiance; lush, junglelike flora; and beautiful lanais. The tropical fantasy decorating theme was tastefully and playfully expressed in every room. The hostess and staff were helpful and welcoming. I loved kayaking and snorkeling in the pristine water of nearby Kealakekua Bay."*
Ron Meadow—Los Gatos, California

**Summary**: The Dragonfly Ranch offers a rich taste of the real Hawaii, where guests are made to feel at home. This unique estate has a view of the ocean and overlooks grazing land that provides a buffer of privacy—there's not a house in sight. This is a soothing and tranquil environment for yoga, and teachers Joyce Anue and Cheri Clampett combine their skills to give you a full and nurturing week. Afternoon planned island adventure is included.

# HANALEI COLONY RESORT KAUAI, HAWAII

*Yoga Retreat with Inez Stein*

## FEBRUARY
### ONE WEEK

The Hanalei Colony Resort is the only resort on Kauai's north shore that is located on the beach. The location is perfect for watching the beautiful sunrises over Hanalei Bay. There are eight two-story buildings housing six to eight condominium units in each building. The resort has a swimming pool and gas barbecue grills and offers free Hawaiian language classes.

Yoga teacher Inez Stein invites people to this Kauai Island resort for her annual yoga vacation. The north shore, with its spectacular waterfalls, lush tropical foliage, and pristine beaches, is nurturing and beautiful. The Hanalei Colony Resort is located on the beach in Haena across the bay from the Princeville cliffs, with mountains on the other side of the road. Winding paths through peaceful gardens connect the condominiums. A few miles past Hanalei Colony Resort is Knee Beach and the entrance to the Kalalau Trail, which winds around the rugged cliffs and lush valleys of the Na Pali Coast.

**Address:** In the Moment Yoga & Adventure Vacations
63 Cherrywood Dr.
Norwood, MA 02062-5502
**Phone:** 800/548-7651
**Fax:** 781/769-9341
**E-mail:** tours@conejo.com
**Web site:** www.conejo.com

**Airport Information:** Hanalei Colony Resort is less than one hour from the Lihue Airport. Transportation is not provided. There are taxi cabs and some bus service. Renting a car at the airport is recommended.

**How to Get There:** Hanalei Colony Resort is in Haena, just past Hanalei on Kauai's north shore.

**Teacher Background:** Inez Stein is a certified Kripalu teacher who has continuing training with Iyengar master teacher Patricia Walden. She has been teaching for more than six years and is the director of In the Moment Wellness Center in Norwood, Massachusetts.

**Style of Yoga:** Kripalu with Iyengar influence. Inez places emphasis on the meditative aspects of yoga leading to self-awareness. She is attentive to detail in yoga poses and sensitive to each individual's capabilities.

**Philosophy of Teacher:** "Yoga is a spiritual practice, bringing us back to the present moment. I stress being mindful of the body: listening to the body's needs and not pushing or straining."

**Student Criteria:** All levels are welcome.

**Disability Access:** No access

*Yoga instructor Inez Stein at Hanalei Colony Resort*

**What to Bring**: Yoga mat (if you have one), loose comfortable clothing, water bottles, hiking boots, and backpacks (if hiking). Mosquito repellent might be helpful.

**Yoga Room Size and Description**: Yoga is practiced close to the ocean in one of the large (approximately 450 square feet) condos with a lanai. Weather permitting, yoga is also practiced on the beach.

**Number of Participants Possible**: 20

**Accommodations**: Participants stay in condominiums that sleep up to four people (one queen-size bed and two twin beds). Each unit comes with a fully equipped kitchen and a private bath. The condos are homey and well furnished with rattan tropical furnishings. The condos have clock radios but no televisions or telephones. A pay phone is available at the office, and local calls on Kauai are free. Beach towels and mats are supplied, and maid service is provided every third day.

**Meals**: Meals are of your own choice and at your own expense. Local supermarkets and farmers' markets allow you to dine quietly in your condo, or the restaurants and hotels nearby provide a variety of cuisines and evening entertainment. One evening the group comes together for a potluck dinner.

**Fee**: Accommodations at Hanalei Colony Resort for the week cost $410 per person (double occupancy) for a garden-view unit and $490 per person (double occupancy) for an ocean-view unit. Call for single, triple, or quadruple occupancy price rates. Tuition for yoga and meditation classes is $95 per person per week. All meals, additional activities, and tours are at additional cost. Call for specific prices.

**Credit Cards**: Mastercard and Visa

**Sample Daily Schedule**:

| | |
|---|---|
| 7:15–8:45 a.m. | Morning yoga, with breathing and meditation |
| 9:00 | Breakfast (on your own) |
| Free time | Exploring the island with group tour adventures or solo activities. |
| 7:00 p.m. | Dinner (on your own) |

**Other Activities**: Guests may avail themselves of virtually any activity possible on the island, such as hiking, snorkeling, sailing, scuba diving, horseback riding, kayaking, helicopter touring, and surfing. Around the island there is plenty to see, do, and buy. Galleries, shops, and eateries are located along the east side of Kauai. For those interested in culture there's the Hawaiian Art Museum in Kilauea and the Kauai Museum in Lihue. The south side has Poipu for snorkeling and the grandeur of Polihale Beach and Waimea Canyon.

**Guest Comment**: *"In the Moment Tours in Hawaii had everything we never had in a group vacation before: yoga, strolls on the beach, kayaking, biking, hiking, exploring beautiful rainforests and waterfalls, and meditation in a beautiful serene environment. The best thing was, you could do it all or do nothing at all. It's your vacation, so relax your own way."*
Connie Villa and Nan Johnson —
San Diego, California

**Summary**: This yoga vacation takes you to the Hawaiian island of Kauai, also known as the Garden Isle. Participants stay in a luxurious resort condominium and enjoy morning yoga on the beach or inside with ocean views. Afternoon free time is allotted each day for island touring and adventure.

# PARADISE POINT RETREAT CENTER
## KONA, HAWAII

*Hawaiian Yoga Adventure with Julia Tindall*

## OCTOBER
### ONE WEEK

Japanese-style gardens amid a profusion of tropical flowers greet you as you enter the grounds of Paradise Point Retreat Center, located on an ancient lava flow on the Kona Coast of the big island of Hawaii. This is a small, exclusive, private retreat and conference center with its own semi-private beach. The secluded estate features Hawaiian elegance with a Japanese-style yoga and meditation room, comfortable dining and kitchen facilities, a swimming pool overlooking the ocean, a koi pond with waterfall, and a staircase providing beach access to Keauhou Bay. Yoga teacher Julia Tindall offers her annual yoga retreat in this private setting off the big island's sunny Kona Coast. The trip includes snorkeling instruction, swimming with turtles and manta rays, a dolphin show at the Hilton, and round-the-island touring.

**Address**: Julia Tindall
P.O. Box 601872
Sacramento, CA 95860
**Phone**: 916/486-4620
**E-mail**: yogajules@aol.com
**Web site**: www.globalff.org/Julia

**Airport Information**: Fly into Kailua-Kona Airport. From the airport rent a car and drive to Paradise Point Retreat Center.

**How to Get There**: Paradise Point Retreat Center is 30 minutes from Kona on the big island of Hawaii.

**Teacher Background**: Julia Tindall is a certified Sivananda yoga teacher, massage therapist, and hypnotherapist. She is the creator of the video *Beginner's Yoga with Julia*, which is based on what she refers to as "Standing Wave Yoga."

**Style of Yoga**: Julia teaches Standing Wave Yoga, which is a gentle beginner practice based on the awareness of breath consciousness in the body. Movements are performed with softness. She incorporates partner yoga, breath work, and Jnana yoga for the mind.

**Philosophy of Teacher**: "Yoga is the consciousness we bring to our lives. It is a tool to help us improve the quality of our lives, to help us to grow and rise to the challenges that life presents with consciousness and awareness. The opportunity that yoga gives us is to bring the awareness learned during practice into everyday living so that eventually, for the yogi, nothing is outside of yoga."

**Student Criteria**: All levels of yoga experience are welcome.

**Disability Access**: No access

**What to Bring**: Yoga mat, comfortable clothes for yoga, shorts and T-shirts, windbreaker, sweater, snorkeling equipment (cheaper to buy it than rent it), swimsuit, beach towel, good walking shoes for the volcano, insect repellent, and rain gear.

**Yoga Room Size and Description**: Yoga is practiced in a large Japanese-screened room. The carpeted room accommodates more than 20 students. While practicing yoga, students listen to the sounds of tropical birds and ocean waves.

**Number of Participants Possible**: 14

**Accommodations**: Paradise retreat has eight rooms available for guests. Most rooms have two twin beds and a private bathroom. There is one room with a king-size bed available. The rooms are simple and clean.

**Meals**: All breakfasts and two dinners are provided during the retreat. Full breakfasts include tropical fruits and egg dishes. The two dinners are by candlelight. All other meals are at your own expense. Nearby hotels offer a variety of restaurant choices.

**Fee**: $895 per person includes one week's accommodations at Paradise Point Retreat Center (double occupancy), breakfast every morning, two dinners, island tour, and all yoga classes with Julia. Not included is airfare, car rental, restaurant meals and drinks, entrance fees, kayak rental, and travel insurance (mandatory).

**Credit Cards**: Not accepted

**Sample Daily Schedule**:
8:00–9:30 a.m.    Hatha yoga practice
9:30                    Breakfast
Following breakfast there are daily excursions to beaches, snorkeling spots, kayak opportunites, hiking in Volcano National Park, shopping in Kona, and other island touring activites. Julia guides these daily tours and recommends her favorite places for enjoying delicious lunches and dinners. Included in the tour is a dolphin show at the Hilton and swimming with dolphins (with luck) at Kealakekua Bay.

**Other Activites**: Snorkeling; swimming; enjoying dolphins, turtles, and manta rays in the ocean; visiting the volcano and coffee plantations; sailing; kayaking; shopping; and island touring. The retreat center has a swimming pool and beach access.

**Guest Comment**: *"Fabulous trip! Full of variety, challenge, and excitement. The retreat center was private and cozy, with a beautiful yoga room and a lovely pool with views over the bay. The yoga was gentle and compassionate yet challenging. I learned breath consciousness for the first time. I am very stiff, but Julia was sweet and patient with me. We swam with dolphins and turtles and explored magnificent coral reefs. I'm going back next year."*
Mark Juarez — Sacramento, California

**Summary**: This trip offers a nice balance of yoga and sightseeing. The secluded retreat estate is set in lush landscaped grounds, complete with swimming pool, koi pond, and private beach. Yoga teacher Julia Tindall leads paticipants on various island excursions each day in addition to teaching morning yoga class.

# MANA LE'A GARDENS
# MAUI, HAWAII

*Seasonal Yoga Retreats*

## YEAR-ROUND

Mana Le'a Gardens is a retreat facility located on 55 acres of privacy and seclusion surrounded by beautiful meadows, grassy knolls, and lush tropical gardens. An ideal setting for yoga groups, Mana Le'a hosts several excellent yoga teachers each year.

The retreat center offers simple and elegantly decorated lodgings, excellent vegetarian food, and the loving "spirit of aloha" shared by a caring, attentive and dedicated staff. A swimming pool with a 75-foot water slide, two hot tubs, and a Watsu pool are beautifully situated beside the pool house, which has showers and massage rooms. A relaxing lounge area off an expansive yoga room has comfortable couches and a fireplace. It opens to the garden rest area, with its tropical pond and waterfall, and to the outdoor dining lanai, where delicious organic meals are served.

**Address**: Mana Le'a Gardens
c/o Michael Corwin
1055 Kaupakalua Dr.
Haiku, Hawaii 96708
**Phone**: 800/233-6467;
in Hawaii 808/572-8795
**Fax**: 808/572-3499
**E-mail**: mlg@maui.net
**Web site**: www.maui.net/~mlg

**Airport Information**: Fly into the Kahului Airport on Maui. The taxi from the airport to Mana Le'a Gardens costs $30.

**How to Get There**: Mana Le'a Gardens is 15 to 20 minutes from the town of Paia, Maui.

**Disability Access**: Limited access

**What to Bring**: Walking shoes or sandals with a good tread, sunscreen, insect repellent, flashlight, sun hat or visor, swimsuit, beach towel, warm jacket or sweatshirt, biodegradable bath articles,

camera with extra film and battery, and your journal.

**Yoga Room Size and Description**: Mana Le'a has a spacious, 1,000-square-foot yoga and meditation hall with hardwood floors and a wall of windows overlooking a lush tropical setting. A full-mirrored wall, a vaulted ceiling with skylights, along with indirect lighting and an excellent sound system all combine to create a peaceful and beautiful environment for Hatha yoga and meditation classes.

**Accommodations**: Rooms are tastefully decorated and accommodate a variety of sleeping arrangements, from private to semi-private to dormitory-style rooms. Sheets, towels, blankets, and pillows are provided.

**Meals**: Delicious gourmet organic vegetarian cuisine is prepared in a variety of styles: Italian, Greek, Asian, Mexican, Mediterranean, and more. Enjoy the fresh baked breads and desserts and homemade salad dressings served with vegetables picked fresh daily from Mana Le'a's own vegetable gardens. Special diets can be accommodated.

**Other Activities**: Hot tub, hiking, and swimming are available at Mana Le'a Gardens. Nearby excursions and activities include snorkeling; scuba diving; sailing; whale watching; trips to Hana and the Seven Sacred Pools, the Haleakala crater, and the botanical gardens; and shopping in Maui.

**Services**: Swedish massage, Watsu, Thai massage, Lomi Lomi, Shiatsu, and other body work methods are available.

**Summary**: This lush tropical Hawaiian setting is secluded and beautiful and provides a nurturing, healing, and rejuvenating environment for yoga. *Mana* means "the spirit of food of life," and *Le'a* is the Hawaiian word for "happiness and joy." Facilities include two hot tubs, a swimming pool, a solar-heated bathhouse situated adjacent to the guest rooms, a Native American sweat lodge on the property, and wonderful hiking opportunities.

# Calendar of Yoga Retreats at Mana Le'a Gardens:

## FEBRUARY
### One Week

**Yoga Teachers**: Rodney Yee and Mary Pafford
**Address**: Piedmont Yoga Studio
c/o Rodney Yee
P.O. Box 11458
Oakland, CA 94611
**Phone**: 510/536-8960
**Fax**: 510/536-8996

**Teacher Background**: Rodney Yee is the codirector, along with his wife, Donna Fone, of the Piedmont Yoga Studio in Oakland, California. He was a ballet dancer with the Oakland Ballet Company and the Matsuyama Ballet Company of Tokyo. He studied philosophy and physical therapy at the University of California at Davis and Berkeley. His Hatha yoga studies include intensives with the Iyengars in India in 1987 and 1989; extensive work with Donald Moyer, Manouso Manos, and Ramanand Patel. He is featured in many award-winning yoga videos and teaches workshops worldwide.

Mary Pafford has studied with many senior Iyengar teachers worldwide and with the Iyengar family in India. Upon completing the teacher training program at the Iyengar Institute in San Francisco in 1985, she taught classes and workshops in California, Hawaii, and other parts of the U.S. and in Europe. Her practices have been influenced by the work of Angela Farmer and her own Vipassana meditation practice, out of which and into which her asana practice flows.

**Style of Yoga**: Iyengar style, drawing on many influences. Both teachers utilize yoga and meditation to cleanse the mind and body, which allows for presence of being.

**Philosophy of Teachers**: "Yoga brings philosophy into action and unveils the natural beauty of our spirits."

**Student Criteria**: Experience with at least six months of yoga practice is recommended.

**Number of Participants Possible**: 30

**Fee**: $1,475 for single occupancy (limited space available), $1,300 for double occu-

*Yoga for the Young at Heart*

*Susan Winter Ward at Mana Le'a Gardens*

pancy, and $1,075 for a dorm (up to four people); $850 for nonparticipating spouses and children age 13 or over, and $450 for children ages 6–12. These prices per person include accommodations, meals, and classes.

**Credit Cards:** Not accepted

**Sample Daily Schedule:**

| 7:00 a.m. | Light breakfast |
| 8:00–11:30 | Yoga |
| 11:00–11:45 | Lunch |
| Free time | |
| 4:30–6:30 p.m. | Yoga |
| 6:45 | Dinner |

**Guest Comment:** *"This was a fabulous trip—Maui in February and yoga with two great and complementary teachers. Mana Le'a is gorgeous, with a great pool (and slide) and good food. The catamaran trip to see the whales up close was a highlight."*
Susan Bierwirth—Healdsburg, California

**MARCH**
**ONE WEEK**

**Teacher:** Susan Winter Ward
**Address:** Awakening in Paradise
P.O. Box 2228
Pagosa Springs, CO 81147
**Phone:** 970/731-9500; 800/558-YOGA
**Fax:** 970/731-9510
**E-mail:** info@yogaheart.com
**Web site:** www.yogaheart.com

**Teacher Background:** Susan Winter Ward, creator of *Yoga for the Young at Heart* (a collection of books and video and audio tapes), is an internationally recognized certified yoga instructor, author, and columnist based in Southern Colorado. Her programs are created and designed especially for seniors and beginners. Susan has been chosen as a cover model for *Yoga Journal* and has appeared in articles in numerous publications and television programs.

**Style of Yoga:** Yoga for the Young at

Heart is a gentle vinyasa or "flow" style of practice. It is a gentle adaptation of the Hatha yoga "Flow Series" as taught at White Lotus Foundation in Santa Barbara, California, and is a beginning practice that is adaptable to anyone's level of ability.

**Philosophy of Teacher:** "I believe in creating a loving atmosphere of self-acceptance, which makes the practice of yoga a personal pleasure and fun to do. I support each student in finding a pathway into their deeper self through Hatha yoga. I believe that the purpose of life is to recognize our own perfection and divinity, to create a foundation of peace within that we extend to the world. Yoga is that doorway to peace."

**Student Criteria:** All ages and levels of practice are welcome.

**Number of Participants Possible:** 25

**Fee:** $1,595 to $1,795, depending on type of room accommodations. Includes yoga classes, lodging, meals, excursions, evening events, one body work session, and surprises. Airfare is at your own expense.

**Credit Cards:** Not accepted

**Sample Daily Schedule:**

| | |
|---|---|
| 7:00–8:00 a.m. | Morning fruit and tea |
| 8:00–9:30 | Yoga for the Young at Heart and meditation |
| 10:00–11:00 | Brunch |
| 11:00–4:00 p.m. | Snorkeling and beach adventure or free time at your leisure |
| 4:45–5:45 | Gentle stretching and pranayama |
| 6:00–7:00 | Dinner |
| 7:30–9:30 | Evening of gentle stretching, pranayama, and guided meditation or Thai massage |

**Guest Comment:** *"The striking beauty and serene energy of Maui in and of itself is a treat. Combining these qualities with Susan Winter Ward's soothing demeanor and gentle yoga, as well as the meticulously kept facilities and delicious, healthy meals at Mana Le'a Gardens, has indelibly marked my heart and mind with the rich benefits of peace, fun, and courage to go within. I gratefully reap these benefits, even now, just by remembering my time on retreat."*
Jen Sobeck — Pagosa Springs, Colorado

# MARCH
## ONE WEEK

**Yoga Teachers:** Cheri Clampett and Joyce Anue
**Address:** 24010 Summit Rd.
Los Gatos, CA 95033
**Phone:** 408/353-6264
**Fax:** 408/353-6476
**E-mail:** joyceaune@aol.com

**Teacher Background:** Cheri Clampett has been teaching and studying yoga for more than 10 years. She has studied with various teachers and received her yoga teacher training certification from the White Lotus Foundation and from Integrative Yoga Therapy. Cheri teaches a flowing yoga class with an emphasis on structure and the healing aspects of yoga. She often incorporates yogassage, partner yoga, and restorative yoga into her classes.

Joyce Anue is an Iyengar-based eclectic teacher. Her background as a physical therapist and body worker has given her a detailed understanding of body mechanics and movement. She has been teaching yoga since 1983 and studied in 1984 with the Iyengars in India. Joyce specializes in yoga for back pain.

**Style of Yoga:** Vinyasa style and Iyengar-based yoga. Both teachers allow freedom to explore internal awareness while in asanas.

**Philosophy of Teachers**: "What we seek we already are. There's nowhere to look but inside."—Joyce

"I attempt to live my life and teach from a place of acceptance, self-exploration, and love."—Cheri

**Student Criteria**: All levels are welcome.

**Number of Participants Possible**: 40

**Fee**: $1,350 per person for a dorm, $1,450 per person for a semi-private room, and $1,550 per person for a private room. Includes accommodations, three meals daily, and all classes with Cheri and Joyce.

**Credit Cards**: Not accepted

**Sample Daily Schedule**:

| | |
|---|---|
| 6:30 a.m. | Optional meditation |
| 7:00–8:45 | Choice of gentle or vigorous asanas |
| 9:00 | Breakfast |
| 9:30–12:30 p.m. | Free time (island adventure or body work) |
| 12:30 | Lunch |
| 1:30–4:00 | Free time |
| 4:00 | Yoga, movement, dance or pranayama class |
| 6:00 | Dinner |
| 7:30–9:00 | Yogassage, partner yoga, sweat lodge |

**Guest Comment**: *"Cheri has a unique combination of grace, softness, and incredible strength that comes through in her teaching. Mana Le'a is the ultimate retreat center in that it's not commercialized. It's elegant yet rustic. The food is excellent, and the walking paths are wonderful."*
Steve Mewhinter—
Santa Barbara, California

≈≋

# SEPTEMBER
## ONE WEEK

**Yoga Teachers**: Elise Miller and Lolly Font
**Address**: P.O. Box 60746

Palo Alto, CA 94306
**Phone**: 650/493-1254
**Fax**: 650/857-0925

**Teacher Background**: Elise Miller is an intermediate senior certified Iyengar yoga teacher from Palo Alto, California. She has an M.A. in Therapeutic Recreation and has been teaching throughout the U.S. and internationally for more than 25 years. She has studied five times with the Iyengars in India and teaches special workshops on back care and scoliosis. Elise's joyous personality, ease of communication, and down-to-earth, precise, and nurturing teaching style endear her to students.

Lolly Font is the director of the California Yoga Center in Palo Alto, California. She has an M.A. in Education and Transpersonal Psychology and has been a certified Iyengar yoga instructor since 1976. Aiming for personal wholeness in her work, Lolly uses yoga and breathing to integrate the physical manifestation of the body with the emotional and spiritual aspects of the individual. Having recovered from arthritis through yoga, Lolly addresses special needs in her classes and in private practice.

**Style of Yoga**: Iyengar yoga

**Philosophy of Teacher**: "To provide the teaching of yoga in a safe environment, with precise instruction and the ability to handle special needs."

**Student Criteria**: Willingness to play and to learn.

**Number of Participants Possible**: 40

**Fee**: $1,195 per person for double occupancy, $1,095 per person to share a room with three to five people. Includes yoga, three vegetarian meals a day, and lodging.

**Credit Cards**: Not accepted

**Sample Daily Schedule:**

7:30–9:30 a.m.   Yoga class
9:30             Breakfast
Late mornings and early afternoons are free, with lunch served at 1:00 p.m.
4:00–6:00 p.m.   Yoga class
7:00             Dinner

**Guest Comment:** *"The accommodations were very comfortable; the food was heavenly!*

*Elise Miller has a unique ability to transform yoga into a very rewarding experience. Her humor, gentle encouragement, and style of yoga are invigorating yet relaxing. I came out of each class feeling mellow and worked out at the same time. I highly recommend these retreats for anyone who is stressed, having physical aches and pains, and would just like to drop out for a week."*

Bonnie Row — Mountain View, California

# LOTUS LIVING ARTS CENTER AT OAK SHORES WALNUT HILL, ILLINOIS

*Yoga Retreats with Marya Mann*

## JUNE, JULY, AND AUGUST

Oak Shores village is a community of homes set on 320 acres of rolling, forested hills and woodlands. The property has three lakes, hiking trails, old-growth forest, flower gardens, songbirds, a den of foxes, and wild blue herons gliding gracefully across morning waters. This natural area located in the heartland of America is the home of the Lotus Living Arts Center, where yoga teacher Marya Mann offers weekend and week-long yoga retreats. The Lotus Living Arts Center was created to provide a blend of education and vacation during which guests, students, and clients find new tools to initiate and sustain a lifelong process of creative personal development. The nonsectarian community of warm and open people provides space and training for the integration of body, mind, and spirit through innovative workshops, seminars, and classes. Yoga is practiced in a studio overlooking one of the lakes. The property has a 260-foot-diameter garden, in the shape of a dream catcher, where you can stroll down pathways past medicinal herbs, fragrant flowers, pools, shrines, and a waterfall.

**Address**: The Lotus Living Arts Center at Oak Shores
c/o Marya Mann
P.O. Box 111
Walnut Hill, IL 62893
**Phone**: 618/735-2280; 800/641-2254
**Fax**: 618/735-2574
**E-mail**: Dreamcat1@aol.com
**Web site**: www.LotusLivingArts.org

**Airport Information**: Nearby airports are St. Louis, Missouri; Mid-America in O'Fallon, Illinois; and the Mt. Vernon Airport. Transport from airports is available.

**How to Get There**: The Lotus Living Arts Center at Oak Shores is located in Walnut Hill Illinois, north of Carbondale and south of Champaign and about one hour east of St. Louis, Missouri. Oak Shores is halfway between Mt. Vernon and Centralia.

**Teacher Background**: From study with B. K. S. Iyengar and Continuum Dance with Emilie Conrad-Da'oud, Marya is experienced in the sacred arts. She was invited to become an initiate of the Agame Hindu tradition in Bali. Mentored by Jose Arguelles, Marya integrated cross-cultural spiritual technologies with dance, theater, and yoga for creative unfoldment.

**Style of Yoga**: Marya Mann has created a unique blend of the sacred arts of yoga, dance, and theater. Yoga Dance flows into precise alignment and focus while maintaining a sense of riding the waves of breath. At lunar times she teaches a tai chi–like Yin yoga, interspersed with stillness and surrender. At solar times her practice is more of a dynamic Yang yoga, or Ashtanga style, where students feel the swift art of placement and challenge the limits of self-control.

**Philosophy of Teacher**: "The purpose of yoga is to remove suffering and bring happiness. In our practice we purify the body and clarify consciousness. In the clear ground of our being we plant good seeds of happiness, abundance, and enlightenment. Concentration on the breath, in the eternal present, awakens the soul. We contact a state of love that exists now. And now. And now. And now. As the scriptures of yoga affirm, no effort is lost on the path."

**Student Criteria**: All that's needed is honesty, openness, and willingness.

**Disability Access**: Yes

**What to Bring**: Bring an open heart, a flexible attitude, a sense of humor, compassion, and friendliness. Also bring loose, comfortable clothing, a hat, sunscreen, a yoga mat, and a sash.

**Yoga Room Size and Description**: Yoga is practiced in a 20' x 30' room overlooking Emerson Lake, on an open-air deck above the water, and in forested glades throughout the land.

**Number of Participants Possible**: 25

**Accommodations**: Lodging at the Lotus includes four bungalows with a total of 10 rooms. Guests sleep in single and double rooms with air conditioning, private baths, and balconies overlooking Emerson Lake. Camping is also available.

**Meals**: Vegetarian meals are available, served privately or community-style.

**Fee**: Weekend yoga retreats are generally $175 per person, depending on room choice (lake view, hot tub, and style).

Bed-and-breakfast arrangements range from $50 to $125 per night. Additional meals cost $10 per meal. Yoga classes are $15 per class. Private yoga sessions are between $40 and $60. Weeklong Yoga Arts programs range from $550 to $750 per person, including room, meals, and classes.

**Credit Cards**: Not accepted

**Sample Daily Schedule**:

| | |
|---|---|
| 7:00 a.m. | Yoga at dawn |
| 8:00 | Breakfast |
| 9:00 | Meditation at a sacred site |
| 10:30 | Dance movement class |
| noon | Lunch, free time |
| 6:00 p.m. | Dinner |
| 8:00 p.m. | Evening Satsang |

**Other Activities**: Swimming, fishing, boating, snorkeling in the lakes, hiking, bird-watching, enjoying the wildlife. Enjoy the nearby tennis courts, golf course, and campgrounds.

**Services**: Massage is available.

**Guest Comment**: *"Coming to the Lotus changed my life. The yoga, the enthusiasm, the beauty of nature, and the visionary weaving of art and nature combine to make the Lotus at Oak Shores an oasis of peace and healing."*
Susan Minor—Walnut Hill, Illinois

**Summary**: Oak Shores is a 320-acre nature preserve with lakes, forest, prairie, wildlife, and woodland hiking trails. The Lotus Living Arts at Oak Shores offers weekend and weeklong yoga retreats as well as other workshops and seminars. Daily yoga, dance, and art are integrated to create the Living Arts lifestyle. Yoga teacher Marya Mann fosters an appreciation of art, movement, and beauty.

# ORBIS FARM
# MAUCKPORT, INDIANA

## *Weekend Hatha Yoga Retreats*

## APRIL, JULY, AND OCTOBER
### WEEKEND RETREATS

Orbis Farm is a meditation center dedicated to the creation of an extended family of like-minded people working on personal growth. Orbis Farm hosts five weekend Hatha yoga retreats every year.

The Orbis Farm began as a dream for owners Helen McMahan and Betty Cole, who opened up their home as a retreat center and workshop facility in 1987. Located on 75 acres of woodland criss-crossed by many walking trails, Orbis Farm sits on beautiful rolling terrain within a valley of the largest hill in Southern Harrison County. The caretakers of this land have designed a large cocreative garden, where vegetables, flowers, and more than 75 herbs are grown. There are benches, chimes, bird feeders and birdbaths in the garden to enhance meditation. The farm is exceedingly private, although easy to find.

**Address**: Orbis Farm
c/o Helen McMahan and Betty Cole
8700 Ripperdan Valley Rd. SW
Mauckport, IN 47142
**Phone**: 812/732-4657
**E-mail**: ORBISFARM@aol.com

**Airport Information**: Fly into Louisville (Kentucky) International Airport.

**How to Get There**: Orbis Farm is situated at the southernmost tip of Indiana, just 40 miles west of Louisville, Kentucky.

**Disability Access**: No access

**What to Bring**: Yoga mats, blocks, belts if you have them (but they are not necessary), and comfortable clothes for yoga.

**Yoga Room Size and Description**: Yoga classes are held in a 20' x 40' car-

peted room overlooking the Orbis Farm garden across a grass meadow.

**Accommodations**: The Yoga Pavilion is a rectangular ranch-style house that has two 15' x 40' dormitories downstairs and a yoga room upstairs. There are 20 beds total: one queen, one double, and the rest singles. The two dormitories are separated by a hallway/vanity area. There is a screened porch with a hot tub off the dorm rooms. Upstairs is the yoga room, two bathrooms with showers, a small kitchenette, and a private room for use by a couple. The place is informal, like Grandma's house, where friends and relatives sleep in spare beds and share the bathrooms; nothing matches, but all the essentials are there: bedding, towels, and the feeling of family. Peaceful views of the garden and woods are seen through windows in every room.

**Meals**: Three vegetarian home-cooked meals are served each day on weekend yoga retreats. Much of the food is grown in the garden and is very appealing, even to people who are not vegetarian.

**Other Activities**: The hiking at Orbis Farm is wonderful. Alligator Trail beckons you to a huge rock outcropping that looks just like an alligator! The Still Point exists in a silent grove of cedars at a natural rock stage. The garden is a nurturing place to visit. Beds of vegetables and splashes of vibrant flowers interspersed with more than 75 herbs allow for beauty in sight and smell. A hot tub on the back porch of Orbis Farm invites aching muscles, pains, and cares to be soaked away.

**Guest Comment**: *"I can't say enough about Orbis. Helen and Betty work very hard to make a place of peace and rejuvenation. The garden is a part of the visit I really enjoyed. We were encouraged to go there to walk and meditate. The woods surrounding the retreat center provided lots of space for everyone who wanted to hike or take time alone."*
Saundra Duffee — Jeffersonville, Indiana

**Summary**: This 75-acre property holds its retreats in a big farmhouse that serves as a place to rest, be nurtured, and grow. The yoga pavilion overlooks the organic garden, the heart of Orbis Farm. Vegetables, flowers, and herbs are grown cocreatively with nature and are used in the meals provided for guests. Weekend Hatha yoga retreats are offered five times each year: two in April, one in July, and two in October.

## CALENDAR OF YOGA RETREATS AT ORBIS FARM:

### APRIL AND OCTOBER
#### WEEKEND RETREATS

**Yoga Teacher**: Amanda McMaine Smith
**Address**: 154 Redwood Dr.
Richmond, KY 40475
**Phone**: 606/624-0413
**Fax**: 702/831-7711

**Teacher Background**: Amanda McMaine Smith has studied the Iyengar method for 10 years and has further enriched her learning under the instruction of Angela Farmer.

**Style of Yoga**: Hatha yoga. Amanda leads her students through breathing meditations and stretches and encourages her students to develop their own yoga practices instead of becoming followers of a particular system. Emphasis is on unfolding the body's own wisdom and needs.

**Philosophy of Teacher**: "Yoga is that discipline which connects us with something far greater than ourselves."

**Student Criteria**: No experience necessary. All are welcome.

**Number of Participants Possible**: 20

**Fee**: $180 per person for a weekend yoga retreat that begins with dinner on Friday at 6:00 p.m. and ends Sunday at 2:30 p.m., after lunch.

**Credit Cards**: Not accepted

**Sample Daily Schedule**:
| | |
|---|---|
| 8:00 a.m. | Breakfast |
| 10:00 | Yoga class |
| 12:30 p.m. | Lunch |
| 4:00 | Yoga class |
| 6:30 | Dinner |

Sessions after dinner are usually devoted to meditation.

## APRIL AND OCTOBER
### WEEKEND RETREATS

**Yoga Teacher**: Lorrie Collins
**Address**: 1741 Minturn Ln.
Indianapolis, IN 46206
**Phone**: 317/253-7302

**Teacher Background**: Lorrie Collins, Ph.D., founded Yoga Alive in Indianapolis. She has taught yoga for more than 28 years and is the author of *Yoga Alive: A Beginner's Manual*.

**Style of Yoga**: Iyengar. Lorrie encourages an exploration of core yoga practice, which involves "energy breathing" and nurturing relaxation and meditation.

**Philosophy of Teacher**: "Yoga unveils the natural beauty of our spirits. Yoga cleanses body/mind to allow our presence of being."

**Student Criteria**: All are welcome.

**Number of Participants Possible**: 20

**Fee**: $180 per person; retreat begins with dinner on Friday at 6:00 p.m. and ends Sunday at 2:30 p.m., after lunch.

**Credit Cards**: Not accepted

**Sample Daily Schedule**:
| | |
|---|---|
| 8:00 a.m. | Breakfast |
| 10:00 | Yoga class |
| 12:30 p.m. | Lunch |
| 4:00 | Yoga class |
| 6:30 | Dinner |

Meditation sessions usually follow dinner.

≋

## JULY
### WEEKEND RETREAT

**Yoga Teachers**: Helen McMahan and Linda Smith

**Address**: 8700 Ripperdan Valley Rd. S.W. Maukport, IN 47142

**Phone**: 812/732-4657

**Teacher Background**: Helen McMahan holds an M.A. in Human Development from the University of Chicago and has more than 25 years experience as a teacher, trainer, and therapist. She teaches Kundalini meditation, Hatha yoga, and tai chi.

Linda Smith, M.Ed., is a Kripalu yoga instructor and a Vipassana meditation teacher.

**Style of Yoga**: Kripalu yoga. Helen and Linda combine postures, breathing exercises, and Buddhist mindfulness meditations to help discover the inner awareness and perspective students essential in facing any of life's challenges with serenity.

**Philosophy of Teacher**: "Yoga is a spiritual discipline dedicated to the discovery of connections . . . between ourselves and our Higher Self."

**Student Criteria**: No experience necessary. All are welcome.

**Number of Participants Possible**: 20

**Fee**: $180 per person for a weekend yoga retreat that begins with dinner on Friday at 6:00 p.m. and ends Sunday at 2:30 p.m., after lunch.

**Credit Cards**: Not accepted

**Sample Daily Schedule**:
| | |
|---|---|
| 8:00 a.m. | Breakfast |
| 10:00 | Yoga class |
| 12:30 p.m. | Lunch |
| 4:00 | Yoga class |
| 6:30 | Dinner |

Sessions after dinner are usually devoted to meditation.

# OPEN DOOR YOGA CENTER
# CAMDEN, MAINE

*Restorative Yoga Retreat for Women with Patricia Brown*

## AUGUST
### WEEKEND RETREAT

Camden is a picturesque coastal town of 5,000 people that draws many visitors in the summer. It is a village where the mountains meet the sea in a dramatic and beautifully rugged landscape. Penobscot Bay, on which Camden sits, is a world-class sailing area. The mountain ranges provide excellent hiking; various peaks offer spectacular vistas of the sea. Yoga teacher Patricia Brown lives in this small coastal town and invites students to her weekend yoga retreat each summer, which provides inspiration for strengthening personal practice. Participants stay in local bed-and-breakfasts located near the yoga studio and enjoy the friendly, casual atmosphere, outdoor activites, and refreshing ocean air of this New England village.

**Address**: Women's Restorative Retreats
P.O. Box 448
Camden, ME 04843
**Phone**: 207/236-6412

**Airport Information**: Fly to Portland, two hours from Camden, and take a bus to Camden. Or fly to Rockland, 15 minutes from Camden, and take a cab to town.

**How to Get There**: Camden is a coastal town on Penobscot Bay in Maine. It is four hours north of Boston on Route 1.

**Teacher Background**: Patricia Brown has been teaching yoga for more than 18 years. She received her nursing diploma from Yale New Haven Hospital and has developed her method of Hatha yoga from a synthesis of the many forms of yoga, movement, and breath work she has studied. She is a practitioner of Vipassana meditation and is a student of Ayurvedic medicine.

**Style of Yoga**: Patricia offers a meditative approach to yoga, blending conscious breathing with clear and sensitive guidance while encouraging students to follow their own ways of finding peace and stillness in the body through the practice of yoga. Her style is a blend of Iyengar, Desikachar with a meditative approach, and a strong emphasis on the breath.

**Philosophy of Teacher**: "To provide students with clear, sensitive guidance while making space for their own understanding of finding peace and stillness."

**Student Criteria**: All levels of yoga experience are welcome. This retreat is for women only.

**Disability Access**: No access

**What to Bring**: Bring layers for changeable Maine coast summer weather, sunscreen, bicycle (if you enjoy biking), and hiking boots for the trails nearby. All yoga props are provided.

**Yoga Room Size and Description:** Yoga is practiced in a 24' x 30' converted barn in the hills of Camden. It is a simple space with skylights and a fully equipped yoga studio.

**Number of Participants Possible:** 20

**Accommodations:** Participants stay in nearby B&Bs in the Camden village. There is a wide variety to choose from. Call Patricia for details regarding B&B options and descriptions.

**Meals:** In the village of Camden, within walking distance from all of the B&Bs, is a variety of cuisine from a dozen or more restaurants. Lobster is always available.

**Fee:** $180 per person includes all yoga classes with Patricia, beginning on Thursday evening and ending Sunday morning. Meals and accommodations are at your own expense. B&Bs range from $65 to $125 nightly for double occupancy.

**Credit Cards:** Not accepted

**Sample Daily Schedule:**
Thursday:
6:00–8:00 p.m.    Restorative pose class and meditation
Friday and Saturday:
9:00–11:00 a.m.    Yoga focusing on classic asanas and breathing
4:00–6:00 p.m.    Yoga Restorative Poses, breathing, and meditation

Sunday:
9:00–11:00 a.m.    Yoga class of classic asana and review of weekend material

**Other Activities:** The area offers hiking, swimming, biking, sailing on windjammers, shopping, exploring restaurants, and picnicking in quiet areas by the sea.

**Guest Comment:** *"Patricia Brown's August Yoga Retreat in Camden, Maine, was the highlight of my summer and had lasting restorative effects. Patricia is a magical teacher, able to create a deep calm and focus in her class. Her emphasis on breathing gave a new rhythm to my yoga practice. Patricia's words are good for the soul, and she also creates a lovely silence in the room. Camden is a delightful New England sea coast town with several good restaurants and lots to do between morning and afternoon yoga sessions. I especially loved going to the lake for a swim and visiting the rocks outside of nearby Rockport. The local inn was also very pleasant, with delicious breakfasts on the porch and a friendly, easy-going atmosphere, which encouraged getting to know our fellow yogis."*
Rose Bodenheimer — Brookline, Massachusetts

**Summary:** The focus of this retreat, offered by yoga teacher Patricia Brown, is renewing and reinspiring your personal yoga practice. The retreat is held in the quaint coastal town of Camden, Maine; participants stay in local B&Bs and dine out in the village restaurants. The area offers wonderful biking, sailing, and quiet time by the sea.

# THE SEWALL HOUSE
# ISLAND FALLS, MAINE

*Kundalini Yoga with Donna Davidge*

## JULY–NOVEMBER

The Sewall House in Island Falls has been entered in the National Register of Historic Places. Built in 1865 for William Sewall, Island Falls's firstborn citizen, it was the community's first post office. By 1870 the home served as a well-known "open house" for travelers who visited Island Falls (among them Theodore Roosevelt). Now, generations later, Sewall's great-granddaughter Donna Sewall-Miller Davidge continues the guest-house tradition and has opened the home up as a yoga and nature retreat house. The retreat offers students from New York City and beyond a chance to commune with nature in a peaceful environment while taking advantage of Donna's expertise as a Kundalini yoga instructor.

Located in northern Maine, Island Falls is close to Canada and near Mount Kathadin. Nearby are forests, lakes, and national parks filled with wildlife such as moose, birds, and loons. The town itself is small and quiet, with an island and waterfall in the center. There is a tranquil fishing lake one mile away that offers opportunities for camping, hiking, canoeing, and meditation.

**Address**: The Sewall House
c/o Donna Sewall-Miller Davidge
Box 254
Island Falls, ME 04747
**Phone**: 888/235-2395
**Fax**: 888/235-2395
**E-mail**: amrita@mindspring.com
**Web site**: www.sewallhouse.com

**Airport Information**: The nearest airport is Bangor. The Sewall House offers limited shuttle (van) service from the airport at an additional cost.

**How to Get There**: The Sewall House is just 30 miles from the Canadian border, 90 miles north of Bangor, right off Highway 95. Buses and rental cars are available in Bangor.

**Teacher Background**: Donna Davidge has been practicing Kundalini yoga

since 1985 and is certified by Yogi Bhajan's 3HO Foundation.

**Style of Yoga**: Kundalini yoga. Donna combines breathing with postures using specific breathing techniques. Mantras are used as well.

**Philosophy of Teacher**: "Kundalini yoga is a powerful tool for people wishing to heal on a soul level and those willing to confront their own denials for personal growth and awareness. Because Sewall House is an intimate experience, people connect on deep levels in a safe environment."

**Student Criteria**: No prior yoga experience is necessary. Students should bring an open mind.

**Disability Access**: Limited access; please call.

**What to Bring**: Comfortable clothes for yoga, hiking and biking clothes, swimsuits, and rain gear.

**Yoga Room Size and Description**: Yoga is practiced in a 25' x 20' converted woodshed adjoining the house.

**Number of Participants Possible**: 12

**Accommodations**: The Sewall House has five private bedrooms, each with double beds. Single mattresses are available for family or friends who want to share the room. There is one bedroom with a half bath on the main floor off the dining room. It contains several photographs of Theodore Roosevelt, including an autographed photograph from his wife. There are four bedrooms on the second floor with a shared full bathroom. The third floor also has a full bathroom for guest use, as well as a massage room and a library. Guests often gather in the living room, which has a cozy fireplace. The parlor room is used for meditation. The kitchen is large and separate from the dining room. There is also a large front porch and a barn. The ambiance is definitely that of history and tradition.

**Meals**: Two meals are offered a day and include garden-fresh, locally grown vegetables as well as chicken and fish options.

**Fee**: $77 per day per person includes overnight accommodations, two meals a day, morning yoga class, and evening meditation class.

**Credit Cards**: Not accepted

**Sample Daily Schedule**:
8:00–9:15 a.m.     Morning yoga
9:30     Breakfast
Activities scheduled individually
6:30 p.m.     Dinner
8:00     Evening meditation

**Other Activities**: In the summer there is hiking, biking, lake tours (which include swimming, fishing, and arranged camping), canoe rentals, boating, and golfing (there is an excellent 18-hole golf course). Some people love to just hang out and sit on the porch watching the world go by. In the winter people cross-country ski, go snowmobiling, and enjoy the small downhill ski slope in town.

**Services**: Various massage and healing techniques are available at specific times.

**Guest Comment**: *"Visiting the Sewall House was an enjoyable and very relaxing experience. Donna is a great yoga instructor and a lovely host. The location is beautiful, the house is special, the food is good, and the yoga classes are great!"*
Katia Bouazza — New York, New York

**Summary**: This retreat getaway provides the environment of a family home that happens to be full of history. Filled with antiques and reminders of a simpler time, this 125-year-old guest house infused health and spirit into a young Teddy Roosevelt. Generations later, yoga teacher Donna Sewall-Miller Davidge continues her family tradition, utilizing the home as a yoga and nature retreat house. The Sewall House offers guests the opportunity to relax and enjoy the small-town ambiance of Island Falls with its surrounding forests, lakes, national parks, solitude, and serenity.

SEE PHOTOS, PAGE 145.

# SEA PASTURES RETREAT HOUSE
# VINALHAVEN, MAINE

*Restorative Yoga Retreat for Women with Patricia Brown*

## LATE SEPTEMBER
### ONE WEEK

Sea Pastures is a rambling old farmhouse on the Island of Vinalhaven in the waters of midcoast Maine. Vinalhaven is the largest island off the coast of Maine with a year-round community. A small village consists of six island stores. The retreat house is situated on a 20-acre peninsula among fields of wildflowers and has views of the sea in almost all directions. Trails from the house lead to the rocky shore and miles of oceanfront walking. The wildlife and daily movements of the sea set the pace for this peaceful island retreat. Yoga teacher Patricia Brown offers a restorative yoga week in this environment that includes days of silence as well as unstructured time for your own reflection.

**Address**: Women's Restorative Retreats
P.O. Box 448
Camden, ME 04843
**Phone**: 207/236-6412

**Airport Information**: The nearest airport is Rockland, Maine—15 minutes from the ferry dock. Portland Airport is two hours away.

**How to Get There**: Vinalhaven is the largest island off the coast of Maine. To reach the island take the ferry from Rockland. The ferry ride is 75 minutes through Penobscot Bay. Cars may be safely left in Rockland at the ferry terminal. Transportation is provided from the ferry on Vinalhaven to Sea Pastures.

**Teacher Background**: Patricia Brown has been teaching yoga for more than 18 years. She received her nursing diploma from Yale New Haven Hospital and has developed her method of Hatha yoga from a synthesis of the many forms of yoga, movement, and breath work she

has studied. She is a practitioner of Vipassana meditation and is a student of Ayurvedic medicine.

**Style of Yoga**: Patricia offers a meditative approach to yoga, blending conscious breathing with clear and sensitive guidance while encouraging students to follow their own ways of finding peace and stillness in the body through the practice of yoga. Her style is a blend of Iyengar, Desikachar with a meditative approach, and a strong emphasis on the breath.

**Philosophy of Teacher**: "To provide students with clear, sensitive guidance while making space for their own understanding of finding peace and stillness."

**Student Criteria**: All levels are welcome; this retreat is for women only.

**Disability Access**: No access

**What to Bring**: Yoga mat, two yoga blankets, comfortable clothes with warm layers (the island is cool in the fall), hat, gloves, and walking shoes.

**Yoga Room Size and Description**: Yoga is practiced in a 35' x 15' room with windows to the sea. The room has wood floors and is heated by a furnace and wood stove.

**Number of Participants Possible**: 10

**Accommodations**: Participants stay in a large three-story Maine farmhouse. Ten bedrooms provide a mix of private and semi-private rooms offering twin or full beds. All rooms are simply furnished in a cottage motif.

**Meals**: Three vegetarian meals daily: a hearty breakfast, light lunch, and full dinner by candlelight. Meals are prepared by a professional whole-foods chef and teacher of vegetarian cooking. The central dining room has beautiful ocean views.

**Fee**: $950 per person includes seven days', six nights' accommodations at Sea Pastures, three vegetarian meals daily, and all yoga classes with Patricia.

**Credit Cards**: Not accepted

**Sample Daily Schedule**:

| | |
|---|---|
| 7:00–8:30 a.m. | Yoga focusing on the classic asanas |
| 8:45 | Breakfast |
| 11:30–12:15 | Midday meditation |
| 12:30 p.m. | Lunch |
| 4:30–5:30 | Restorative poses and breathing |
| 6:00 | Dinner |
| 8:00 | Evening meditation |

Three or four days during the middle of the retreat will be spent in silence.

**Other Activities**: Nature surrounds you on this island. There are opportunities for walking, bicycling, beachcombing, freshwater and saltwater swimming, and napping on the front porch hammock.

**Guest Comment**: *"Patricia Brown's retreat on Vinalhaven Island was an experience I will cherish for a long time. Sea Pastures is located on a beautiful peninsula with many paths to Vinalhaven's rocky shore, where you can watch lobstermen hard at work, see beautiful sunrises and schooners under full sail, or walk for hours. Patricia is a very knowledgeable and eloquent yoga instructor who cares very deeply about yoga and her students. I felt that I was able to deepen my yoga practice, focus more inward, and become more aware of what I need in my life to feel energized, healthy, and contented. This is the second retreat of Patricia's that I have attended, and I would highly recommend any of her retreats."*

Kitty Fenn — Westbook, Maine

**Summary**: This women's retreat is the place to come for solitude by the sea and undisturbed time to deepen into yourself through the practice of yoga. Quiet and rustic, Sea Pastures on Vinalhaven Island offers extensive oceanfront walking, freshwater quarries, nature trails, and wonderful night sky viewing. Yoga teacher Patricia Brown invites women to experience this peaceful island setting for a week of rest, reflection, silence, meditation, and restorative yoga.

# MAR-LU RIDGE CONFERENCE CENTER
# JEFFERSON, MARYLAND

*A Weekend Yoga Retreat with Hillary Blackton, Sarabess Forster, Simone Heurich, and Kathy Rowly*

## SEPTEMBER
### WEEKEND RETREAT

Four women who teach yoga in the metro Washington, D.C., area combine their expertise in offering this yearly mountain yoga retreat at the Mar-Lu Ridge Conference Center in Jefferson, Maryland. This mountain retreat center is private and isolated and includes 50 acres of woodlands. The conference center is a two-story wooden frame building that has guest rooms on both floors. The top floor has the main meeting room, which has views of the surrounding mountains. There is a swiming pool on the grounds, although it may not be available for use in September. The hiking trails are well maintained and nice for running and walking.

**Address**: Sunflower Yoga Company
c/o Sarabess Forster
1305 Chalmers Rd.
Silver Spring, MD 20903
**Phone**: 301/445-3882
**E-mail**: sarabess@juno.com

**Airport Information**: Fly into Ronald Reagan National Airport in Virginia.

**How to Get There**: The Mar-Lu Center is 45 minutes away from Ronald Reagan National Airport and 15 minutes northwest of Frederick, Maryland.

**Teacher Background**: Hillary Blackton is the past president of the Mid-Atlantic Yoga Association and present director of Divine Life Yoga in Gaithersburg, Maryland. Hillary's gentle wisdom, along with her disciplined approach, merge the meditative with the precise, expanding her teachings beyond the boundaries of any one tradition.

Sarabess Forster, M.Ed., is certified by Sivananda Yoga International and teaches Hatha yoga in Silver Spring, Maryland. She is the host of the TV cable show *The 20-Minute Yogi* and author of *God is Now Here* and *Yoga is Not Yogurt*, books and videos for yoga practice.

Simone Heurich has been finding balance and discovering the peace and joy within through the many facets of yoga for 20 years. She received certification from Janana at Evergreen Yoga and the Yoga Center in Columbia, Maryland, and has attended many workshops and retreats with teachers from a variety of traditions. Her style is a blend of all she has experienced.

Kathy Rowley has 20 years of teaching experience as a certified yoga instructor and is past president of the Mid-Atlantic Yoga Association. Having taught throughout the metropolitan D.C. area, she is widely respected for her style of teaching, which is drawn from many diverse schools of training.

**Style of Yoga**: These teachers teach, collectively, Hatha yoga, Raja yoga, Mantra yoga, vegetarian cooking, and meditation.

**Philosophy of Teachers**: "In common we have a warmth and caring and personalized approach to sharing yoga with people and animals and creatures."

**Student Criteria**: All levels are welcome.

**Disability Access**: Limited access

**What to Bring**: A yoga mat, two blankets, a stretch strap, and a meditation cushion. These items will also be available for purchase.

**Yoga Room Size and Description**: Two rooms are used for yoga practice. The main room is very spacious and holds about 75 people. This room is carpeted and has windows on three sides, which provides lots of light. The smaller room is not carpeted and opens on a porch that looks out on the mountains.

**Number of Participants Possible**: 45 to 50

**Accommodations**: There are 20 guest rooms. Rooms are double or triple occupancy; all have private bathrooms. They are carpeted but not deluxe. Each guest room is furnished with a couch, a table, and a chair. Some of the rooms have an outside deck.

**Meals**: Two vegetarian meals are served each day. Tea, fruit, and snacks are available throughout the weekend. The dining room is on the first floor of the conference building.

**Fee**: $210 per person for triple occupancy, and $225 per person for double occupancy. Includes lodging, meals, and all classes.

**Credit Cards**: Not accepted

**Sample Daily Schedule**:

| | |
|---|---|
| 7:00 a.m. | Wake up |
| 7:30–8:00 | Morning meditation |
| 8:15–10:00 | Beginning and intermediate asana classes |
| 10:00 | Brunch |
| 11:00–2:00 p.m. | Free time |
| 2:00–3:45 | Vegetarian cooking class |
| 4:00–5:45 | Beginning and intermediate asana classes |
| 6:00–7:00 | Dinner |
| 7:00–8:30 | Evening program: Chakras/Healing |
| 9:00–9:30 | Evening meditation |
| 10:00 | Lights out |

**Other Activites**: The property allows for plenty of walking and hiking on well-marked trails. There are many secluded areas for meditation. There is also a swimming pool at the conference center.

**Guest Comment**: *"I had a wonderful time at the Mar-Lu Ridge Yoga Retreat. Having the opportunity to take classes with four different professional yoga teachers meant that we learned many new things. Each teacher was special in her own way. I also enjoyed the 'extra' classes (including vegetarian cooking and foot reflexology). The setting was lovely and not far away. The cost was reasonable. I was concerned about sharing a room with someone I had not met, but that worked out fine, too. I can't wait to go back next time!"*

Debra Levy—Silver Spring, Maryland

**Summary**: This retreat offers participants the opportunity to study with four differerent yoga teachers, who collectively guide you toward a weekend of rest, relaxation, and renewal in the spirit of yoga. Each day begins and ends with meditation. The Mar-Lu Conference Center is an older facility set in the mountains.

# MARTHA'S VINEYARD
# CHILMARK, MASSACHUSETTS

*Yoga and Meditation with Patricia Lotterman*

## OCTOBER AND MAY
### WEEKEND RETREAT

Martha's Vineyard, a small island off the coast of Cape Cod in Massachusetts, attracts tourists year-round. Patricia Lotterman offers her yoga retreats in a large private home in the town of Chilmark. The house was built in 1994 and has beautiful wood floors, lots of windows, and brightly painted walls. The house sits next to three acres of conservation land that has well-marked trails for hiking. On the island are maple, oak, and tupelo trees, among others. One can sometimes spot rabbits and deer in the backyard of the house, and bird-watchers may catch glimpses of wild turkeys, geese, and swans. Spring-time brings lots of wildflowers (poison ivy, too). The beach is one mile from the house.

**Address**: Patricia Lotterman
7 Pomeroy St.
Allston, MA 02134
**Phone**: 617/782-1571
**E-mail**: plotto@msn.com

**Airport Information**: Fly into Boston and take the Puddle Jumper to Martha's Vineyard. Arrange with Patricia to be picked up at the airport. The house is 10 minutes away.

**How to Get There**: The ferry ($10 round-trip) leaves Wood's Hole, Falmouth, at 7:45 p.m. for Martha's Vineyard. Parking at Wood's Hole is $7.50/day. Keep in mind that traffic is heavy on Friday evenings. The group will be met by a hired van and driven to the house.

**Teacher Background**: Patricia Lotterman holds a teaching certificate from the Sivananda Yoga Vedanta Centers and is a licensed massage therapist. She has been teaching yoga for seven years. She

is working on her masters in education in Health Counseling.

**Style of Yoga**: Hatha yoga, with each class including strength, flexibility, and balance poses, pranayama, and partner poses. Patricia feels strongly about the importance of warming up before moving into asanas. Relaxation is incorporated throughout the class, with an extended guided relaxation at the end.

**Philosophy of Teacher**: "Participants are encouraged to work at their own pace, gentle or challenging, depending on the moment."

**Student Criteria**: Some experience with Hatha yoga and meditation is helpful but not required.

**Disability Accessible**: No access

**What to Bring**: Personal needs, meditation cushion, blanket, comfortable clothes for yoga, walking shoes, and a bathing suit. Yoga mats and towels are provided. Participants who choose to sleep on the carpeted floor need to bring their own sleeping bag.

**Yoga Room Size and Description**: Yoga is practiced in a large room with a quasi-cathedral ceiling, hardwood floors, skylights, and a wall of windows that overlook lots of greenery and the ocean and fill the room with natural light. There is a fireplace on one end where an altar is constructed.

**Number of Participants Possible**: 10

**Accommodations**: One enters the house on the ground floor, where there are three bedrooms, a full bath, a laundry facility, and an open, carpeted sleeping area for four people (with their own sleeping bags). One bedroom has two single futons, one bedroom has a queen-sized futon, and one bedroom has a double bed. Participants share two bathrooms, one on each floor. One bathroom has a tub/shower, and one has a shower and steam; there is also a partially enclosed shower outdoors. All of the sleeping quarters on the bottom floor of this two-story house look out on trees, shrubs, and a lawn, where a hammock beckons an afternoon nap.

**Meals**: Two vegetarian meals are served each day (brunch and dinner), with nondairy and nonwheat options. Meals are prepared by Patricia herself, who grew up in a family of chefs and makes her own sauces, fresh salads, and main dishes with love. Participants are asked to help with cleanup after meals (Karma yoga).

**Fee**: $130 per person, or $110 if sleeping on the floor in the common room. This cost does not cover your ferry ticket.

**Credit Cards**: Not accepted

**Sample Daily Schedule**:
Participants arrive Friday evening for fruit, tea, and introductions.

| | |
|---|---|
| 6:30 a.m. | Meditation |
| 8:00–10:00 | Hatha yoga |
| 10:00 | Brunch |

Free time to explore, walk, bike, enjoy the hot tub, nap, and read.

| | |
|---|---|
| 4:00–6:00 p.m. | Hatha yoga |
| 6:00 | Dinner |
| 8:00 | Satsang |

The program ends after brunch on Sunday. Satsang includes a 20-minute sitting meditation, followed by the chanting of Sanskrit prayers, as well as hymns, folk songs, and whatever the group brings to the experience; then there is a group discussion sparked by reflection on "blessing cards." Satsang finishes with Arati, a light ceremony.

**Other Activities**: On Martha's Vineyard there are all kinds of activities: kayaking, horseback riding, biking, hiking, visiting artists' studios, and shopping. Participants can enjoy walks on the beach or through the woods or can just rest in the hammock with a good book. Nearby is an old-fashioned local store, where people sit on the front porch in rocking chairs watching island life go by. The landscape includes flower gardens, horse farms, an organic nursery, and quaint vineyard homes.

**Guest Comment**: *"The boat ride over from Wood's Hole, Massachusetts, to the island was special, with the sea separating me from routine and daily responsibilities as I entered into 48 hours of yoga asanas, meditation, rest, walks, chanting, sharing, and nature."*
Peggy Ryan—Somerville, Massachusetts

**Summary**: This weekend yoga and meditation retreat on Martha's Vineyard offers quiet time in a large private home near conservation land, productive farms, and the sea. The house has a huge deck with a whirlpool, and when the fog lifts you can see the ocean. Yoga teacher Patricia Lotterman incorporates satsang, discussion, and ritual, creating an intimate and peaceful weekend.

# KRIPALU CENTER FOR YOGA AND HEALTH
# LENOX, MASSACHUSETTS

## YEAR-ROUND

Founded on the yogic principles that all humanity belongs to one family and that the divine dwells within each of us, Kripalu Center for Yoga and Health is a spiritual retreat and program center in the Berkshire Hills of western Massachusetts. The center is located on 300 acres of forests, meadows, and rolling hills, and the moment you step onto the grounds there is a sensation of calm and quiet.

The main building that houses Kripalu, previously a Jesuit seminary, is a sprawling facility covering approximately four acres. Kripalu's staff is friendly and welcoming, transforming the overwhelming facility into a warm, pleasant environment. The Kripalu staff facilitates instruction of yogic principles through a large number of yoga, self-discovery, holistic health, and spiritual programs. The facility is also used for seasonal retreats by various yoga teachers outside the Kripalu staff. (Call for catalog of events.)

**Address:** Kripalu Center for Yoga and Health
P.O. Box 793
Lenox, MA 01240
**Phone:** 800/741-7353
**Fax:** 413/448-3274
**Web site:** www.kripalu.org

**Airport Information:** Fly into the Albany (New York) airport. Kripalu offers a reduced-fare limousine service every Friday and Sunday from the airport to Kripalu at 3:00 p.m. and from Kripalu to the airport at 1:30 p.m.

**How to Get There:** Kripalu Center is a two-hour drive from Boston and three hours from New York City.

**Teacher Background:** Staff members of Kripalu take turns leading yoga postures and meditation sessions and assist in teaching various courses.

**Style of Yoga:** Kripalu yoga uses prolonged holding of asanas to go inward and discover what blocks people from living joyfully and in alignment with their body's natural rhythms.

**Philosophy of Teachers:** "Kripalu yoga is both a practical and a spiritual approach to yoga. Its primary purpose is to bring you, the practitioner, to an integrated experience of body, mind, and spirit. This methodology respects the physical, mental, emotional, and energetic needs that are unique to each one of us as individuals. It also reflects the commonality that we share as fellow human beings."

**Student Criteria:** No prior experience is necessary.

**Disability Access:** There are some rooms with handicap accessibility — please call ahead.

**What to Bring:** Yoga mat if desired.

**Yoga Room Size and Description:** There are seven yoga rooms of various sizes available for simultaneous programming. Each room is equipped with audio and video capability and has windows with views of an apple orchard.

**Number of Participants Possible**: 100

**Accommodations**: Simple, dorm-style rooms with bunk beds for 4 to 24 people or standard rooms for two (8' x 12'), with either two twin beds, a double bed, or a queen. Bathrooms are down the hall. Standard-plus rooms are slightly larger, and some have private baths. Bedding and basic bath linens are provided. There is no maid service; you make your own bed. Towels are replaced daily, and linens after 10 days. Additional towels are available at a nominal fee.

**Meals**: Three vegetarian meals are provided daily; no eggs, fish, or meat of any kind are served. Meals can be taken in the main cafeteria-style dining room or in smaller, silent dining areas. Breakfast is a silent meal in every room. Lunch is the major meal at Kripalu where vegetarian cuisine ranges from good to incredible.

**Fee**: Dormitory with hall bath is $85, and a room for two with hall bath is $95 per night. A semi-private (two people) room with hall bath is $130, and a semi-private room with private bath is $155 per night. A private room (one person) with hall bath is $160, and a private room with private bath is $170 per night. There is a two-night minimum-stay requirement. The above are weekend rates. Rooms cost slightly less midweek. Specific programs have additional tuition cost. (Call for brochure.)

**Credit Cards**: Not accepted

**Sample Daily Schedule**:

| | |
|---|---|
| 6:00–7:25 a.m. | Kripalu yoga, pranayama, and meditation |
| 7:30–8:30 | Breakfast |
| 8:30–11:30 | Session |
| noon–1:30 p.m. | Lunch |
| 1:30–4:00 | Program session |
| 4:15–5:45 | Kripalu yoga and meditation |
| 5:45–6:45 | Dinner |
| 7:30–9:00 | Satsang, concert, or other evening event |

A special meditation room is available for use 24 hours a day.

**Other Activities**: There are 300 acres of forests and meadows here, with beautiful walking and hiking trails, meditation gardens, and a private beach on Lake Mahkeeac. Inside the Kripalu building is a sauna, whirlpool bath, and exercise room available for guests.

**Services**: Kripalu Health Services offers treatment options such as Kripalu body work, reflexology, shiatsu, craniosacral therapy, and energy balancing.

**Guest Comment:** *"It meant a lot to me that I didn't have to do anything, only what I felt comfortable doing. There was no pressure to accomplish any specific goal."*
Wendy Patitucci—New York, New York

**Summary**: Kripalu is one of the largest centers for yoga and health in the country. Dedicated to self-discovery through yoga and holistic health, Kripalu Center is a safe setting for self-exploration, rest, and renewal. The huge four-story facility is staffed with various program options, classes, and services, so there is plenty to experience in the way of healing and instruction. The vegetarian food is simple and nourishing and the accommodations are plain, but everything is clean. Yogic principles are clearly stated and enforced, making shared spaces a peaceful and pleasant experience. Outdoors color and beauty abound in every season. Enjoy the center's 300 acres of forests, meadows, rolling hills, and views of Lake Makeenac.

# TEMENOS
# SHUTESBURY, MASSACHUSETTS

*Indian Summer Yoga Retreat for Women*

## SEPTEMBER
### WEEKEND RETREAT

Temenos is a rustic and remote retreat center nestled in 78 acres of forest on a small New England mountain. Its Quaker founders chose the name Temenos, which is a Greek word referring to the sanctuary space surrounding an ancient temple or altar. Their vision was to create a simpler lifestyle and to help people cultivate more harmonious relationships and live in balance with nature.

In accord with this vision, yoga teachers Puja Sue Flamm and Marilyn Hart offer this annual Indian Summer Yoga Retreat weekend exclusively for women. Participants stay in cozy cabins in the woods, far away from city lights, electricity, and telephones. Thousands of acres of woodland belonging to the Quabbin Reservoir watershed border Temenos on three sides. The spacious lodge has ample room for cooking, eating, dancing, yoga, and sitting by an open-fire Franklin stove.

**Address**: New England Center for Yoga and Healing Arts
c/o Puja Flamm
17 Kellogg Ave.
Amherst, MA 01002
**Phone**: 413/256-0604
**Fax**: 413/253-7037
**E-mail**: pujas@aol.com
**Web site**: www.pujayoga.com

**Airport Information**: Temenos is about one and one-half hours from Hartford, Connecticut (fly into Bradley Airport), and a little more than two hours from Boston (fly into Logan Airport).

**How to Get There**: The nearest town is Shutesbury. The nearest large town is Amherst, which is 25 minutes away.

**Teacher Background**: Puja Sue Flamm is the codirector of the New England Center for Yoga and Healing Arts in Amherst. She spent six years on staff at Kripalu Center for Yoga and Health, where she acted as program director. Puja is a certified yoga teacher, a licensed massage therapist, and a body-centered counselor. She has practiced yoga for more than 20 years and teaches internationally.

Marilyn Hart is director of the Green River Yoga Center in Greenfield, Massachusetts. She has been teaching yoga and practicing meditation since 1985. Marilyn has studied the Iyengar method intensively, is a certified Kripalu yoga teacher, and practices Holotropic and other forms of breath work. Marilyn spent time in India practicing Vispassana meditation and studying Ashtanga Vinyasa yoga with Pattabhi Jois.

**Style of Yoga**: Eclectic—Iyengar, Kripalu, Ashtanga.

**Philosophy of Teachers**: "We create a safe, supportive environment for guiding participants to deeper levels of self through sessions of Hatha yoga, breathing, and meditation. We offer support, healing, and empowerment for women."

**Student Criteria**: Women only

**Disability Access**: No access

**What to Bring**: Sleeping bag or bedding, comfortable clothes for yoga, toiletries, a flashlight, candles, matches, warm clothing for nighttime, good walking shoes, and rain gear.

**Yoga Room Size and Description**: The yoga space is about 600 square feet, with a large skylight and several windows looking over the forest of deep green pines.

**Number of Participants Possible**: 25

**Accommodations**: There are five cabins at Temenos; two to six people sleep in a cabin. All the cabins have wood stoves, small propane burners for cooking, sinks, and basic kitchen supplies. The cabins are very simple and rustic but clean and charming with lots of light. Guests use three outhouses on the property. There is one shower in the main lodge, but people are encouraged to take sponge baths in their cabins to conserve water.

**Meals**: Three vegetarian meals are served each day. The food is mostly organic and prepared by a gourmet vegetarian chef. All meals are eaten in silence, consciously. Special diets are accommodated. Participants eat together in the main lodge.

**Fee**: There is a sliding-scale fee of $190 to $295 per person based on annual income. This includes a two night stay, all meals, and classes.

**Credit Cards**: Not accepted

**Sample Daily Schedule**:

| | |
|---|---|
| 7:30–8:30 a.m. | Walk and outside meditation (optional) |
| 8:30–9:30 | Breakfast |
| 9:30–1:00 p.m. | Yoga session |
| 1:00–3:00 | Lunch, free time |
| 3:00–5:30 | Yoga session |
| 5:30–7:00 | Dinner |
| 7:00–9:30 | Fire ceremony |
| 10:30 | Lights out |

Registration begins Friday at 4:00 p.m., and the retreat ends with a closing circle on Sunday at 2:00 p.m.

**Other Activities**: Temenos is surrounded by beautiful forested areas for hiking, with well-marked trails. When exploring, you may discover the jizo rock carving of the Buddha created by a Zen Buddhist nun while on the three-month retreat at Temenos. There is also a pine grove surrounding a fire circle where many outdoor rituals are held. There is a small pond for swimming, which is fed by natural mineral springs. Two minutes from the pond, next to the lodge, sits a wood-heated sauna.

**Guest Comment:** *"I loved Temenos, the visual beauty of the cabin as well as the quiet of nature without electricity. I appreciated the meditative presence and focus that Puja and Marilyn brought to the retreat. Magical moments included hugging the earth, quotes from Rumi, and the combination of yoga practice with meditative practice."*
Kathy Conyers—Manchester, Connecticut

**Summary**: This weekend retreat at Temenos, for women only, offers a safe and supportive environment in the woods for exploring deeper levels of self. Yoga teachers Marilyn Hart and Puja Flamm guide participants in becoming present in nature, eating consciously, practicing Hatha yoga, breathing, and meditating. The retreat atmosphere is supported with social silence, plus free time to walk, write, read, and rest.

# ARC RETREAT COMMUNITY STANCHFIELD, MINNESOTA

## *Yoga Retreat with Maryann Parker*

### APRIL AND OCTOBER
#### WEEKEND RETREATS

The ARC Retreat Community is an ecumenical community and retreat center committed to hospitality and welcoming persons who are on spiritual journeys of search and renewal. The letters ARC stand for action, reflection, and celebration. ARC is situated on 73 acres of beautiful pine and hardwood forest. A spring-fed creek pours into a nearby undeveloped lake. There is a screened-in gazebo, a lovely garden where vegetables and herbs grow, and a solitary cabin hermitage. Retreats are held in the comfortable cedar log house. ARC has a chapel, library, book nook, and large and small meeting rooms with fireplaces. This retreat setting offers a quiet place and reflective atmosphere for individuals and groups seeking to slow down the pace of life and restore balance. Yoga teacher Maryann Parker holds two annual yoga weekends at this place of stillness, which, she says, "beckons one to delve into the true nature of existence."

**Address**: Maryann Parker
4517 Moreland Ave.
Minneapolis, MN 55424
**Phone**: 612/927-9380
**Fax**: 612/922-5762

**Airport Information**: Fly into Minneapolis-St. Paul International Airport. Maryann will arrange transportation from the airport to the ARC Retreat Community for participants who make arrangements with her ahead of time.

**How to Get There**: ARC Retreat Community and Retreat House is located eight miles northwest of Cambridge, Minnesota.

**Teacher Background**: Maryann has an eclectic yoga background, including Himalayan Institute training and Iyengar (she studied one month at the Iyengar Institute in India) and Kripalu yoga.

She has more than 18 years of teaching experience and has been leading yoga retreats for six years.

**Style of Yoga**: Maryann's classes include breathing, structurally correct posture work, and relaxation. Internal awareness and the joy of doing yoga are emphasized.

**Philosophy of Teacher**: "Because yoga is done with mindfulness, an inner awareness is cultivated, and concentration is sharpened. Internal awareness and the joy of doing yoga are emphasized in my teaching."

**Student Criteria**: All levels of experience are welcome.

**Disability Access**: Yes

**What to Bring**: Yoga mat, bottled water, comfortable clothes for yoga, sweaters and socks for warmth, personal toiletries, walking or hiking shoes.

**Yoga Room Size and Description**: Yoga sessions are held in the third-floor library. The room has a vaulted ceiling and a large floor-to-ceiling window looking into the treetops. The room is carpeted, so students use yoga mats. Ten students fit comfortably into this space. With a larger group, two sessions accommodate 20 people.

**Number of Participants Possible**: 20

**Accommodations**: The comfortable cedar-log retreat house has 12 single rooms and three double rooms. Linen and towels are furnished. There is one bathroom for each three rooms, with sinks in every room. Rooms are simply decorated —log walls, wooden furniture, and hand-sewn quilts complete the mountain cabin atmosphere. Each room has a desk and rocking chair. Windows look out onto the woods. The space is quiet and simple.

**Meals**: Three meals are served daily and are healthy, wholesome, and simple. Most meals are vegetarian and include home-baked breads and desserts as well as fresh vegetables and herbs from the garden. The dining room has four large round tables where meals are served. The simple yet tasty meals respect the global view that encourages us to live more with less.

**Fee**: $300 per person for the weekend includes shared room, three meals daily, and all yoga classes with Maryann.

**Credit Cards**: Not accepted

**Sample Daily Schedule**:

| | |
|---|---|
| 8:30 a.m. | Breakfast |
| 9:30 | Yoga and relaxation class |
| noon | Lunch |

Free time for walks, quiet reflection, reading in the library, naps

| | |
|---|---|
| 3:30 p.m. | Restorative yoga poses |
| 5:30 | Dinner |

Evening discussion (yoga theory, nutrition, vitamin supplements, tension relief, breathing exercises, meditation)

**Other Activities**: The property offers wonderful walking and hiking trails, skiing trails in season, and canoeing on the lake. There is plenty of space on the property and in the retreat house for quiet, reflective, personal time and rest.

**Services**: Professional massage can be arranged for an additional fee.

**Guest Comment**: *"This quiet, wooded setting is an ideal place to unwind, forget the outside world, and listen to the challenges that our unique bodies present."*
Faye Younger—Minneapolis, Minnesota

**Summary**: This weekend yoga retreat offered by teacher Maryann Parker takes place in an environment that offers an atmosphere of deep stillness and silence. The comfortable cedar-log retreat house, which is tucked in among huge oak trees, has a protected, homey quality and feeling. Participants snuggle into log beds each night covered by handmade quilts and go to sleep to the gentle sound of the wind blowing through the trees. The ARC Community Retreat is a spiritual environment ideal for yoga, rest, and relaxation.

# COBBLESTONE CABINS
# TOFTE, MINNESOTA

*Iyengar Yoga Retreat with Kristin Chirhart and Lee Sverkerson*

## MAY AND OCTOBER
### WEEKEND RETREATS

Highway 61 on the way to Cobblestone Cabins is a gorgeous drive, the road shaded by hardwood forests. Cobblestone Cabins, located on the north shore of Lake Superior—the largest freshwater lake in the United States—offers an atmosphere of quiet, natural beauty and clean, pine-scented air. The rustic, pine-paneled resort cabins face the lake.

Twice each year, yoga teachers Kristin Chirhart and Lee Sverkerson offer a weekend of Iyengar yoga in this serene setting. The budding of new life in spring invigorates, and the fall colors of the surrounding forest display variety and beauty. In both seasons retreat participants enjoy challenging and rewarding yoga classes as well as the cobblestone beach, walking the lake, and deep relaxation in the wood-burning sauna. The natural beauty and serenity of the setting encourage a focus on reflection, meditation, and rest.

**Address:** Kristin Chirhart and Lee Sverkerson
B. K. S. Iyengar Yoga Center
2736 Lyndale Ave. S
Minneapolis, MN 55408
**Phone:** 612/872-8708
**Fax:** 612/872-1893
**E-mail:** chirh001@tc.umn.edu

**Airport Information:** Fly into Minneapolis-St. Paul. Cobblestone Cabins is a four-hour drive from Minneapolis. Participants usually carpool.

**How to Get There:** Cobblestone Cabins is located on the north shore of Lake Superior, 85 miles north of Duluth on Highway 61.

**Teacher Background:** Kristin Chirhart has been practicing Iyengar Yoga since 1979. She is certified and has made several trips to Pune, India, to study with B. K. S., Geeta, and Prashant Iyengar.

Lee Sverkerson has been practicing Iyengar yoga since 1981. He has been teaching since 1988, is certified, and studies regularly with B. K. S., Geeta, and Prashant Iyengar. Both Kristin and Lee teach full time at the B. K. S. Iyengar Yoga Center in Minneapolis, Minnesota.

**Style of Yoga:** Iyengar method.

**Philosophy of Teachers:** "Our philosophy is based on the classical yoga of Patanjali as commented on and developed by B. K. S. Iyengar."

**Student Criteria:** At least six months study of Iyengar yoga is helpful, although all levels are welcome.

**Disability Access:** No access

**What to Bring:** Yoga mat, three yoga blankets, and a belt. Comfortable clothing for yoga, swimsuit, walking shoes, a flashlight, and food for cooking your own meals.

**Yoga Room Size and Description**: Yoga is practiced in a 700-square-foot room overlooking Lake Superior. The room is pine paneled and has wood floors.

**Number of Participants Possible**: 20

**Accommodations**: Guests stay in rustic, nonsmoking cabins on Lake Superior. Seven of the cabins have full cooking facilities, including propane oven, refrigerator, and ample dishes and cookware. The two smaller cabins have partial cooking facilities, including refrigerator. All the cabins have electricity and propane heat. Bathrooms include a shower, toilet, and sink. The cabins are furnished simply but comfortably. Towels, sheets, and blankets are provided. There are two bedrooms in each cabin, accommodating four people per cabin.

**Meals**: Participants bring their own food for cooking. The group eats together at a vegetarian potluck held on Saturday night.

**Fee**: $140 per person includes two nights lodging (four to a cabin) at Cobblestone Cabins and four yoga classes with Kristin and Lee.

**Credit Cards**: Not accepted

**Sample Daily Schedule**:
Friday evening
6:00–8:00 p.m.    Yoga class
Saturday
9:00–11:00 a.m.    Yoga class
6:00–8:00 p.m.    Yoga class

8:00             Vegetarian potluck
                 dinner
Sunday
8:00–10:00 a.m.   Yoga class
10:30            Check out

**Other Activities**: Cobblestone Cabins provides row boats, canoes, kayaks, and a ball field and playground area. There are wonderful opportunities for hiking, biking, bird-watching, swimming, and fishing. The Superior Hiking Trail and the Boundary Waters Canoe Area are close at hand. There is a wood-burning sauna on the property, which is only 15 feet from the cold water of Lake Superior.

**Guest Comment**: *"It's fall in Minnesota, on the shores of Lake Superior. There are charming, rustic cabins and pleasant trails in the woods. Long walks and time for relaxation are built into the weekend experience. This is an exhilarating place for a weekend of yoga. Kristin and Lee are a great team. Their teaching creates the right kind of atmosphere for gaining confidence in the practice of yoga."*
Ruth Murphy—St. Paul, Minnesota

**Summary**: This retreat setting is perched on top of a cliff on the edge of Lake Superior. The breaking waves on the rocky shore below Cobblestone Cabins provide a soothing and peaceful ambiance for yoga in an environment of lush and mature trees. Iyengar yoga teachers Kristin Chirhart and Lee Sverkerson offer three days of intensive yoga, during which students are positively encouraged to push past the point of comfort into the poses, gaining confidence and progression. Students cook their own meals and share a vegetarian potluck on Saturday night.

# FEATHERED PIPE RANCH
# HELENA, MONTANA

*Feathered Pipe Yoga Specialty Weeks*

## JUNE–SEPTEMBER

Nestled against the tree-covered Rocky Mountains and surrounded by thousands of acres of Forest Service land, the Feathered Pipe Ranch is a retreat center providing learning experiences that inspire healthy living. A potpourri of yoga instructors representing a diversity of yogic traditions are scheduled each year, as are other programs that nurture wholeness and interconnectedness with all of life. Feathered Pipe offers only one program at a time so that guests can benefit fully without distractions. Each instructor is unique and has achieved a level of teaching excellence that has earned national or international recognition within his or her tradition. (Please call for a catalog to find out about current scheduled instructors.)

Equal to the beauty that surrounds it, Feathered Pipe has a wonderful, nurturing atmosphere. The staff is dedicated to making guests feel comfortable and at home. Masterfully crafted log lodges, simple cabins, yurts, and teepees offer a variety of lodging options. The 110-acre ranch property has a sparkling private lake, pristine water, clean air, abundant wildlife, and healing plants that flourish in the mountain setting. There are miles of hiking trails in the adjoining national forest and a hidden meditation garden next to a rushing stream. The retreat sits on land that was once inhabited by a Native American tribe and was named after the tradition of passing the sacred feathered pipe to connect all beings in the circle of life and receive guidance from the Great Spirit.

**Address**: Feathered Pipe Ranch
P.O. Box 1682
Helena, MT 59624
**Phone**: 406/442-8196
**Fax**: 406/442-8110
**E-mail**: fpranch@met.net
**Web site**: www.featheredpipe.com

**Airport Information**: Fly into Helena. Van service is available from the airport for $35 round trip.

**How to Get There**: The ranch is 13 miles from Helena.

**Teacher Background**: Many different yoga teachers visit Feathered Pipe Ranch.

Many teachers have a background in Iyengar and/or Ashtanga yoga. Please call for a catalog and for questions regarding the different yoga intensives offered.

**Style of Yoga**: Hatha, Ashtanga, and Iyengar. Some teachers offer a soft, gentle approach to yoga, while others teach a more dynamic, challenging form. Please call for a catalog and for questions regarding the different yoga intensives offered.

**Philosophy of Teachers**: Varies according to individual teachers.

**Student Criteria**: All levels are encouraged to come.

*Laughing Water at Feathered Pipe Ranch*

**Disability Access:** Yes, fully accessible.

**What to Bring:** Yoga props are provided. Bring comfortable clothes for yoga, walking shoes, and sweaters or long-sleeved shirts for cool mountain nights.

**Yoga Room Size and Description:** 40' x 60'. The yoga room has hardwood floors, a stone fireplace, and large glass windows that face the mountains and overlook the lake.

**Number of Participants Possible:** 36

**Accommodations:** You may choose to stay indoors or outdoors. Teepees, tents, and yurts provide the outside accommodations and are spread apart on the land to give each camper abundant privacy. Indoors, guests can stay in a variety of cabins (semi-private) or in the lodge dormitory (up to four people in a room). A lovely cedar bathhouse holds bathroom facilities for campers along with a hot tub and sauna for everyone's use. Cabins come with or without a bath.

**Meals:** Gourmet natural food is a specialty at the ranch. Organically grown ingredients are used whenever possible. The menu is primarily vegetarian, but occasionally chicken or fish is served. Special diets can be accommodated. Food is served banquet-style and includes a smorgasbord of delightful dishes three meals a day.

**Fee:** From $800 to $1,200 per person per week (call for catalog), depending on the program. This includes all instruction, lodging, meals, and general use of bathhouse and ranch facilities. A double room with a private bath is an additional $250 per person. A double room with a shared bath is an additional $150 per person.

**Credit Cards:** Mastercard and Visa

**Sample Daily Schedule:**
6:30–8:00 a.m.    Breakfast

| | |
|---|---|
| 9:00–noon | Yoga class |
| noon–1:30 p.m. | Lunch |
| 2:00–5:00 | Yoga class |
| 6:00–7:30 | Dinner |
| 7:00–10:00 | Class (evening program) |

**Other Activities:** The ranch lands include fabulous wilderness hiking and secluded places for meditation in nature. You'll be able to see millions of stars on a clear night. Sauna and hot tub in the cedar bathhouse.

**Services:** A professional massage staff is at hand for appointments.

**Guest Comment:** *"Feathered Pipe exceeded all my expectations for class content, location, accommodations, and food. I thought I was going on a vacation with yoga classes worked in, but it ended up being an important journey where the discovery was all about me—physically and spiritually."*

Dottie Lentz—Austin, Texas

**Summary:** Located in the heart of Montana's Rockies, Feathered Pipe Ranch is designed with natural log and stone buildings set in a wilderness area that feels like a million miles from everything. Fresh, clean mountain air, clear blue skies, pure drinking water, and a natural wilderness setting make this yoga retreat a place where you can melt into nature and get recentered. The staff is warm and gracious; the yoga instructors are nationally and internationally renowned. Seven- and ten-day retreats are available June through September. The Feathered Pipe Foundation also sponsors yoga retreats and tours throughout the world, which vary each year (please call for information).

# ROCK CREEK RESORT
# RED LODGE, MONTANA

*Yoga Retreats with Elizabeth and David Klarich*

## JUNE, JULY, AND AUGUST
### SIX-DAY RETREATS

Rock Creek Resort is a conference and retreat facility located on the Beartooth Highway in Montana. The resort is tucked in a beautiful canyon just below Beartooth Pass and is only five miles from Red Lodge, a tourist- and skiing-oriented community. Creeks, mountains, and views surround this luxurious resort. Facilities include two main lodges, townhouses, condominiums, tennis courts, and a health club with indoor swimming pool, sauna, and Jacuzzi. A nearby campground on the creek is available for those who choose to camp instead of stay at the resort.

**Address**: Elizabeth Klarich
937 N. 24th St.
Billings, MT 59101
**Phone**: 406/245-6256
**Fax**: 406/657-3245
**E-mail**: yogareflex@aol.com

**Airport Information**: Fly into Logan International Airport in Billings, Montana (67 miles north of Red Lodge), or Yellowstone Regional Airport in Cody, Wyoming (67 miles south of Red Lodge). A shuttle bus from Billings is approximately $40 per person.

**How to Get There**: Rock Creek Resort is five miles from Red Lodge, and 65 miles from Billings. It is just off the Beartooth Highway by Rock Creek.

**Teacher Background**: Elizabeth and David Klarich are both certified Ananda yoga teachers with eclectic backgrounds and training, including studies with Self-Realization Fellowship, Iyengar teachers, Desikachar teachers, Kripalu teachers, and Sivananda teachers.

**Style of Yoga**: Individualized, flowing movement that is meditative, gentle, energizing, and calming, allowing students to stretch, strengthen, and balance. Elizabeth and David focus on breathing, comfort, upliftment, and enjoyment so that everyone's needs are met.

**Philosophy of Teachers**: "To be caring, loving, honoring to our bodies, minds, and souls as we deepen our sense of connectedness within ourselves and our community (circle of retreat participants) through sharing in movement, stillness, dialogue, and music."

**Student Criteria**: All levels are welcome.

**Disability Access**: Some access; please call.

**What to Bring**: Props are provided. Bring warm clothes for evening mountain strolls, comfortable clothes for yoga, hiking shoes, a swimsuit, a tennis racquet, and personal items.

**Yoga Room Size and Description**: Two meeting rooms are used for yoga, one 37.5' x 30' and the other 37' x 19'. Both rooms are carpeted and have high ceilings and an abundance of windows with views of Rock Creek.

**Number of Participants Possible**: 30

**Accommodations**: Various rooms, apartments, suites, townhouses, condos, and cabins are available at Rock Creek Resort. Most rooms have balconies or patios that overlook the mountains. Kitchenettes are available in the apartments, condos, townhouses, and cabins. All accommodations are first class, with twin, queen, or king beds and private baths.

**Meals**: A light breakfast is served daily. Lunches and dinners are on your own. The resort has two restaurants on the premises. Some rooms have kitchenettes.

**Fee**: Tuition for the yoga classes is $385 per person. This fee includes a light breakfast. Lodging costs range from approximately $88 per night (for a double-occupancy room) to $250 per night (for a cabin that sleeps six). Roommate coordination can be arranged for those who want to share lodging expenses.

**Credit Cards**: Not accepted for yoga tuition. Rock Creek Resort accepts Visa, Discover, Mastercard, and American Express.

**Sample Daily Schedule**:

| | |
|---|---|
| 7:00–8:00 a.m. | Sadhana |
| 8:00–8:45 | Light breakfast (provided) |
| 8:45–10:30 | Asana class |
| 10:30 | Brunch (on your own) |
| 11:30–5:00 p.m. | Free time and organized outings |
| 5:00–6:00 | Dinner break |
| 7:30–9:30 | Evening program (yoga, music, dialogue, sharing, playtime, meditation) |

**Other Activities**: On-property indoor facilities include a health club with a heated swimming pool, Jacuzzi, exercise room, and sauna. Outdoor facilities include tennis courts, a soccer field, a playground, and volleyball courts. You can also play horseshoes, and fish for trout in Rock Creek. Red Lodge offers many restaurants, shopping opportunities (including art galleries), and a golf course.

**Services**: Massage, facials, reflexology treatments, and babysitting are available.

**Guest Comment**: *"I loved my experience at the yoga retreat held at Rock Creek Resort in Red Lodge. Elizabeth's style of teaching yoga is dynamic and effective in releasing tension in the body and bringing in spiritual awareness. Elizabeth teaches from the heart with a priceless knowledge of yoga. The Rock Creek resort felt like heaven on earth. The scenic views and trails, with the creek flowing in front, provided a tranquil, pleasing experience. I can't wait for the next retreat!"*
Mary Cavanaugh — Billings, Montana

**Summary**: This retreat, held in Montana's beautiful Beartooth Mountains, combines yoga with outdoor activities, including hiking, biking, tennis, and touring. Families are welcome, and babysitting is provided with advance arrangement. Instructors Elizabeth and David Klarich have an extensive yoga background and offer an eclectic, creative approach to teaching.

# WHITE MOUNTAINS
# GORHAM, NEW HAMPSHIRE

## *Yoga Backpacking Trip with Gillian Kapteyn Comstock and Russell Comstock*

## MAY, JULY, AND SEPTEMBER
### FIVE-DAY RETREATS

Meeting at the Wild River trailhead in the wilderness of the White Mountains, guides Gillian Kapteyn Comstock and Russell Comstock take people three miles along this vibrant river to an exquisite camping spot on Cypress Brook in a protected grove. Near deep and sunny pools and among maples and beeches, Cypress Brook is a beautiful place for enjoying the wilderness and deepening the practice of yoga. Yoga is taught three times a day. On the third day the group experiences the purifying effect of a day of silence and fasting while continuing yoga practice. With the rhythm of yoga three times a day, meditation walks in silence, sleeping on the earth, and open-hearted sharing, participants cultivate a spirit of belonging to nature and all of life.

**Address**: Earth Island Expeditions/ The Maitri Foundation
201 Ten Stones Circle
Charlotte, VT 05445
**Phone**: 802/425-4710; 800/793-4770
**Fax**: 802/425-4004
**E-mail**: earthexped@aol.com

**Airport Information**: Fly into Portland, Maine, and drive 90 miles. Manchester, New Hampshire, is three and one-half hours away.

**How to Get There**: The camping site is located in the easternmost part of the White Mountains along the border of New Hampshire and Maine. It is 90 miles northwest of Portland, Maine, 40 miles north of Conway, New Hampshire, and 15 miles south of Gorham, New Hampshire. Specific directions and a map will be sent. Participants must arrange their own

transportation to and from the trip meeting site.

**Teacher Background**: Gillian Kapteyn Comstock, codirector of Earth Island Expeditions, is a holistic psychotherapist, a certified Kripalu yoga instructor, and a Phoenix Rising yoga therapist with a private practice in the Champlain Valley of Vermont. She holds an M.A. in Counseling Psychology and a B.A. in Human Ecology and is a certified Wilderness First Responder.

Russell Comstock, codirector of Earth Island Expeditions, is an active student and teacher of wilderness living skills. He holds a B.A. in Human Ecology and has trained as a Quest Guide with Earth Rise Foundation and at the School of Lost Borders and as a wilderness guide through outdoor leadership training seminars. Russell is a licensed New York state guide and is a nationally certified Wilderness Emergency Medical Technician.

**Style of Yoga**: Kripalu yoga

**Philosophy of Teachers**: "We are dedicated to discovering with others the spirit of wilderness in mind, body, and earth. When we discover the connection between the inner and outer wilderness, we satisfy our wild soul and become more sensitive to the wild places on earth."

**Student Criteria**: All levels are welcome. Previous backpacking/camping experience or peak physical fitness is not required, although good health of body and mind are important.

**Disability Access**: No access

**What to Bring**: Participants will be given a complete and specific list of suggested equipment and clothing needed for this backpacking trip, which has been "field tested" for enjoying whatever weather conditions happen to occur.

**Yoga Room Size and Description**: The earth in a lovely grove of beeches and maples is our yoga room.

**Number of Participants Possible**: 8

**Accommodations**: Participants camp in the backcountry. The group will set up tents and tarp canopies as shelters for sleeping, eating, and practicing yoga. Participants will find their own tent sites at the camping site. The Wild River is just minutes down the trail, and streams provide excellent opportunities for refreshing dips.

**Meals**: All food and cooking gear are provided. Guides delight in working with participants to create delicious meals in the wild. Three vegetarian meals a day are prepared from organi-

cally grown whole foods. The third day of the retreat is a day of fasting. Meals are cooked over the open campfire and often include homegrown and fresh fruits and vegetables as well as wild edibles. Special dietary needs can be accommodated.

**Fee**: $450 per person includes guided backpack trip (four nights and five days of camping), three meals daily, and yoga/meditation instruction.

**Credit Cards**: Not accepted

**Sample Daily Schedule**:

| | |
|---|---|
| 6:30 a.m. | Wake-up drum, campfire, and hot tea |
| 7:00–8:30 | Morning yoga (gentle) |
| 8:30–9:30 | Breakfast and dream sharing |
| 9:30–11:30 | Personal free time |
| 11:00–12:30 p.m. | Midday yoga |
| 12:30–1:30 | Lunch |
| 1:30–4:00 | Personal free time |
| 4:00–5:30 | Late afternoon yoga (vigorous) |
| 6:00–7:00 | Dinner |
| 7:00–8:30 | Evening council circle (sharing, ritual, song, and story) |

The third day includes fasting, silence, and periods of solitude and meditation.

**Other Activities**: Living simply outdoors, solitude in nature, learning wilderness living skills, sitting by the campfire at night, enjoying the boundless sky. The waterfalls, streams, pools, forest wildflowers, birds, wildlife, and the forested grove all offer poignant moments for play and reflection.

**Guest Comment**: *"A magical experience. Russell and Gillian brought together a diverse group of strangers and through the power of yoga, the wilderness, and open-hearted sharing created a unified family of kindred spirits. I came away from this remarkable experience feeling uplifted and immeasurably enriched."*
Norma Maege — Stowe, Vermont

**Summary**: This backcountry camping experience takes place in the wilderness setting of the White Mountain National Forest. Participants enjoy community meals, yoga, and sharing, along with times of solitude in a protected grove at Cypress Brook. Here clear pools, waterfalls, and mossy rocks bring beauty and inspiration for yoga and meditation. In the stillness and enchantment of this environment, practicing yoga in the grove helps cultivate a spirit of belonging to life and to all of earth.

SEE PHOTOS, PAGE 146.

# THE HARD AND THE SOFT ASHTANGA YOGA CENTER EAST HAMPTON, NEW YORK

*Power Yoga with Beryl Bender Birch and Thom Birch*

## JUNE–SEPTEMBER
### ONE WEEK EACH MONTH

The Hard and The Soft Ashtanga Yoga Center in East Hampton is adjacent to the home of yoga instructors Beryl Bender Birch and Thom Birch, who offer yoga retreats here from June through September. Their center is a secluded spot on two acres of land surrounded by scrub oak and pine trees, meditation gardens, birds, and a swimming pool with a lovely deck and relaxing lounge chairs. Approximately one mile from town and one mile from the beaches, the center provides bikes for guests to use. There are three resident white Siberian huskies on the premises who, like their owners, eat only organic foods and are very clean and sweet.

**Address**: Beryl Bender Birch and Thom Birch
325 East 41st St. #203
New York, NY 10017
**Phone**: 212/661-2895
**Fax**: 516/329-5221
**E-mail**: yoga@power-yoga.com
**Web site**: www.power.yoga.com

**Airport Information**: LaGuardia and JFK airports are approximately 95 miles away, and Islip (Long Island) is approximately 55 miles away. The trip from LaGuardia and JFK can take from two to four hours. The trip from Islip can take from one and one-half to two and one-half hours. All three airports connect to East Hampton via the Hampton Jitney, 516/283-4600 or 800/936-0440.

**How to Get There**: East Hampton is 100 miles east of New York City, almost at the end of Long Island.

**Teacher Background**: Beryl Bender Birch and Thom Birch have been offering yoga

vacations internationally since 1985. They are both students of Krishnamacharya and Patanjali and have studied Ashtanga yoga directly with Sri K. Pattabhi Jois. Beryl has been teaching yoga for more than 25 years, and Thom has been teaching for more than 15 years. Thom began his yoga career as a runner; he and Beryl now teach their Power yoga classes at the New York Runners Club, an organization of runners with more than 30,000 international members.

**Style of Yoga**: Ashtanga or Power yoga. Beryl Bender Birch first coined the term *Power yoga* as a user-friendly word for the Western mind. Power yoga is a strong practice (as opposed to softer and better-known forms of yoga) that utilizes strength and heat in the body, giving the body a workout. Beryl and Thom teach Power yoga in a way that is tailored to each individual's needs and abilities.

**Philosophy of Teachers**: "We are classical teachers of Patanjali's yoga, or Ashtanga yoga—the eight-limbed path, and we use asana and pranayama as our basic daily practice."

**Student Criteria**: All are welcome.

**Disability Access**: No access

**What to Bring**: Yoga mat, comfortable clothes for warm, humid weather, sweater for cool evenings, swimsuit, beach towel, running/walking shoes.

**Yoga Room Size and Description**: The studio is a light-filled room with hardwood floors and windows on four sides.

**Number of Participants Possible**: 12

**Accommodations**: The main house, which belongs to Beryl and Thom, has three bedrooms and three bathrooms and sleeps up to five people. Participants sleep two to a room unless they request a single. There is limited availability for camping in the backyard. Campers need to bring their own camping equipment. The private home next door is also available—it has three bedrooms and two bathrooms and sleeps up to five people.

**Meals**: Two vegetarian meals per day (brunch and dinner) are prepared by a gourmet natural-foods chef who cooks everything fresh each day using all organic foods.

**Fee**: $1,200 per person per week includes two yoga classes per day plus two meditations, pranayama, and lecture; two meals per day; accommodations; and use of bikes for trips to town or the beach.

**Credit Cards**: Not accepted

**Sample Daily Schedule**:

| | |
|---|---|
| 7:00 a.m. | Meditation and breathing |
| 8:00 | Yoga practice |
| 11:00 | Brunch |

Free time for hiking, swimming, biking, relaxing on the beach, reading

| | |
|---|---|
| 3:30 p.m. | Afternoon lecture |
| 6:30 | Dinner |
| 8:00 | Evening program |

**Other Activities**: This small upscale resort town has beautiful beaches and no hotels or commercial buildings on the beaches. The area offers hiking trails and great roads for in-line skating, biking, and running. East Hampton tends to be a playground for the rich and famous in the summertime and offers plenty of fabulous upscale shopping, tennis, and golf. Thom and Beryl have a pool, deck, and hot tub at their home. There are great trails for biking and exploring nearby wetland areas where you may see a variety of water birds.

**Guest Comment**: *"The yoga was challenging and expertly assisted. The small group created a special intimate environment conducive to diving deep into the practice of yoga. By week's end, I felt as if I had traded my body in for a new one. The hospitality and accommodations were exceptional. The daily bike trips to the beach were full of fun and laughs. The food was exquisitely fresh, organic, lovingly prepared, and worth the trip in and of itself. The guitar playing and singing was food for the soul. By far the best of the best. I look forward to returning next year."*

Colby Lewis—
Stockbridge, Massachusetts

**Summary**: Beryl Bender Birch and Thom Birch hold weeklong Ashtanga Power yoga vacations at their yoga center in East Hampton. One mile from the beach, this elegant private house is surrounded by pine and oak trees and has a lovely pool, deck, and light-filled yoga room. This vacation offers an opportunity to stay in the actual home of these internationally renowned teachers, who offer intimate classes and morning meditations on the beach.

# ANANDA ASHRAM
# MONROE, NEW YORK

## YEAR-ROUND

Nestled in the foothills of the Catskill Mountains, Ananda Ashram is the country center of the Yoga Society of New York, Inc. Founded in 1964 by Ramamurti S. Mishra, M.D., later known as Shri Brahmananda, the ashram functions as a universal center for spiritual research, East-West cultural exchange, and the living application of the teachings of yoga. The ashram offers retreat facilities for guests year-round and residential accommodations for staff and students.

With 85 acres of woods, rolling meadows, and orchards and a beautiful lake with an island, the grounds provide a serene, natural environment for spiritual retreat and healing. In the spirit of the founder, the programs offered at the ashram are nonsectarian, with an emphasis on self-analysis and promotion of peace through mutual understanding. The ashram strives to be a common ground where the cultures and philosophies of East and West—both ancient and modern—may come together to form a vital and peaceful whole. To this end, individuals and groups of all faiths, creeds, origins, and orientations are welcomed at the Ashram.

**Address**: Ananda Ashram
13 Sapphire Rd.
Monroe, NY 10950
**Phone**: 914/782-5575
**Fax**: 914/782-6688
**Web site**: www.anandaashram.org

**Airport Information**: From New York and New Jersey airports take a shuttle bus to the Port Authority. From the New York City Port Authority take the Shoreline Bus to Monroe (1 hour 20 minutes) and then take a cab to Ananda Ashram (10 minutes).

**How to Get There**: The ashram is located in Monroe, New York, 50 miles from New York City.

**Teacher Background**: Yoga classes and weekend programs are facilitated by ashram teachers who are senior disciples and students of Shri Brahmananda.

**Style of Yoga**: Hatha yoga with daily meditation, Sanskrit chanting, and discussion of yoga philosophy.

**Philosophy of Teachers**: "We follow Pantajali's eight-fold path."

**Student Criteria**: All levels of experience are welcome.

**Disability Access**: There are no ramps, but many buildings have one floor and are at ground level. Please call ahead of time for further information.

**What to Bring**: Comfortable clothing for meditation and yoga, warm clothing and firm shoes for outdoors, a flashlight, an alarm clock, toiletries, a notebook, and a yoga mat.

**Yoga Room Size and Description**: Yoga is practiced in two rooms. One is 15' x

18', the other 12' x 16'. The larger room, in the lake house, is carpeted and has windows overlooking the lake. The smaller room is in the main house and has windows looking out on the lake and trees. This room is also carpeted.

**Number of Participants Possible**: 40

**Accommodations**: Three guest houses provide simple dormitory and semi-private rooms. Dormitories have bunk beds and sleep up to six people per room. A semi-private room has two beds. All the rooms have windows and pleasant views, some overlooking the lake. Bathrooms are shared. Camping is available in season.

**Meals**: The ashram serves lacto-vegetarian meals in a variety of cuisines three times daily on weekends and holidays. During the winter and early spring, only one formal meal, lunch, is served on weekdays; breakfast and dinners are informal. Three meals daily are included in the room rate.

**Fee**: Costs are $50 per person per weekend night, $40 per weekday night, $230 per week, $400 per two weeks, and $530 for a three-week stay. This includes meals, morning and evening satsang, cultural programs, Sanskrit classes, and one movement class a day. A 10-percent discount is given to students over 18, seniors, members, and sponsors. Please inquire about youth rates and family rates.

**Credit Cards**: Discover, Mastercard, and Visa

**Sample Daily Schedule**:

| | |
|---|---|
| 7:00 a.m. | Yoga class |
| 8:00 | Breakfast |
| 9:00 | Satsang program |
| 10:30 | Sanskrit class |
| 12:30 p.m. | Lunch |
| 4:00 | Yoga class |
| 5:30 | Dinner |
| 7:30 | Satsang program |

The satsang program includes a Vedic fire ceremony, silent meditation, and Sanskrit chanting followed by a presentation and discussion of yoga philosophy.

**Other Activities**: Walk on the ashram's nature paths and enjoy its variety of plants and wildlife. There is a swimming pool and eucalyptus sauna on the premises. A silent healing temple is maintained for personal prayer and meditation throughout the day.

**Services**: The ashram healing center offers Swedish, deep tissue, and trigger-point massage, shiatsu, acupressure, facials, foot reflexology, relaxation training, and electro-magnetic and crystal healing.

**Guest Comment**: *"I have been coming to Ananda Ashram for over 10 years. Each year I look forward to many beautiful aspects of Ananda: the genuine warmth and friendliness of the staff and guests, the delicious vegetarian meals, and the area of lush, natural beauty. I appreciate the casual informality of Ananda Ashram. I know I speak for others when I say that I feel totally safe and free to be myself."*
Elizabeth Page—San Rafael, California

**Summary**: Ananda Ashram is a beautifully wooded property of 85 acres that includes gardens, a lake, and several resident and guest houses. Emphasis at this yoga community is on quiet relaxation, natural beauty, meditation, cultural entertainment, and physical, mental and spiritual comfort. Besides the daily morning and evening meditation programs, the ashram offers a variety of classes and workshops on topics, including Hatha yoga, Sanskrit, East-West dance, music, and art.

# SIVANANDA ASHRAM YOGA RANCH
# WOODBOURNE, NEW YORK

## YEAR-ROUND

A wonderful escape from the noise, smog, and business of the city, the Sivananda Yoga Ashram Ranch is located in the New York Catskills on 77 acres of rolling fields, wooded hills, and open skies. The hilltop countryside is abundant with wildlife and nature trails and has a swimming pond for use in the summer. In winter enjoy the beauty of white snow, brisk invigorating air, and silent forests to glide through on cross-country skies.

The ranch offers a complete daily schedule of yoga based on the traditional yogic teachings of Sivananda and infused with Vedanta philosophy. The ranch is open 365 days a year, and programs include weekend yoga getaways, five-day mini yoga vacations, and other special events and trainings. Guests are required to participate fully in all scheduled classes and meditations and can make reservations for any length of stay year-round.

**Address**: Sivananda Ashram Yoga Ranch
Catskill Mountains
P.O. Box 195, Budd Rd.
Woodbourne, NY 12788
**Phone**: 914/436-6492
**Fax**: 914/434-1032
**E-mail**: yogaranch@sivananda.org
**Web site**: www.sivananda.org/ranch.htm

**Airport Information**: Fly into LaGuardia or JFK in New York City.

**How to Get There**: Woodbourne is 100 miles from New York City, which takes a little more than two hours to drive. The bus from New York's Port Authority goes to Woodbourne, and you will be picked up in town by the ranch staff if you call.

**Teacher Background**: Classes are taught by ashram staff on a rotating basis. All staff teachers have been trained in the Sivananda yogic teachings and philosophy.

**Style of Yoga**: Classical yoga, which includes a synthesis of Raja, Hatha, Karma, and Bhakti yoga. Classes are taught by ashram staff and follow teachings set by Swami Sivananda. Twelve main asana positions are used. Devotional practices such as silent meditation, chanting, prayers, and Sanskrit verses are used daily to help cultivate the teachings.

**Philosophy of Teachers**: "Vendanta philosophy, exploring the nature of self and truth. Five basic principles of health: proper exercise, proper breathing, proper relaxation, proper diet, positive thinking, and meditation. Discipline can provide physical, psychological, and spiritual balance and harmony."

**Student Criteria**: No experience necessary. All guests must participate in the daily schedule.

**Disability Access**: No access

**What to Bring**: Yoga mat (can be rented), swimsuit, towel, good walking shoes or boots, comfortable clothes for yoga class.

**Yoga Room Size and Description**: Two indoor rooms are used for yoga. The temple can accommodate about 22 people, and a large hall holds up to 50 or 60. In the summer three outside platforms are also used for yoga; one holds 55 people, another holds 35, and the smallest holds 12.

**Number of Participants Possible**: 140

**Accommodations**: There are two guest buildings; one is a turn-of-the-twentieth-century farmhouse, the other a small 1920s three-story hotel. The farmhouse has three baths that guests share and 11 rooms holding 26 beds. Most rooms have two beds each, some three or four. The other guesthouse has 22 rooms and 49 beds. There are also seven apartments with private baths on the first floor. Each apartment has two to four beds. All rooms are very simple and rustic. When the weather permits, tent space is available.

**Meals**: An organic garden and greenhouse supply a good portion of the food. Meals are strictly vegetarian. Dairy products are used sparingly. No eggs, fish, fowl, garlic, onions, or caffeinated beverages are served. Two buffet-style meals are served each day. In the summer people eat outside.

**Fee**: Shared rooms, Sunday through Thursday, cost $40 per night per person; rooms cost $5 more on Friday and Saturday. The weekly rate is $250. Apartments with a private bath cost $10 more per person per night. Camping (bring your own tent) Sunday through Thursday costs $30 per person per night and $5 more on Friday and Saturday. The weekly rate is $190. Holiday rates are an additional $10.

**Credit Cards**: Visa and Mastercard

**Sample Daily Schedule**:

| | |
|---|---|
| 5:30 a.m. | Wake-up bell |
| 6:00 | Satsang |
| 8:00 | Hatha yoga class |
| 10:00 | Brunch |
| 11:00 | Karma yoga |
| 1:00 p.m. | Workshop |
| 4:00 | Dinner |
| 8:00 p.m. | Meditation, chanting, and talk |

Satsang includes chanting, meditation, readings, and discussion. Attendance at classes and meditations is mandatory.

**Other Activities**: There is a Russian sauna, organic gardening, sweat lodges, music and dance concerts, cross-country skiing in the winter, fields of flowers in the spring, swimming in the pond in the summer, brilliant colors in autumn, and hiking in every season.

**Guest Comment**: *"The Sivananda Ranch is a place that encourages beginners and at the same time is serious and challenging for more experienced practitioners. The staff and residents truly pursue a spiritual lifestyle, which is inspiring to guests."*
Gail Lichter—New York, New York

**Summary**: Simple, rustic, and clean, the Sivananda Yoga Ranch offers programs based on the traditional yogic teachings of Sivananda. Emphasis is on personal discipline in the practices that results in finding inner silence and peace. Participation in program activities is mandatory. The ranch is a hilltop retreat with 77 acres of woodlands and panoramic views of the Catskill Mountains. The main meeting facility is a 100-year-old farmhouse. In the summer yoga is done outside on platforms. The staff is warm and welcoming. You may arrive on any day and stay as long as you wish.

# GLADE MOUNTAIN RETREAT CENTER
# ASHEVILLE, NORTH CAROLINA

*A Weekend of Yoga, Massage, and Natural Foods with*
*Mary Lou Buck, Brian Federal, Jan Noble, and Lynn Hogue*

## MAY AND NOVEMBER
### WEEKEND RETREATS

Glade Mountain Retreat is a quiet mountainside farm and five-bedroom conference center built on 78 acres overlooking a valley near Leicester, North Carolina. The retreat setting is a gorgeous spot, landscaped with rocks, beautiful flowers, and colorful trees. As the sun rises each morning over the woodlands and meadows, guests awaken to the songs of birds. The property offers country dirt roads for hiking through woods, by pastures, and along a lovely stream with waterfalls.

Twice a year, four facilitators join together to give a weekend retreat at Glade Mountain, combining their talents in offering classes in yoga, massage, and natural foods. The weekend is designed to blend both private instruction with group learning experiences, giving participants personal quiet time and sharing times together.

**Address**: Mary Lou Buck
3406 Mar Vista Circle
Charlotte, NC 28209
**Phone**: 704/525-2293
**E-Mail**: Maryloubuc@aol.com

**Airport Information**: Fly into Asheville, North Carolina. From the airport you will have to rent a car or take a taxi to Glade Mountain Retreat.

**How to Get There**: Near Leicester, North Carolina, Glade Mountain Retreat Center is 30 miles west of Asheville and three hours from Charlotte, North Carolina.

**Teacher Background**: Mary Lou Buck, B.S. Physical Education, is a full-time yoga instructor and creator of *Yoga for Life*, a 56-minute practice tape available in audio and video. She is certified by the Kripalu Center for Yoga and Health and has had advanced teacher training.

Her career has evolved from a personal practice and love of yoga, which began in 1972, and from her experience in physical education and recreation.

Brian Federal is a certified Kripalu body worker and yoga teacher living and practicing in Charlotte, North Carolina. His style of body work incorporates techniques such as Swedish, deep tissue, shiatsu, as well as spa body treatments, skin care, and aromatherapy.

Jan Noble and Lynn Hogue are both creative chefs who enjoy inventing low-fat vegetarian meals and sharing recipes with others.

**Style of Yoga**: Kripalu yoga, a balanced flow of postures that develop greater body awareness, strength, endurance, and flexibility. Breathing techniques are included.

**Philosophy of Teachers**: "Our emphasis is on balance of mind, body, and spirit."

**Student Criteria**: All levels welcome.

**Disability Access**: No access

**What to Bring**: Two blankets and a yoga mat; comfortable, loose fitting clothing (T-shirt and shorts, sweatshirt and pants, socks to layer for warmth, jacket, slippers, and walking shoes); a sleeping bag or bedding; towel; wash cloth; toiletries; a large bath towel for massage class; a journal or notebook for writing; and fruit to share.

**Yoga Room Size and Description**: The room used for yoga is a round, carpeted room with round windows looking out at the mountains. The room measures 800 square feet.

**Number of Participants Possible**: 10

**Accommodations**: Glade Mountain Retreat Center offers five double-occupancy rooms in all. Generally there are two single beds in each room, although it can be arranged for three beds in one room. Guests share shower and bathroom facilities.

**Meals**: Participants at the retreat help with meals (optional) as an informal instruction in natural-foods cooking. Snack food, including fruit, is available during the day.

**Fee**: $250 to $275 per person includes two yoga classes each day, individual instruction, a back rub and a foot rub, natural-foods cooking instruction, meals, and accommodations.

**Credit Cards**: Not accepted

**Sample Daily Schedule**:

| | |
|---|---|
| 8:45 a.m. | Wake-up yoga class |
| 9:45 | Breakfast |
| 11:00 | Body awareness |
| noon | Yoga class |
| afternoon | Private yoga instruction or massage |
| 5:00 p.m. | Food preparation (participants help in the kitchen) |
| 6:00 | Dinner |
| 8:00 | Group foot massage with partners Friday evening; back massage Saturday evening. The retreat ends on Sunday at 2:00 p.m. |

**Other Activities**: The retreat grounds allow for lovely walks. A meditation path at the back of the property leads to two streams and a waterfall. Colorful trees and flowers adorn the garden. There are also open pastures and wooded country roads to explore.

**Guest Comment**: *"My experience of yoga at Glade Mountain Retreat Center was truly wonderful and spiritually sustaining in many ways. The yoga, taught by three different teachers in addition to the master teacher Mary Lou, was top notch and inspired. It's wonderful to experience yoga through the perspective of different teachers. The food was delicious vegetarian cuisine. Also included was an hour-and-a-half massage as well as a session of aromatherapy. This was a new experience for me, and it was enlightening and wonderful. I would highly recommend this retreat. The setting is spectacular, nestled in the North Carolina mountains overlooking a picturesque valley. I was inspired to sit and sketch the scene . . . so beautiful."*

Debbie George— Charlotte, North Carolina

**Summary**: This retreat, in a lovely mountaintop setting, offers a weekend of yoga classes, massage classes, individual yoga instruction, and guidance in vegetarian cooking with four informative facilitators. The land and trees surrounding the retreat provide a peaceful energy and beautiful views.

# LAKE JUNALUSKA
# BLUE RIDGE MOUNTAINS, NORTH CAROLINA

*Fourth of July Yoga Retreat*

## JULY
### ONE WEEK

Every year the Lighten Up Yoga and Wellness Center, founded by Lillah Schwartz, sponsors a weeklong yoga retreat with internationally renowned teachers at Lake Junaluska Assembly in the mountains of western North Carolina. Lake Junaluska is a year-round conference and retreat center that serves the United Methodist community. The beautiful 200-acre lake is surrounded by rolling hills, exquisite gardens, and a walking path lined with breathtaking roses. There is a bridge that spans the lake, from which people enjoy watching and feeding the many ducks and swans that swim by.

One of the special features of this retreat is that children are welcome. A Children's Activity Program is provided by the Lake Junaluska Child Care Ministry for kids up to 11 years of age. Preteens and teens are welcome to use the recreation room, pool, and other facilities on their own. Children are housed in larger hotel rooms with their parents and remain under the supervision of the Juneluska children's staff during yoga classes. Child care for two evening yoga programs should be prearranged.

**Address:** Lighten Up Yoga—
East Coast Yoga Vacation
60 Biltmore Ave.
Asheville, NC 28801
**Phone:** 828/254-7756
**Fax:** 828/254-3797

**Airport Information:** The Asheville Airport is only 50 minutes from Lake Junaluska. An additional fee of $30 per person will cover round-trip van transportation to the assembly. Cooper Travel Service is the travel agent recommended by Lighten Up Yoga for this retreat. Call toll free 800/627-1644.

**How to Get There:** Lake Junaluska Assembly is two miles north of Waynesville and five miles east of Maggie Valley. The retreat center is just 26 miles west of Asheville, with easy access to Interstate 40.

**Teacher Background:** Teachers vary from year to year. Call Lighten Up Yoga to get current announcement for this year's retreat.

**Style of Yoga:** Mostly Iyengar teachers lead the retreats. Sometimes teachers with other styles lead as well. Please call for this year's schedule.

**Philosophy of Teachers:** Varies with each individual teacher.

**Student Criteria:** Beginners who have had at least three months or more of yoga practice and those at intermediate levels. An intermediate student has a regular inverted practice, can push up into a full back bend with arms straight, and can perform a handstand with the support of a wall.

**Disability Access**: No access

**What to Bring**: Yoga mats, blankets, straps, and blocks.

**Yoga Room Size and Description**: The yoga room is air-conditioned, carpeted, large (900 to 1,000 square feet) and private, with windows on two sides.

**Number of Participants Possible**: 50

**Accommodations**: The yoga group stays in a full-service hotel and historic inn with a charming antebellum atmosphere, air-conditioned rooms, private baths, TVs, phones, and a 24-hour switchboard. The inn provides double-occupancy rooms for all yoga participants (some variations are available for couples and families).

**Meals**: Lake Junaluska provides the yoga group with a vegetarian menu in a private dining room. A mixed buffet of vegetarian entrees is served and includes nondairy dishes whenever possible. For those who want nonvegetarian meals, there is another dining hall that serves meat dishes.

**Fee**: $990 per person for adults includes seven nights', six days' accommodations (double occupancy), meals, and yoga classes. Nonparticipating spouses deduct $160. For children staying in deluxe rooms with parents, the fee is $382 for ages 12–17, $168 for ages 5–11, and $95 for children 4 and under.

**Credit Cards**: Not accepted

**Sample Daily Schedule**:
(Participants are divided into two groups: general and intermediate levels.)

| | |
|---|---|
| 7:00–8:30 a.m. | Breakfast |
| 7:30–9:30 | Group 1 yoga class |
| 9:45–11:45 | Group 2 yoga class |
| noon–1:30 p.m. | Lunch |
| 3:00–4:30 | Group 1 yoga class |
| 4:45–6:15 | Group 2 yoga class |
| 6:00–7:00 | Dinner |
| 8:00 | Evening programs |

**Other Activities**: Lake Junaluska offers hiking and jogging trails, biking, walking in the gardens, tennis, shuffleboard, a beautiful golf course, canoeing in the lake, and swimming and sunning by the pool. Nearby sightseeing attractions include the Great Smoky Mountains National Park, the Blue Ridge Parkway, the Biltmore Estate, and the Cherokee Indian Reservation. There will be fireworks and a celebration of the Fourth of July.

**Guest Comment**: *"I have thoroughly enjoyed attending East Coast Yoga Vacation at Lake Junaluska for the past eight years. The mountains of western North Carolina are an ideal setting for a yoga vacation experience. There are many opportunities to explore the mountain trails and waterfalls in the area, and a trip into Asheville is rewarding as well. The quality of yoga instruction has always been exceptional, with highly skilled, well-known teachers. Each year I look forward to my week in the North Carolina mountains with my yoga friends, many of whom return year after year, as I do."*
Larry Schonhofen—Clemmons, North Carolina

**Summary**: This weeklong yoga residency at Lake Junaluska accommodates the whole family. Children are welcome, appreciated, and well cared for. An annual event sponsored by the Lighten Up Yoga Center in Asheville each year brings opportunities to study with accomplished yoga teachers, many of whom are of the Iyengar tradition. Set on a gorgeous Lake Junaluska, the retreat center offers swimming, canoeing, biking, and a wonderful rosebush-lined walking path. A great place to enjoy yoga while taking the time to stop and smell the roses!

# BUCKHORN SPRINGS RETREAT CENTER ASHLAND, OREGON

## *Yoga with Julie Lawrence*

### AUGUST
### SIX DAYS, FIVE NIGHTS

Buckhorn Springs Retreat Center is a 120-acre mineral-springs resort located on Emigrant Creek in Southern Oregon. This quiet retreat sits in a secluded valley at the confluence of the Siskiyou and Cascade Mountains. Listed on the National Register of Historic Places, the century-old lodge and 12 cabins are being completely and authentically restored. The revival of Buckhorn Springs began in 1989 and now offers a restored lodge with eight unique guest rooms, a restaurant serving healthy, hearty meals, and four creek-side cabins. Yoga teacher Julie Lawrence holds her August retreat each year at this historic hot springs hotel. Although the hot springs are not fully functioning at this time, the peaceful forest setting is ideal for yoga, meditation, and relaxation. Known as a place where Native American tribes once gathered for sacred healing rites, the ambience of Buckhorn Springs is one of beauty and tranquility.

**Address**: Julie Lawrence
1020 S.W. Taylor St., Suite 780
Portland, OR 97205
**Phone**: 503/227-5524
**E-mail**: PouncerLW@aol.com
**Web site**: www.jlyc.com

**Airport Information**: Fly into Medford, Oregon.

**How to Get There**: Buckhorn Springs Retreat Center is 20 minutes from Ashland, Oregon.

**Teacher Background**: Julie Lawrence, director of the Julie Lawrence Yoga Center in Portland, Oregon, is a certified Iyengar yoga instructor and has studied many times with the Iyengars in Pune, India. Julie has taught in the United States and internationally for more than 20 years.

**Style of Yoga**: Iyengar yoga. Julie's style of teaching integrates Eastern practice of yoga with our Western lifestyle.

**Philosophy of Teacher**: "Yoga is a process of making oneself whole. By working the body, controlling the breath, and quieting the mind, we create a stable, calm framework in which to live our lives."

**Student Criteria**: All levels of experience are welcome.

**Disability Access**: Yes

**What to Bring**: Yoga props are necessary. Bring three firm yoga blankets, a yoga mat, a block, and a strap. Bring your favorite poetry for the after-dinner poetry reading on the deck. Also bring comfortable clothes for yoga, a warm sweater, a swimsuit, walking shoes, a flashlight, insect repellent, sunglasses, suntan lotion, personal hygiene items, and clothes for town if you choose to go to a Shakespearean play in Ashland.

**Yoga Room Size and Description:** The room used for yoga is the large living room of the main lodge. The room has a beautiful wood floor, some windows that look out on nature, and high ceilings. It is approximately 900 square feet.

**Number of Participants Possible:** 25

**Accommodations:** The main lodge has multiple newly redecorated rooms. Some have single beds; some have double, queens, or kings. In addition, separate cabins are available. All rooms in the lodge have their own private bath. Most of the cabins have a private bath as well, although a few share a nearby bathhouse. Guests sleep two to a room; single rooms are available for an extra fee.

**Meals:** Three homemade vegetarian meals are served daily. Much of the food is grown in the garden on the property. Special dietary needs are cheerfully accommodated.

**Fee:** $735 per person includes five nights' lodging (double occupancy) at Buckhorn Springs, three daily vegetarian meals, and two yoga classes each day with Julie. Single rooms are available at an additional fee.

**Credit Cards:** Not accepted

**Sample Daily Schedule:**

| | |
|---|---|
| 7:30–8:30 a.m. | Light breakfast |
| 9:30–noon | Yoga class |
| 12:30 p.m. | Lunch |
| 4:00–6:00 | Yoga class |
| 6:30 | Dinner |
| 8:15 | Discussion and/or free time |

One evening the group will hold an after-dinner poetry reading on the deck.

**Other Activities:** The area offers fabulous hiking on more than 100 acres of forest land, swimming in nearby lakes, horseback riding, and fishing (current license required). Buckhorn Springs is only 20 minutes away from the Ashland Shakespeare Festival, which runs all summer. Dinner is finished in time for participants to go into Ashland for a play. Sleeping, reading, and just doing nothing are also encouraged.

**Services:** Professional massage is available.

**Guest Comment:** *"The concentration and intensity of yoga instruction in the yoga vacation was worth 18 weeks of classes all in one week. As a teacher, Julie inspires as she instructs. She is gentle and kind as she pushes you to your edge. Her explanations, demonstrations, and humor helps you understand what you need to do to reach a pose. Her emphasis on the little things helps you achieve the pose more easily. When I returned home I was stronger in both spirit and body."*
Amy Duncun — Portland, Oregon

**Summary:** This yoga vacation provides Iyengar yoga, pranayama, meditation, and friendship in the serenity of an Oregon forest. Participants enjoy swimming in nearby mountain lakes or catching a Shakespearean play at the festival in Ashland. Yoga teacher Julie Lawrence is warm and encouraging as well as precise in her yoga instruction.

# THE HIMALAYAN INSTITUTE
# HONESDALE, PENNSYLVANIA

## YEAR-ROUND

Founded in 1971 by Sri Swami Rama, the Himalayan Institute of Yoga Science and Philosophy is situated in a serene, wooded setting on 400 acres in the rolling hills of the Pocono Mountains of northeastern Pennsylvania. Combining Eastern wisdom with Western technology, the institute offers a wide variety of seminars and programs in Hatha yoga, meditation, yoga philosophy, psychology, holistic health, and related topics.

The 400-acre campus, rich in wildlife, offers beautiful vistas; woodland hiking trails; vegetable, herb, and flower gardens; an orchard; and a waterfall near a spring-fed pond. Originally built as a Catholic seminary, the institute's three-story main building offers clean and comfortable facilities. Yoga instruction is provided by professional and dedicated residents. Research into ancient healing and self-development techniques by the resident faculty is used as the basis for many of the programs offered. Biofeedback is linked with the practice of yoga and Eastern philosophy to create a mind/body approach to living.

**Address**: The Himalayan Institute
RR 1, Box 400
Honesdale, PA 18431
**Phone**: 800/822-4547
**Web site**: www.himalayaninstitute.org

**Airport Information**: The Himalayan Institute is one and one-half hours from the Wilkes-Barre/Scranton Airport and three hours from New York City airports (add an extra hour if driving during rush hour).

**How to Get There**: The Himalayan Institute is located in northeastern Pennsylvania, six miles north of the town of Honesdale on Route 670.

**Teacher Background**: Trained staff members of the Himalayan Institute take turns leading Hatha yoga classes and assist in teaching the various courses.

**Style of Yoga**: Raja yoga. The study and practice of Raja yoga techniques for

body, breath, mind, and spirit are taught in a systematic and comprehensive manner following the eight-limbed system of Ashtanga yoga.

**Philosophy of Teachers**: "The teachings at the Himalayan Institute help people grow physically, mentally, and spiritually and become more self-reliant by combining the best knowledge of both the East and the West."

**Student Criteria**: Generally there are no prerequisites; some classes require participants to have a regular Hatha/meditation practice. Please call for information.

**Disability Access**: Depends on the disability. There are no elevators in the building, only stairs. Please call with concerns.

**What to Bring**: Yoga mat, casual, comfortable clothing, robe, slippers, sweater or shawl for cool evenings, toiletries (including soap), alarm clock, flashlight, and umbrella.

**Yoga Room Size and Description**: Four different rooms are utilized for Hatha yoga classes; each has carpet and windows.

**Number of Participants Possible**: 15 to 50

**Accommodations**: Simply furnished rooms have one or two twin beds and a sink. Single rooms are limited and may be unavailable for some programs. Dormitories (separate men's and women's) accommodate 18 in bunk beds. Guests share hall bathrooms. Limited accommodations for families with children may be available by prior arrangement.

**Meals**: Three nutritionally balanced vegetarian meals are served each day, cafeteria style. Nondairy options are available. Breakfast is hearty. The main meal is served at lunch, and a light meal is served at dinner. A tea room serves herbal brews (noncaffeinated) that vary from day to day. Coffee is not served at the institute.

**Fee**: For two nights in a single room pay $130 per person; for seven nights, $455. For two nights in a double room pay $110 per person; for seven nights, $385. For two nights in the dorm pay $90 per person; for seven nights, $315. Seminars and programs have additional fees. Call for a catalog. The Meditation Retreat Program is included in these rates, as are meals.

**Credit Cards**: Visa and Mastercard

**Sample Daily Schedule**:

| | |
|---|---|
| 6:45 a.m. | Hatha yoga |
| 8:00 | Breakfast |
| 10:00 | Lecture/workshop |
| 12:30 p.m. | Lunch |
| 3:30 | Lecture/workshop |
| 6:00 | Dinner |
| 7:30 | Lecture/workshop |
| 9:00 | Meditation |

**Other Activities**: Hiking trails, cross-country skiing and ice skating in the winter, tennis, handball, basketball and biking. There is also exercise equipment available.

**Services**: Therapeutic massage, pancha karma, biofeedback, holistic health services, and psychological counseling are available. A bookstore/gift shop and homeopathic pharmacy are also available.

**Guest Comment**: *"We love the quiet, tranquil environment at the Himalayan Institute. The food, the instruction, the clean pleasant facilities were a plus. Residents maintain beautiful flower gardens. A true sanctuary in the Pennsylvania mountains."*
Terry and Susan McDonald —
Walpole, New Hampshire

**Summary**: The Himalayan International Institute of Yoga Science and Philosophy uses Hatha yoga, biofeedback, aerobic exercise, breathing, meditation, diet, and fasting to help people to reduce stress in their daily lives. Surrounded by trees and flowers, rabbits, deer, and wooded hiking trails, this mountaintop setting and its serene atmosphere provide the appropriate environment for exploring mind and body healing.

# INNER HARMONY RETREAT CENTER
# INNER HARMONY, UTAH

*Inner Harmony Yoga Retreats*

## MARCH, JUNE, JULY, AUGUST, AND SEPTEMBER
### WEEKLONG RETREATS

At 9,300 feet, nestled in the aspen-covered mountains of southern Utah, Inner Harmony Retreat Center has spectacular vistas enhanced by the seasons. Summer and fall offer walks and challenging hikes around the 70-acre grounds. Winter brings cross-country skiing. Combine these outdoor activities with yoga and you've got an energizing vacation. That's just what owners John and Lynn Epert had in mind when they started hosting weekend yoga retreats at Inner Harmony in 1991. Since that time they have expanded to offering eight weeklong yoga retreats each year. All retreat presenters are acclaimed in their field of expertise and are certified instructors. Teachers John Friend, Mary Beth Markus, and Elise Miller are regulars at Inner Harmony. Please call Inner Harmony for specific guest teacher retreat dates.

**Address**: John and Lynn Epert
P.O. Box 87390
Phoenix, AZ 85080
**Phone**: 800/214-0174; 800/347-5633
**Fax**: 602/566-2659
**E-mail**: jepert@Azonline.com
**Web site**: www.ihretreat.com

**Airport Information**: Fly into Cedar City from Salt Lake City via Delta's Skywest airlines. Transportation is provided to and from the airport at no cost to participants. Some people fly into Las Vegas, Nevada, because flights are more reasonably priced, and then rent a car and drive three hours to Inner Harmony.

**How to Get There**: Inner Harmony is four miles from Bryanhead Ski Resort in southern Utah, 30 miles from Cedar City, 186 miles from Las Vegas (a three-hour drive), and 250 miles from Salt Lake City.

**Teacher Background**: John Friend has been a seriously playful instructor of yoga since 1973. His system of Anusara yoga is heart oriented, spiritually based, and yet uses profoundly effective bio-mechanical principles to help students align with optimal health. It's an all-inclusive yoga in which each student's various abilities and limitations are deeply respected and honored.

Mary Beth Markus teaches in the Iyengar tradition, with a special focus on opening the heart and centering the mind. Director of Desert Song Yoga and Massage Center in Phoenix, Arizona, Mary Beth has been a student of yoga and massage for 20 years.

Elise Miller is a certified intermediate senior Iyengar yoga teacher with an M.A. in Therapeutic Recreation. Elise's classes are designed to meet the challenges of students with a variety of back difficulties, including scoliosis, or students who engage in strenuous physical activity. Her energized teaching approach encourages students not only to use their inner "knowing" to guide the healing process but also to go beyond their perceived limitations.

**Style of Yoga**: Anusara, Iyengar

**Philosophy of Teachers**: Varies with teachers.

**Student Criteria**: All levels are welcome.

**Disability Access**: No access

**What to Bring**: All yoga props are provided. Bring casual, comfortable clothes, personal toiletries, extra layers for warmth, and hiking boots.

**Yoga Room Size and Description**: Yoga is practiced in a 32' x 56' (nearly 1,800 square feet) room with oak floors. Glass windows fill the room with lots of light.

**Number of Participants Possible**: 40

**Accommodations**: Inner Harmony offers 12 spacious semi-private rooms with full bathrooms, nine dorm-style sleeping quarters in partitioned areas with bunk beds, and limited tent sleeping arrangements in the summer. People who sleep in dorms and tents use a shared Scandinavian bathhouse.

**Meals**: Three vegetarian meals are served each day. Meals are prepared by a gourmet vegetarian chef who cooks mostly vegan dishes, with some dairy options. Special diets are accommodated. All meals are prepared with wholesome ingredients, using natural foods for health and well-being.

**Fee**: $545 to $995 per person, depending on sleeping arrangements, for a seven-day retreat. Includes lodging, meals, and yoga classes.

**Credit Cards**: Visa and Mastercard

**Sample Daily Schedule**:

| | |
|---|---|
| 6:00 a.m. | Wake up |
| 6:30–7:30 | Pranayama and meditation |
| 7:30–8:30 | Breakfast |
| 8:30–11:30 | Asanas |
| 11:30–12:30 p.m. | Lunch |
| 12:30–4:00 | Free time for outdoor activities or rest |
| 4:30–6:30 | Asanas |
| 6:30–7:30 | Dinner |
| 7:30 | Evening program |
| 10:00 | Quiet time |

**Other Activities**: Inner Harmony has acres of scenic areas ideal for hiking, biking, cross-country skiing, mountain biking, and rock climbing. Nearby excursions include Cedar Breaks, Bryce Canyon, and Zion National Parks as well as the Shakespeare Festival in Cedar City. You can also just relax between classes in the outdoor Jacuzzi and sauna.

**Guest Comment**: *"The week I spent at Inner Harmony was wonderful. The love, inspiration, and vision created there seeped through every moment of my stay."*
Karen Sillas—Santa Monica, California

**Summary**: This privately owned center offers a limited number of participants the opportunity to participate in eight yoga retreats each year. With an abundance of outdoor activities, Inner Harmony creates an invigorating and rejuvenating yoga vacation. Spectacular vistas are enhanced by the seasons in this mountain setting. Quality retreat presenters lead the yoga, while owners John and Lynne Epert are warm and gracious hosts.

# SATCHIDANANDA ASHRAM (YOGAVILLE) BUCKINGHAM, VIRGINIA

## YEAR-ROUND

Satchidananda Ashram, which is also known as Yogaville, is a spiritual center and community where people of diverse faiths come together to practice the principles of Integral yoga as taught by Sri Swami Satchidananda. The ashram sits on 750 acres of woodland along the James River in the foothills of the Blue Ridge Mountains. One of the unique landmarks of Yogaville is the Light of Truth Universal Shrine, also known as LOTUS, which serves as a central gathering place for people of all backgrounds and beliefs to worship, meditate, or sit in contemplation according to their individual traditions together under one roof. The shrine is built in the shape of a lotus flower and set amid the peace and calm of a 16-acre lake, with the Blue Ridge Mountains in the background. It is adorned with pools, waterfalls, and a grand cupola topped with a golden spire.

Programs at the ashram include retreats, meditation, Hatha yoga workshops, teacher trainings, and scriptural studies. Each summer a two-week residential program is available for children ages eight to 16. Activities include Hatha yoga, swimming, sports, arts and crafts, drama, hiking, and campfires.

**Address**: Satchidananda Ashram
Buckingham, VA 23921
**Phone**: 804/969-3121
**Fax**: 804/969-1303
**E-mail**: iyi@yogaville.org
**Web site**: www.yogaville.org

**Airport Information**: Charlottesville is the closest city with an airport, Amtrak, and Greyhound service. There is no public transportation from Charlottesville to Yogaville. You can rent a car or contact the Ashram Reservation Center (800/858-9642) to arrange transportation ($25 one way).

**How to Get There**: Yogaville is 40 miles from Charlottesville, Virginia.

**Teacher Background**: Various staff members who have been trained under the teachings of Satchidananda take turns leading Hatha yoga classes, meditation, and related courses and the ashram.

**Style of Yoga**: Integral yoga

**Philosophy of Teachers**: "Be good, do good, serve all. Be easeful, peaceful, and useful. Paths are many; truth is one."

**Student Criteria**: Openness to learning. All levels are welcome.

**Disability Access**: Yes, fully accessible.

**What to Bring**: Yoga mats, indoor/outdoor Hatha yoga blanket or towel, loose comfortable clothing, personal toiletries, swimsuit and beach towel, flashlight, alarm clock, indoor slippers, slip-on shoes, sun hat, and umbrella.

**Yoga Room Size and Description:**
Three rooms are used for yoga. One is large enough to accommodate 30 people; the other two accommodate 20 people each. All three rooms are carpeted and have heat and air-conditioning.

**Number of Participants Possible:** 60

**Accommodations:** Two dormitories are available (Vivekananda Vihar and Ramalinga Nilayam) and are air-conditioned and convenient to meals and programs. Semi-private rooms for singles, married couples, and families are also available. Each dormitory has a shared bathroom, shower, and laundry facility nearby. The Lotus Inn, consisting of six units, is adjacent to the dormitories and offers private rooms. Each unit contains a fully-equipped kitchenette, full bath, one double bed, a sofa bed, and individually controlled heat and air-conditioning. The third option for sleeping arrangements is tenting. Set off in a quiet wooded area are 12 campsites, including some platforms. Campers bring their own tents, bedding, and towels. People in tents have use of the bathroom/shower house. To keep the focus on spiritual goals, unmarried men and women are housed separately and asked to observe celibacy during their stay.

**Meals:** Three nutritious lacto-vegetarian meals are served each day. Lunch is the main meal of the day. Breakfast and dinner are light and nourishing. No meat, poultry, fish, or eggs are permitted at the ashram.

**Fee:** Rates vary depending upon length of stay and choice of accommodations. A weekend stay runs approximately $220 per person, which includes the weekend program, dorm accommodations, and three meals daily. Midweek rates are slightly lower.

**Credit Cards:** Visa and Mastercard

**Sample Daily Schedule:**

| | |
|---|---|
| 5:00–6:15 a.m. | Meditation |
| 6:20–7:20 | Meditation |
| 6:20–7:35 | Multilevel yoga classes |
| 8:00–9:00 | Breakfast |
| 8:30 | Karma yoga (optional participation in the work schedule at the ashram) |
| 11:45 | Shuttle to LOTUS (the Light of Truth Universal Shrine) |
| noon | Meditation at LOTUS |
| 12:45 p.m. | Lunch |
| 1:30–5:30 | Karma yoga |
| 6:00 | Meditation |
| 6:30–7:30 | Dinner |
| 7:30 | Evening program |

**Other Activities:** Peaceful nature walks along the river, sauna, hot tub, swimming in the lake and nearby river.

**Services:** Massage therapy is available.

**Guest Comment:** *"I could never put into words the magnificence of Satchidananda Ashram—Yogaville. It is a wonderful retreat and teaching center. It has an ecumenical vibration, welcoming all people. 'Perfection in action' comes to mind, remembering my stay at Yogaville. It is very nurturing to your body, mind, and spirit. Yogaville is a working, viable community that serves as an inspiration and model, moving us by its example toward world peace."*
Josie Tulya McLaughlin —
Chico, California

**Summary:** This year-round spiritual center is located in a rural area of Virginia adjacent to the James River. Based on the teachings and practice of Integral yoga as taught by founder Swami Satchidananda, the ashram invites guests to stay for a few hours, several days, or longer. The Light of Truth Universal Shrine, located at the center of Yogaville, is dedicated to the light of all faiths and world peace.

# THE KENMORE INN
# FREDERICKSBURG, VIRGINIA

*Spring Break Yoga Retreat with Ren Fields*

## MARCH
### WEEKEND RETREAT

Fredericksburg is one of America's most historic cities. It is located on the scenic Rappahannock River, where people enjoy ferry and canoe rides or walking for hours along the river paths. The city allows visitors to step back in time: many of its original homes and buildings—examples of architecture ranging from pre-Revolutionary to Victorian—are open to the public.

The Kenmore Inn, home of this weekend yoga retreat, has the ambiance of a colonial bed-and-breakfast. The inn is located just blocks from the visitors center, from which guests are guided to several historic sites and more than 150 antique and specialty shops. Yoga teacher Ren Fields enjoys combining this historic ambiance with a weekend of yoga practice to give participants a relaxing and educational vacation.

**Address**: Ren Fields
The Yoga and Healing Arts Center
P.O. Box 7
Fredericksburg, VA 22404-0007
**Phone**: 540/371-4555
**E-mail**: ren4yoga@yahoo.com

**Airport Information**: Fly into Dulles or Ronald Reagan National Airport in Virgina or Baltimore Washington International in Maryland. There are trains and shuttle service to Fredericksburg. Arrange to have someone pick you up in Fredricksburg and take you to the Kenmore Inn.

**How to Get There**: Fredericksburg is 50 miles south of Washington, D.C.

**Teacher Background**: Ren Fields has practiced yoga since 1968 and has been teaching since 1982. Her main influence came from the teachings of Vishnu Divananda. She has certificates in Intuition/Energy Medicine and Chi Kung.

**Style of Yoga**: Mindful yoga. Ren exposes her students to a wide variety of teachings and techniques of Hatha yoga, including Classical, Ashtanga, Kundalini, meditation, pranayama, and yoga philosophy.

**Philosophy of Teacher**: "I follow the Ashtanga, eight limbs of yoga. Energy is a focus in all of the retreats."

**Student Criteria**: All levels are welcome. People with medical limitations need a doctor's permission where warranted (heart condition, high blood pressure, and medications).

**Disability Access**: Full access

**What to Bring**: Yoga mat and blanket, comfortable clothes for yoga, walking shoes for sightseeing.

*Tom Price, HIS Moments*

*Yoga instructor Ren Fields*

**Yoga Room Size and Description**: Some of the classes are held at an old, nice-but-not-fancy local church two blocks from the inn. Built in the early 1900s, the church has a large, 50-foot room with a 20-foot ceiling, tile floors, and 15-foot frosted glass windows.

**Number of Participants Possible**: 35 to 50. With more participants the group is split into separate level-one and level-two classes. Guest teachers join the retreat to teach extra classes.

**Accommodations**: Rooms at the Kenmore Inn range from deluxe suites with fireplaces and cathedral ceilings to beautifully appointed shared or private rooms. Every room has its own bathroom. There are 12 rooms in the inn.

**Meals**: The Kenmore Inn is a bed-and-breakfast. Hearty breakfasts of cereals, fruits, juices, teas, and coffees are served each morning. Lunch and dinner are at your own expense. There is a restaurant in the inn as well as more than 30 to choose from downtown.

**Fee**: Accommodations range from $65 to $150 per person per night. Call the Kenmore Inn (540/371-7622) to make your own reservations. The yoga weekend program is $145 per person and includes three yoga and meditation sessions and an evening concert, often given by concert guitarist Peter Fields, who is Ren's husband.

**Credit Cards**: The Kenmore Inn accepts Visa, Mastercard, American Express, Diner's Club/Carte Blanch. Credit cards are not accepted for the yoga program.

**Sample Daily Schedule**:
Friday
| | |
|---|---|
| 5:00–6:00 p.m. | Mindful yoga practice: meditation and breath in motion |
| 6:45–7:30 | Dinner and sharing |
| 7:45–9:00 | Meditation and healing |

Saturday

| | |
|---|---|
| 9:00–11:00 a.m. | Yoga practice |
| 11:00–3:00 p.m. | Free time |
| 3:00–5:00 | Yoga practice |
| 5:00–7:30 | Free time |
| 7:30–9:00 | Exploration in meditation: discussion and practice |

Sunday

| | |
|---|---|
| 8:00–9:30 a.m. | Mindful yoga practice |
| 9:45–10:30 | Group brunch at the Kenmore Inn |
| 10:30–12:30 | Closing circle |

**Other Activities**: Historic Fredericksburg is filled with gorgeous architecture, museums, mansions, historical exhibits, galleries, buildings, homes, and tour opportunities. For Civil War buffs, there are tours of Civil War battlefields. Many tourists like riding through the streets of "old town" on the trolley or by horse and buggy. Other attractions are ferry rides along the river and more than 150 antique and novelty shops.

**Guest Comment**: *"Great weekend! I enjoyed the flow, the variety. It was interesting; just enough challenge, and the concert topped it off. Rooms were wonderful."*

Christine Barton — San Diego, California

**Summary**: This yoga retreat is held in a luxurious colonial inn located in the heart of Fredricksburg's historic downtown district. The weekend offers exploration of American history with the calming aspects of yoga, breath work, and meditation practice. Yoga instructor Ren Fields offers a wide variety of yoga styles and healing topics.

# ROXBURY MILL BED & BREAKFAST
# FREDERICKSBURG, VIRGINIA

*Autumn Yoga Retreat with Ren Fields*

## OCTOBER
### WEEKEND RETREAT

Roxbury Mill was built as the working mill for Roxbury Plantation in the early 1700s. The plantation consisted of 14,000 acres from the Po to the Ni River. The land was a grant to Larkin Chew from the King of England. The Chews were a prominent Virginia family and played an important part of the early history of the area. In 1969 George and Joyce Ackerman purchased the Roxbury Mill and had it renovated as a residence. Today the picturesque and tranquil setting of this eighteenth-century grist mill is a warm and inviting bed-and-breakfast. It has a spacious great room that is large enough for stretching, and yoga teacher Ren Fields holds her annual autumn yoga retreat here. Nestled among the full colors of fall, the grounds have many sitting gardens. The Po River rushes through the millrace, while herons and lazy turtles sun on the dam and crooning frogs, crickets, and songbirds perform.

**Address**: Ren Fields
The Yoga and Healing Arts Center
P.O. Box 7
Fredericksburg, VA 22404-0007
**Phone**: 540/371-4555
**E-mail**: ren4yoga@yahoo.com

**Airport Information**: Fly into Dulles and Ronald Reagan National Airport in Virginia or Baltimore Washington International in Maryland. Trains and shuttle services are available to Fredericksburg. Transportation in Fredericksburg to Roxbury Mill B&B can be arranged.

**How to Get There**: Roxbury Mill is 14 miles south of Fredericksburg, Virginia, in historic Spotsylvania county on the Po River and Route 1 South. The mill is 64 miles south of Washington, D.C.

**Teacher Background**: Ren Fields has 30 years of experience in yoga and is a cer-

tified yoga instructor. She also holds Certification in Intuition from Carolyn Myss, Ph.D, and Norman Shealy, M.D., two highly regarded researchers and teachers of the chakra system.

**Style of Yoga**: Classes focus on bringing our physiological and emotional self (chakras) into balance with the use of pranayama (breath work), Hatha, Asana, Vinyasa, Ashtanga, and Kundalini yogas, acupressure, and meditation.

**Philosophy of Teacher**: "I follow the Ashtanga, eight limbs of yoga."

**Student Criteria**: All levels are welcome. People with medical limitations need a doctor's permission where warranted (heart condition, high blood pressure, and medications).

**Disability Access**: Yes

**What to Bring**: Yoga mats, blankets, and comfortable clothes for yoga.

**Yoga Room Size and Description**: Classes, talks, and lectures are held in the "great room"—a 20' x 30' room with 12-foot ceilings and a large stone fireplace. Some classes and talks are given outdoors by the river.

**Number of Participants Possible**: For the retreat, 30. The Roxbury Mill accomodates 20. Others stay at a nearby hotel.

**Accommodations**: The Roxbury Mill Bed & Breakfast has a 900-square-foot master suite with beds for six people and room enough for 14 dorm campers with their own cots and mats.The suite offers a view of the river and a private deck extending over the dam and mill pond. It is warmly furnished and has eighteenth-century decor and wide pine floors and beams. Some participants choose to stay at a nearby Holiday Inn. These participants are picked up in the morning and taken back at the end of the day if they prefer not to drive back and forth on their own.

**Meals**: Hearty vegetarian and vegan meals are served. On both Friday and Saturday participants enjoy a sit-down dinner, and on Saturday and Sunday mornings brunch is provided by the mill's renowned caterer and owner. Hot and cold drinks and snacks are provided throughout the day.

**Fee**: Accommodations and meals for the weekend at Roxbury Mill B&B cost $100 per person for a dorm bed and $70 per person if you bring your own cot and mattress. Otherwise, brunches cost $10 each, and dinners are $15. Snacks and drinks are included. The yoga program costs $145 per person and includes classes in yoga, meditation, chakras, and vibrational healing.

**Credit Cards**: Not accepted

**Sample Daily Schedule**:
Friday:
| | |
|---|---|
| 5:00 p.m. | Yoga class |
| 7:00 | Dinner |
| 8:00 | Chakras discussion |

Saturday:
| | |
|---|---|
| 9:00–11:00 a.m. | Yoga and chakra-balancing meditation |
| 11:00 | Brunch |
| 3:00–5:00 p.m. | Yoga and chakra-balancing meditation |
| 5:00 | Dinner |
| 7:00 p.m. | Evening singing |

Sunday:
| | |
|---|---|
| 9:00 a.m. | Yoga class |
| 11:00–1:00 p.m. | Brunch and closing circle |

**Other Activities**: The Roxbury Mill B&B is just 15 minutes south of historic Fredericksburg, which is filled with gorgeous architecture, museums, mansions, historical exhibits, galleries, buildings, homes, and tour opportunities. Walking tours of battlefields, trolley and buggy rides, ferry rides along the river, and over 150 antique and novelty shops make this town an exploration into American history and an adventure.

**Services**: Massage is available on site.

**Guest Comment**: *"The food was excellent, and the hostess was very nice. The yoga classes, informative discussions, and visualization exercises were wonderful. We were allowed ample time to work through what we learned on our own—the 'quiet room' was very effective. I liked everything."*
Denise Ramsbotham—
King George, Virginia

**Summary**: Yoga teacher Ren Fields offers mindful yoga (movement meditation) in this tranquil and serene bed-and-breakfast next to the Po River. This gorgeous property, with its lovely gardens, chirping birds, and singing river was once a plantation. The retreat focuses on energy work with the chakras, using yoga as a tool.

# THE YOGA LODGE ON WHIDBEY ISLAND GREENBANK, WASHINGTON

## YEAR-ROUND

Situated on five secluded acres at the end of a private lane not far from the village of Greenbank, the Yoga Lodge is a bed-and-breakfast that includes a yoga lesson and the use of a sauna. Weekend guests receive a private or semi-private lesson suitable to their experience; midweek guests join one of the ongoing small group classes. There are two small orchards on the property, an organic vegetable and flower garden, a small pond, woodland walks, and the wood-fired sauna nestled in trees. The natural surroundings provide habitat for wildlife such as deer, rabbits, herons, owls, woodpeckers, eagles, coyotes, and a chorus of songbirds. The serenity and peacefulness of this setting creates an atmosphere conducive to contemplative yoga practice or just spending quiet time amid the wonders of nature.

**Address**: The Yoga Lodge on Whidbey Island
c/o Gail Malizia
3475 Christie Rd.
Greenbank, WA 98253
**Phone**: 360/678-2120
**E-mail**: citroen@whidbey.com
**Web site**: www.disinclair.com/dsin/yoga

**Airport Information**: Sea-Tac International Airport is about two hours by shuttle to the ferry dock. From the ferry dock the lodge is another 20 minutes. There is free bus service on the island.

**How to Get There**: Whidbey is considered the largest island in the continental United States and is accessed by ferry from Seattle or via Deception Pass from Bellingham and points north.

**Teacher Background**: Gail Malizia is a certified Iyengar yoga teacher, has a master's degree in psychology, is director of the Seattle School of Yoga, and is proprietress of the Yoga Lodge. Gail has taught locally as well as in Alaska, Canada, Europe, and India. Her principal teachers have been B. K. S. Iyengar for Hatha yoga and Dr. Michael Gladych for Raja yoga.

**Style of Yoga**: Iyengar Hatha yoga. Gail's teaching blends anatomy, physiology, and yoga philosophy with a good dose of imagery and humor. She accents the interrelatedness of all beings.

**Philosophy of Teacher**: "Yoga is a way of life based on respect for all life forms. It is an avenue to self-discovery that enriches our lives regardless of age, occupation, or belief."

**Students Criteria**: Self motivation and sincerity.

**Disability Access**: No access

**What to Bring**: A sleeping bag and towel help to cut down on laundry (the Yoga Lodge is on a communal well). Be sure to bring comfortable clothing in layers, walking shoes, and a rain jacket.

The Yoga Lodge

*Yoga instructor Gail Malizia at the Yoga Lodge*

**Yoga Room Size and Description**: The yoga room is a little more than 600 square feet and feels airy and comfortable. The room has radiant floor heat and large sliding glass doors that open out onto the lawn and orchard and is fully equipped with yoga props,

**Number of Participants Possible**: 20 to 22

**Accommodations**: There are three dorm-style bedrooms that sleep three to four people each. Each room has sleeping lofts as well as ground-floor beds — singles and one double bed. Rooms are simple but comfortable and have lots of light and views of the woodland orchard. Each room has its own private entrance from the outside. There is also lots of space for pitching tents in good weather.

**Meals**: Continental breakfast is included with overnight stays. For personal retreats (three-day minimum stay), three vegetarian meals are served daily.

**Fee**: For an overnight stay, which includes continental breakfast, one yoga class, and use of the sauna rates are as follows: $65 single room, $110 double room with shared bath is. Deduct $5 if you bring a sleeping bag and bath linens; deduct $10 if you also pitch a tent. Personal retreats (minimum three- to five-day stay) are $75 per person per day, which includes daily yoga instruction (group or private), three vegetarian meals, private lodging, and use of the sauna.

**Credit Cards**: Not accepted

**Sample Daily Schedule**:
8:00–10:00 a.m.   Continental breakfast
10:00–11:30       Yoga lesson
Free time
The sauna is available for guests before or after dinner. Bed-and-breakfast guests may partake in weekday yoga classes.

**Other Activities**: The property is only two miles from South Whidbey State Park and an easy drive or bike ride to Ebby's Landing, the Port Townsend ferry, Beachcomber's Beach, and other attractions of Whidbey Island. The village of Langley is an artist's mecca and has a number of museums and fine clothing stores. Easy hiking along the bluffs allows you to view beautiful scenery. There is a wood-fired sauna in the woods at the lodge.

**Guest Comment**: *"Lovely, quiet lodge in the woods. Excellent, insightful private yoga lesson. Loved the wood-burning sauna."*
Floye Nui Sumida—Seattle, Washington

**Summary**: The Yoga Lodge is founded on the principles of nonviolence, generosity, simplicity, and humanitarian service. This secluded lodge offers bed, breakfast, and yoga class for personal retreat or casual overnight stay. Owner and yoga teacher Gail Malizia invites people to experience the peace and quiet of nature amid fresh sea air. The Yoga Lodge maintains a scholarship fund and work-study program for those on limited income.

# SLEEPY CREEK RETREAT
# BERKELEY SPRINGS, WEST VIRGINIA

*Customized Yoga Retreat with Susan Segall*

## APRIL–NOVEMBER
### MIDWEEK OR WEEKEND RETREATS

Sleepy Creek Retreat, located on the eastern panhandle of West Virgina, is a sanctuary for spiritual renewal for people who want to relax, heal, and experience personal transformation. Situated on 20 acres, Sleepy Creek offers spectacular mountain views, serene walks in the woods along a peaceful stream, hiking in nearby hills, and quiet meditation under a tree by the pond. There is also a meditation circle on the property overlooking a mountain range. The main building offers lovely guest rooms with country elegance. The house has lots of decks and windows through which you can view the mountains. Bird feeders surround the decks and are placed in the nearby woods. Yoga teacher Susan Segall (Sharda) invites individuals, couples, or groups of three to enjoy a customized yoga vacation in this pristine mountain retreat environment.

**Address**: Susan Segall
P.O. Box 736
Berkeley Springs, WV 25411
**Phone**: 304/258-9082; 800/838-9360
**Web site**: www.wellnesstraining.com

**Airport Information**: Hagerstown Airport in Maryland is 45 minutes away. Baltimore Washington International, Ronald Reagan National Airport, and Dulles in Washington, D.C., are 90 miles away. Transportation can be arranged with a four-week notice.

**How to Get There**: Sleepy Creek Retreat is 10 miles outside of Berkeley Springs, West Virginia. It is two hours from Washington and Baltimore.

**Teacher Background**: Susan Segall, M.Ed. in Counseling Education, has been teaching yoga for more than 25 years. She is certified by the Jain Meditation International Center in New York

as a practitioner of integrated health and wellness. Susan has studied a variety of yoga disciplines and is a founding member of the Yoga Teachers Association of Pittsburgh.

**Style of Yoga**: Vinyasa flow Hatha yoga and adaptive yoga for people with special needs. Susan also specializes in women's issues and has designed a sequence of asanas for women experiencing menopause.

**Philosophy of Teacher**: "With the tools of Eastern and Western philosophy, psychology, and practice, I offer self-care programming that emphasizes the experience of rootedness and connectedness."

**Student Criteria**: All levels of experience are welcome.

**Disability Access**: No access

**What to Bring**: Yoga mat; loose, comfortable clothing; hiking shoes; and a journal.

**Yoga Room Size and Description**: Yoga is practiced in a small conference room in the main house. The room is carpeted and has panoramic views of the mountains. Standing poses are sometimes practiced outside.

**Number of Participants Possible**: 3

**Accommodations**: Participants stay in three private guest rooms with private baths on the lower level of the main house. Two of the rooms have queen beds and whirlpool bathtubs. The other room has two single beds. All rooms are nicely appointed with a country elegance and have views of the mountains.

**Meals**: Meal plans are optional and at an additional fee. Participants can choose to have one, two, or three meals served daily. Supervised fasting is also an option. There are restaurants nearby, and a kitchenette is available for use for those who bring snacks. Customized meals include vegetarian or vegan. Vegetarian cooking demonstrations are also available.

**Fee**: $180 per person per night includes lodging at Sleepy Creek Retreat, two yoga classes daily with Susan, and one body work session. Discounts are given to couples or traveling companions. Customized meal plans are extra. Call Susan for prices and details.

**Credit Cards**: Not accepted

**Sample Daily Schedule**:
| | |
|---|---|
| 7:30–9:00 a.m. | Yoga class |
| 9:00 | Breakfast |
| Free time | |
| noon | Lunch |
| 4:00 p.m. | Customized body work session: choice of Swedish massage, acupressure, reflexology, Jin Shin Do, or combination |
| 5:30 | Dinner |
| 7:30–9:00 | Yoga class |

**Other Activities**: The retreat property offers wonderful hiking and secluded places for meditation. Activities such as horseback riding, paddleboating, swimming, golf, antique shopping, and fine dining are five to 15 minutes away. Nearby Berkeley Springs is known for its healing mineral waters. Cacapon State Park is just five minutes away and offers wonderful hiking trails. Cacapon Mountain is one of the oldest mountains in the world. Crystals are found all around this area.

**Guest Comment**: *"I have been to many spas and retreats, but the ones I have enjoyed and gained the most benefits from were working with my 'personal trainer,' Susan Segall. I recently had a colonoscopy, and my yoga breathing, which Susan taught me, helped me get through."*
Anne Dittman—Hagerstown, Maryland

**Summary**: This retreat opportunity designed for one, two, or three people is ideal for those who want a private, customized yoga experience. Body work and optional customized meals are included. Susan Segall offers retreats of various lengths, ranging from one day to one week. Sleepy Creek—steeped in country elegance and situated on 20 acres of quiet mountain beauty—lends itself nicely to this individualized, personal retreat.

# CRESS SPRING FARM
# BLUE MOUNDS, WISCONSIN

## YEAR-ROUND

Cress Spring Farm is a unique center that links the practices of sustainable agriculture, community living, environmental activism, and Hatha yoga. The center was founded in 1988 by Roger Eischens, who has created an instructional system of yoga called High Energy yoga. The farm hosts various activities throughout the year, including High Energy yoga, agriculture, Ayurvedic counseling, and sports training programs.

Unlike most of the Midwest, the land at Cress Spring Farm is not flat. Deep valleys and high hills dot the landscape. The yoga center is tucked into one of the valleys. The farm's namesake, Cress Spring, bubbles up crystal-clear drinkable water all year round. Over two thirds of the farm's 200 acres are wild, split evenly among woods and prairie. Plenty of hiking trails are available. Biking is stunning; low-traffic roads weave about the farmland.

**Address**: Cress Spring Farm
4035 Ryan Rd.
Blue Mounds, WI 53517
**Contact**: Scott Anderson
**Phone**: 608/767-3876
**Fax**: 608/767-3932
**E-mail**: Saayog@aol.com
**Web site**: http://members.aol.com/cresspring/cress.html

**Airport Information**: Fly into Madison. Transportation from the airport or bus depot is available with prior arrangement. There is also train service to Madison.

**How to Get There**: Cress Spring Farm is nestled in a valley in Vermont Township, eight miles from Mount Horeb, 35 miles from Madison, 200 miles from Chicago, and 250 miles from Minneapolis.

**Teacher Background**: The yoga staff at Cress Spring Farm comes out of an Iyengar asana background and a Zen sitting practice.

**Style of Yoga**: High Energy yoga is an instructional system based on the teachings of B. K. S. Iyengar. Classes emphasize individualization of the work and a balance between physical practice (asana) and sitting practice (dyana and pranayama). Transformational work, a sequence, meditation, pranayama, and chakra chanting constitute the elements of a High Energy yoga practice. The format of the classes involves much partner work and small group experience.

**Philosophy of Teachers**: "We come from a history of alternative education. The focus here is getting the teacher out of the spotlight and getting the student to a place where he or she can make his or her own discoveries and conclusions. The teachers here are devout practitioners, but we're active in many other facets of simple living, too. The yogis here are farmers, stewards of livestock, mechanics, etc. There is no pretense, nor holiness. Just a very earthy approach to this most fascinating practice."

**Student Criteria**: Students should be self-starters. There are no amenities or pampering. Students make their own beds and prepare their own meals. They will feel welcome and have all resources available; however, they must not be shy about asking for what is needed.

**Disability Access**: No access

**What to Bring**: Sleeping bag or bedding, slippers, mud boots or snow boots, health and beauty aids, reading material, and any special foods.

**Yoga Room Size and Description**: The yoga room is 18' x 40'. Large south-facing windows invite the sunshine in. Floors are maple-wood finished in non-toxic materials. Props are provided and include wall ropes, blankets, mats, blocks, belts, back benders, spine bags, and weights.There is a deck adjacent to the yoga room that is a common hangout space after practice.

**Number of Participants Possible**: 20

**Accommodations**: A co-ed dormitory on the renovated third floor of the farmhouse has a dozen beds and several privacy screens. The dorm is carpeted and has a big skylight and several windows. It includes a bathroom and access to the tiny rooftop deck. There are two other bathrooms in the house, each with showers. A private room is available on occasion. Camping space is available during the warmer months.

**Meals**: Meals are not provided. Students bring their own food or buy food at Cress Spring Farm. Everyone cooks together—staff, residents, and guests—and everyone eats together. The food is almost exclusively organic, much of it produced on the property and prepared simply. The kitchen is meat-free. Ayurvedic principles of food choices permeate the residents' and staff members'

individual diets. Counseling in Ayurvedic typology and diet is available.

**Fee**: There are no fees for overnight guests, although donations are accepted. Charges are for yoga instruction only. Classes cost between $10 and $15 per person per class. All-day workshops are $35. Private sessions are $45 per hour.

**Sample Daily Schedule**:

| | |
|---|---|
| 6:15 a.m. | Sitting meditation |
| 8:00 | Asana practice |
| 10:00 | Breakfast |

The rest of the day is free for individual instruction, hiking, gardening, or other activities.

| | |
|---|---|
| 1:00 p.m. | Lunch |
| 7:00 | Dinner |

**Other Activities**: Miles of hiking, great road biking, cross-country skiing in the winter, food preservation/canning during harvest season—there's always tons of garden work to be done—and Cress Spring Farm is an ideal place for just being. The nearest town is Mount Horeb, which offers coffee shops, antique shops, a co-op grocery store, library, and a bookstore. There are lots of books on a myriad of subjects at Spring Cress Farm.

**Guest Comment**: *"Cress Spring Farm is the best of a retreat center, a community, and a yoga school. The setting makes it an ideal place to learn, to spend time alone, or to be with other like-minded folks."*

Andrej Peterka—
Minneapolis, Minnesota

**Summary**: Cress Spring Farm is 200 acres of land housing a working farm and community. Residents practice High Energy yoga on a daily basis and host activities that include yoga instruction, organic farming, bioregional activism, and counseling. Guests have the opportunity to experience community living, the sharing of work, healing, and activism.

# International Yoga Vacations and Retreats

# SIVANANDA YOGA RETREAT HOUSE
# REITH BEI KITSBUHEL, AUSTRIA

## YEAR-ROUND

The Sivananda Yoga Retreat House sits on the sunny slopes of Reith, an oasis of peace in the mountains of Kitzbuhel in the high Alps. This traditional three-story alpine house looks like it belongs in a storybook, with its large, wood-floor rooms, big beams, and windows with gorgeous views. Enchanting hiking paths and picturesque cross-country ski trails are just down the hill from the Retreat House. A few miles away lies the city of Kitzbuhel, with its storybook charm, pedestrian village, hot baths, and boutiques.

Swami Durgananda is the director of the Sivananda Yoga Retreat House and a longtime disciple of Swami Vishnu Devananda. The programs at the Retreat House are based on Swami Vishnu Devanandas's five points for a holistic evolution of body, mind, and soul, which include proper exercise, proper breathing, proper relaxation, proper diet, and positive thinking and meditation.

**Address**: Sivananda Yoga Retreat House
Am Bichlachweg 40 A
A-6370 Reith bei Kitzbuhel
Austria
**Phone**: 001-43-5356 67404
**Fax**: 001-43-5356 67405
**E-mail**: tyrol@sivanda.org
**Web site**: www.sivanada.org

**Airport Information**: Fly into Munich, Germany, or Innsbruck, Austria. If you fly into Munich, take the train to Innsbruck. Guests will be picked up at the train station.

**How to Get There**: The Sivananda Yoga Retreat House sits on a slope above Reith, four kilometers from the village of Kitsbuhel.

**Teacher Background**: Classes are taught by ashram staff on a rotating basis. All staff teachers have been trained in the Sivananda yogic teachings and philosophy.

**Style of Yoga**: Classical yoga, which includes a synthesis of Raja, Hatha, Karma, and Bhakti yoga. Classes are taught by ashram staff and follow teachings set by Swami Sivananda. Twelve main asanas are used. Devotional practices, such as silent meditation followed by Sanskrit mantra chanting, are used daily to help cultivate the teachings.

**Philosophy of Teachers**: "Vendanta philosophy, exploring the nature of self and truth. Five basic principles of health: proper exercise, breathing, relaxation, diet, positive thinking, and meditation. Discipline can provide physical, psychological, and spiritual balance and harmony."

**Student Criteria**: No experience necessary. All guests must participate in the daily schedule. Cigarettes and alchohol are not allowed.

**Disability Access**: No access

**What to Bring**: Blanket and meditation shawl, comfortable clothing, walking shoes and house shoes, rain gear, flash-light, swimsuit, and beach towel. Yoga articles are available in the Retreat House boutique.

**Yoga Room Size and Description**: Yoga is practiced in two separate rooms on the first and third floors of the Retreat House. One room has golden/reddish handmade wood floors, walls, and ceiling with big beams and windows looking out on the mountains and meadows. One yoga room has a wall made of stone with a gentle waterfall trickling down it.

**Number of Participants Possible**: 150

**Accommodations**: Guests stay in Hotel Florian, a family hotel across the street from the Retreat House. Rooms accommodate 2–4 people and have private baths. Private single rooms are available as well. Each room has a balcony with a view. Room service is included, and there is a sauna in the hotel.

**Meals**: Two buffet-style vegetarian Ayurvedic meals are served daily: brunch and dinner. Meals are prepared according to yogic and Ayurvedic dietary principles. Food is prepared without meat, eggs, onions, or garlic. Coffee is not served.

**Rates**: $45 per person per night includes yoga classes, meditation, and lectures. A one-week stay is $315 per person. Children up to 5 years stay free; children 6–10 years stay for 50 percent of regular cost; and children 11–14 years stay for 75 percent of regular cost. Child care is not provided.

**Credit Cards**: All major credit cards are accepted.

**Sample Daily Schedule**:

| | |
|---|---|
| 5:30 a.m. | Wake up |
| 6:00 | Meditation, chanting, lecture |
| 8:00 | Asanas and pranayama |
| 10:00 | Brunch |
| 2:00 p.m. | Lecture/workshop |
| 4:00 | Asanas/pranayama |
| 6:00 | Dinner |
| 7:30 | Meditation, mantra chanting, and lecture |

Attendance at the two daily meditations and asana classes is mandatory.

**Activities**: A renowned spot for winter sports in the Alps of Kitzbuhel, the region also offers summer sporting activities—miles and miles of hiking trails, swimming in local lakes, and more. Bicycles are available for rent. During the winter, enjoy picturesque cross-country ski trails just down the hill from the Retreat House. For down-hill skiing, there are various ski stations nearby. A five-minute drive from the Retreat House is a bird sanctuary and wetlands preserve.

**Guest Comment**: *"I loved the quiet. I was there during the winter season, and there was a lot of snow and sunshine—and beautiful, big mountains. I enjoyed the yoga classes and all the silent walks in the mountains."*
Mary Ann Powell—Munich, Germany

**Summary**: The Yoga Retreat House, nestled in the sunny slopes of Reith, Austria, is a beautiful and peaceful place to study yoga. The Alps are right at your doorstep. Along with miles and miles of hiking trails and skiing opportunities, guests experience a thorough, step-by-step yoga program that embraces the teachings of Swami Sivananda and Swami Visnu Devananda. Each day begins with the serenity of early medita-tion. The storybook charm of the Retreat House and the nearby village adds to the ambience of pure life energy and health.

# ISLAND OF BALI
# SANUR AND UBUD, BALI

*Yoga in Bali with Ann Barros*

## FEBRUARY AND JULY
### TWO-WEEK VACATION

Halfway around the world at the tip of Java, just south of the equator, lies the little island of Bali. Iyengar yoga instructor Ann Barros has been leading yoga vacations in Bali since 1985. This two-week vacation opportunity to become enmeshed in the rich Hindu culture of Bali is enhanced with daily yoga classes, language and cultural orientation, and guided insight. Ann's tour package includes three nights' stay by the ocean at Sanur's Beach Village and 10 nights in Ubud, Bali's cultural center. Excursions include walks through rice fields, visits to temples and sacred shrines, meeting Balinese artists, three traditional dance performances, and optional visits to traditional healers.

**Address**: Ann Barros
341 26th Ave.
Santa Cruz, CA 95062
**Phone**: 831/475-8738
**Fax**: 831/474-8738
**E-mail**: abarros@pacbell.net
**Web site**: www.baliyoga.com

**Airport Information**: Airfare from Los Angeles via Singapore Airlines is included in Ann's fee. If you're flying from San Francisco there is no extra charge. Ann can also arrange reduced "through fares" for domestic flights with United, TWA, Delta, and American airlines.

**How to Get There**: Ann will meet you at the airport for transport to Sanur's Beach village.

**Teacher Background**: Ann Barros has been teaching Iyengar yoga in the Santa Cruz area for more than 20 years, including five years at UCSC. She studied with B. K. S. Iyengar in India in 1976 and again in 1980, and longtime study with Ramanand

Patel continues to inspire her advanced practice. Ann visited Bali in 1980 and fell in love with the culture. Later that year she graduated as a certified Iyengar instructor from the Iyengar Institute in San Francisco. She has a strong dance background and love of art, music, yoga, and Hinduism.

**Style of Yoga**: Iyengar

**Philosophy of Teacher**: "I give lots of individual attention and pay close attention to alignment details in the poses."

**Student Criteria**: Some yoga experience. Interest in Balinese culture.

**Disability Access**: No access

**What to Bring**: Yoga mat and belt. Lightweight clothes, basic amenities, vitamins, sunscreen, and mosquito repellent.

**Yoga Room Size and Description**: In Candi Dasa yoga is practiced in an open-air pavilion overlooking the ocean.

© Roger Zessin

*Yoga in Bali with Ann Barros*

In Ubud yoga is practiced in an open-air pavilion set in lush tropical gardens. Both pavilions have tile floors and are clean and beautiful.

**Number of Participants Possible**: 24

**Accommodations**: During the first three days the group stays in lovely oceanside bungalows in Sanur. The area has lush green banana, papaya, and coconut trees. In Ubud, accommodations are set in lavish gardens, with views of terraced rice fields and the sacred volcano, Mount Agung. The rooms (bungalows) are deluxe and have marble bathtubs, hot water, electricity, and balconies; breakfast is served at your doorstep every morning. There is a swimming pool on the property.

**Meals**: All breakfasts and two lavish dinner feasts are included in the tour. Breakfast usually consists of eggs, toast, fruit salad, and coffee or tea. Twice during the tour participants gather to enjoy

an exotic traditional Balinese dinner. You choose and pay for lunches and all other dinners. Finding vegetarian options in Bali is easy.

**Fee**: $2,900 per person, based on two persons sharing a room with twin beds and a private bath. This includes predeparture videotape orientation in the United States with round-trip airfare from Los Angeles to Bali, several days of language instruction and orientation upon arrival, all accommodations, all breakfasts, two Balinese dinners, tickets to two Balinese dances, daily yoga classes with Ann, and local transportation to and from airport and bungalows in Candi Dasa and Ubud.

**Credit Cards**: Not accepted

**Sample Daily Schedule**:
In Candi Dasa:
| | |
|---|---|
| 7:00–8:30 a.m. | Morning yoga |
| 8:30 | Breakfast |
| 1:00 p.m. | Language and cultural orientation |

4:00–5:30      Afternoon yoga
                     (restorative postures)
Between classes there is free time for snorkeling, sailing, strolling on the beach, and resting.

In Ubud:
7:00–8:30 a.m.    Morning yoga
8:30               Breakfast
Excursions to visit Balinese artists at work
4:00–5:30 p.m.    Afternoon yoga
                     (restorative poses)
Some evenings include traditional dance performances.

**Other Activities:** The arts abound in Bali. Creating beauty is considered a religious service to society. The group will visit many Balinese artists, including painters, woodcarvers, basket weavers, tapestry weavers, and mask makers. Participants will also probably encounter spontaneous village festivals that include dance performances, ceremonies, cremations, and feasts. Exploring Ubud's many shops, cafés, museums, temples, and shrines is a treat. There is also free time to relax by the pool or take walks in the rice fields.

**Guest Comment:** *"Selamat everything! Ann is a master yoga teacher who combines the spiritual realm with an appreciation of the sensual world of Bali. She has the proper proportion of Balinese knowledge and American sophistication to create a memorable tour that satisfies all needs and leaves her participants fulfilled."*
Carole Baral—Carmel, New York

**Summary:** Bali is a magical place filled with gracious people, beautiful scenery, and a deeply rooted spirituality. Ann Barros's yoga tour gives participants a balance of rich cultural experience enhanced by the pleasure of practicing yoga. Ann's expertise in the areas of language, culture, and customs of Bali places participants in good hands. This excursion offers enough time for a two-day tour of Bali's temples and shrines.

# ISLAND OF BALI
# SAYAB, NEAR UBUD, BALI

## *Yoga in Bali with Bob and Shannon Smith*

## MARCH
### ONE TO FOUR WEEKS

This trips begins in Penestanan, a small village outside Ubud where yoga teachers Bob and Shannon Smith have hosted small groups each year since 1991. Participants stay in family compounds in the village and witness the rich and vibrant culture of the Balinese people. Each morning begins with meditation and Hatha yoga in a spectacular setting on a high plateau among rice fields. A number of evenings are spent sharing Balinese feasts, watching dance performances, visiting temples, and enjoying the grace and simplicity of the village life. Bob and Shannon have a second home in Sayan, another small village outside of Ubud, and are well acquainted with the language, culture, and traditions of the Balinese people. The experience of being with the Balinese people will open your eyes to new ways of bringing ritual and spirituality into daily life. Participants experience a blend of the practice of yoga and the rhythm of Balinese life.

**Address**: Hatha Yoga Center
4550 11th Ave. NE
Seattle, WA 98105
**Phone**: 206/632-1706
**Fax**: 206/362-8517

**Airport Information**: Fly into Denpasar International Airport.

**How to Get There**: Take a taxi to Ubud (approximately one and one-half hours).

**Teacher Background**: Bob and Shannon Smith have been teaching yoga and offering yoga vacations for more than 20 years. Bob is the author of *Yoga for a New Age*.

**Style of Yoga**: Eclectic, flowing Hatha yoga. Inner awareness is the key focus for all posture and pranayama work.

**Philosophy of Teacher**: "Connect deep within and move from the core. Breath work, energy work, and meditation are crucial elements in the asana practice."

**Student Criteria**: At least six months experience with Hatha yoga.

**Disability Access**: No access

**What to Bring**: Yoga mat, good walking shoes, and swimsuit. Pack lightly—most of what you will need you can buy very inexpensively in Bali.

**Yoga Room Size and Description**: Yoga classes are held in a large covered pavilion in Penestanan Village situated amid rice paddies on the hill that dominates Ubud.

**Number of Participants Possible**: 30

**Accommodations**: Most participants stay at Malati's, a family-run guest compound

Hatha Yoga Center

*Yoga in Bali with Bob and Shannon Smith*

in Penestanan village that offers thatched-roof bamboo bungalows with tiled floors. All of the bungalows have hot water and incredible views of rice fields or of the nearby mountains. Rooms are simple, have two or three beds each, and are set along tropical paths lined with lush vegetation. Malati's has a swimming pool and café/bar. Lower-cost rooms (some without hot water) are available at other nearby family compounds for those on a tight budget.

**Meals**: Breakfast, served after morning yoga, is included with bungalow rooms and generally consist of trays of fresh tropical juices, ginger tea, thick coffee, eggs, toast, and jam. Other meals are at your own expense. There are many nearby restaurants that serve traditional Asian, Italian, North American, and European cuisine. Vegetarian options are easy to find. Plan on spending approximately $10 a day for meals.

**Fee**: Bob and Shannon charge $200 per

person per week for yoga instruction. The cost for two weeks of study is $400, for three weeks, $550, and for one month, $650. Estimated costs for lodging is $100 to $200 a week. Meals cost $6 to $10 a day.

**Credit Cards**: Not accepted

**Sample Daily Schedule**:

| | |
|---|---|
| 7:30–9:30 a.m. | Yoga and meditation |
| 10:00 | Breakfast |
| Free time | |
| 4:30–6:00 p.m. | Yoga and meditation every other day (Monday, Wednesday, Friday, and Sunday) |

**Other Activities**: There are wonderful dance performances to attend in the evenings and shadow-puppet plays and temple tours to enjoy during the afternoons. You can rent a bicycle, take music lessons, or take batik-making or woodworking classes. Participants enjoy exploring Ubud and the many temples and villages within a few hours' drive.

**Guest Comment:** *"Yoga is, at the very least, a generative experience for most people, no matter where it is practiced. But if you are drawn toward experiences that test the edge, you should go to Bali with Bob and Shannon Smith. Generous and gracious hosts, Bob and Shannon are also excellent teachers who make sure you are challenged even as they support you. You will practice in an inspirational setting, live in charming quarters, eat lots of delicious food, sweat like a rainforest, and return home permanently altered. The experience is worth much more than it could ever cost you."*
Yasmine Rafi—Seattle, Washington

**Summary:** Bob and Shannon Smith invite students to study Hatha yoga in the rich land of Bali. Students discover new ways of bringing ritual and spirituality into their daily lives. Participants can come for one week, 10 days, two weeks, or up to four weeks for independent study. The Hatha yoga and meditation practice will add a structure to your time in Bali, enabling you to meet other like-minded individuals as you learn about the beautiful island's culture.

# Sivananda Ashram Yoga Farm, Grass Valley, California

*See description on pages 16–17.*

Sivananda Ashram Yoga Farm

Sivananda Ashram Yoga Farm

# The Expanding Light, Nevada City, California

*See description on pages 23–24.*

The Expanding Light

The Expanding Light

# The Sewall House, Island Falls, Maine

*See description on pages 78–79.*

The Sewall House

The Sewall House

# Yoga Backpacking Trip, White Mountains, New Hampshire

*See description on pages 99–101.*

Earth Island Expeditions

Guides Gillian Kapteyn Comstock & Russell Comstock/Earth Island Expeditions

# Sivananda Ashram Yoga Camp, Val-Morin, Québec, Canada

*See description on pages 171–172.*

Sivananda Ashram Yoga Camp

Sivananda Ashram Yoga Camp

# Sivananda Ashram Yoga Retreat, Paradise Island, Bahamas

*See description on pages 173–174.*

Sivananda Ashram Yoga Retreat

Sivananda Ashram Yoga Rerreat

# Pura Vida Retreat Center, San José, Costa Rica

*See description on pages 189–190.*

Pura Vida Retreat Center

Pura Vida Retreat Center

# Sivananda Yoga Vedanta Dhanwanthari Ashram, Kerala, India

*See description on pages 195–196.*

Sivananda Yoga Vedanta Dhanwanthari Ashram

Sivananda Yoga Vedanta Dhanwanthari Ashram

# Yoga in Ireland with Kevin Gardiner

*See description on pages 197–198.*

© Sharon Smith

© Sharon Smith/ Man of Aran Cottage

# Ananda Assisi, Assisi, Italy

*See description on pages 201–203.*

Ananda Assisi

Ananda Assisi

# Yoga with Gayna Uransky, Zihuatanejo, Guerrero, Mexico

*See description on pages 210–211.*

© Gayna Uransky

© Berkley Fogelsonger

# Hotel Na Balam, Isla Mujeres, Quintana Roo, Mexico

*See description on pages 212–215.*

Hotel Na Balam

Hotel Na Balam

# Rio Caliente Hot Springs Spa, La Primavera, Jalisco, Mexico

*See description on pages 216–219.*

# Villas Shanti, Puerto Morelos, Quintana Roo, Mexico

*See description on pages 224–231.*

Villas Shanti

Villas Shanti

# Maya Tulum, Tulum, Quintana Roo, Mexico

*See description on pages 232–236.*

# Wilka T'ika Garden Guest House, Urubamba, Peru

*See description on pages 243–245.*

© Terry Cumes

# ISLAND OF BALI
# UBUD, THE NORTH COAST, AND BIMA, BALI

## *Bali Living Arts Yoga Journey with Marya Mann*

### OCTOBER AND NOVEMBER
### ONE- AND TWO-WEEK YOGA JOURNEYS AND RETREATS

Yoga teacher Marya Mann of Bali Living Arts offers one- and two-week yoga journeys and retreats during which participants immerse themselves as pilgrims in the sacred arts of yoga, dance, and painting. The yoga journeys involve travel and touring through Bali. The group stays in Ubud for several days, visiting sacred temples and studying with Ubud artists and village healers. From Ubud participants embark on a three-day boat cruise through a remote archipelago to behold primeval animals and plants, including healing herbs. While staying in secluded seaside villas you'll have opportunities to climb sacred volcanoes, swim in the Java Sea, and live in communion with nature among a close-knit Balinese clan. Following the tour Marya offers a one- or two-week yoga intensive on the north coast of Bali, where students stay in one village the entire time.

**Address**: Bali Living Arts
c/o Marya Mann
P.O. Box 111
Walnut Hill, IL 62893
**Phone**: 618/735-2280; 800/641-2254
**Fax**: 618/735-2574
**E-mail**: Dreamcat1@aol.com
**Web site**: www.LotusLivingArts.com

**Airport Information**: Fly into Denpasar International Airport.

**How to Get There**: Marya will meet you at Ngurah Rai Airport near Denpasar.

**Teacher Background**: From study with B. K. S. Iyengar and of Continuum dance with Emilie Conrad-Da'oud, Marya's experience in the sacred arts has always brought her back to Bali, where she was invited to become an initiate of the Agame Hindu tradition. Mentored by Jose Arguelles, Marya has integrated cross-cultural spiritual technologies with

dance, theater, and yoga for creative unfoldment. Bali Living Arts grew out of Marya's 1986 field research on the art, community, and temple practice of Bali.

**Style of Yoga**: Yoga dance flows into precise alignment and focus while maintaining a sense of riding the waves of breath. At lunar times Marya Mann teaches a tai chi–like Yin yoga interspersed with stillness and surrender, and at solar times her practice is more of a dynamic Yang yoga, or Ashtanga style, during which students feel the swift art of placement and challenge the limits of self-control.

**Philosophy of Teacher**: "The purpose of yoga is to remove suffering and bring happiness. In our practice we purify the body and clarify consciousness. In the clear ground of our being, we plant good seeds of happiness, abundance, and enlightenment. Concentration on the breath in the eternal present awakens

Bali Living Arts

*Bali Living Arts: A Balinese temple ritual*

the soul. We contact a state of love that exists now. And now. And now. And now. As the scriptures of yoga affirm, no effort is lost on the path."

**Student Criteria**: People should be in a reasonable state of fitness for yoga, a few long stretches of travel, and hiking.

**Disability Access**: Special assistance may be available. Please call.

**What to Bring**: Lightweight clothing that dries quickly and is comfortable and loose. Shorts should be long (modesty in dress will, in part, determine your acceptance by the local people); shirts should cover the shoulders. One long-sleeved shirt, long pants, and socks are recommended for protection against mosquitoes. Bring a light jacket, swimsuit, towel, sun hat, sunscreen, closed-toe walking shoes, sandals, insect repellent, toiletries, and notebook and pen.

**Yoga Room Size and Description**: Yoga

is practiced in many outdoor places: near family temples and shrines, on remote white-sand beaches in the Lesser Sunda Islands, and on a raised platform in an open-air pavilion.

**Number of Participants Possible**: 12

**Accommodations**: Participants stay in beautiful Balinese bungalows with in-room toilets. Bungalows overlook either flowered courtyards or the Java Sea. Except for the three days on the luxurious boat cruise, private rooms are available. On the boat guests sleep in cabins with bunk beds (four to a room).

**Meals**: During the journey most meals are included and are vegetarian. Meat lovers will enjoy Bali's curried chicken and *babi guling*, a traditional roast pig beloved by the Balinese and used as part of their ceremonial cycle. During the intensive, meals are not included.

**Fee**: Tour price is $3,000 per person,

which includes two weeks' lodging (double occupancy), all yoga and cultural instructions, ceremonies, and most meals. The yoga intensive on the north coast costs $650 per person for one week and $1,250 per person for two weeks, including lodging and yoga classes.

**Credit Cards:** Not accepted

**Sample Daily Schedule:**

| | |
|---|---|
| 6:00 a.m. | Pranayama |
| 8:00 | Breakfast |
| 10:00–noon | Meditation at sacred sites |
| 12:30 p.m. | Lunch |
| 1:30–5:00 | Cultural tours and activities |
| 6:00 | Dinner |
| 7:00 | Balinese dance performances, temple ceremonies, visits to |

Balinese friends, satsang, language lessons, or free time

**Other Activities:** Balinese dance, painting, mask-making, scuba diving, swimming, boating, snorkeling, hiking, bird-watching, hot springs, and shopping.

**Guest Comment:** *"I can't imagine a better way to be in Bali. On every level, physical, emotional, mental, and spiritual, I was nourished and heightened. I unconditionally recommend it!"* LeRoy Peterson—Parkland, Florida

**Summary:** Yoga teacher Marya Mann invites yoga participants to experience Bali as pilgrims, exploring the artistic, spiritual, and social underpinnings that have made the Balinese a people whose culture promotes balance, harmony, and beauty with both natural and supernatural forces.

# ISLAND OF BALI
# UBUD AND THE VILLAGE OF SIDEMAN, BALI

*Yoga and the Culture of Bali with Mark Horner and
Laughing Duck Tours*

## MAY AND JUNE
### TWO WEEKS

Bali residents Jean and William Ingram and the Balinese families of Wayan Sudarta (Darta) and Made Maduarta (Pung) have been organizing yoga and cultural tours to Bali since 1990. They pride themselves on personal service, high standards, and the orchestration of opportunities for deep and personal interactions between group members and the Balinese. Yoga teacher Mark Horner joins these resident tour guides to offer a two-week yoga excursion in Bali. Included in the trip are introductory talks on Balinese lifestyle, rituals, ceremony, and traditional herbal medicine given by Wayan Sudarta and friends. Classes in Balinese cooking will be led by Darta's wife in their family home. Guided walks through villages and rice fields with Made Maduarta offer the chance to learn about temples, flora and fauna, and rice farming. The "touchstone" of twice-daily yoga classes with Mark will also bring you closer to the refined Balinese culture, as both Bali and yoga have their spiritual roots in the same Hindu traditions.

**Address**: Mark Horner
475 Chalda Way
Morago, CA 94556
**Phone**: 925/927-7279
**E-mail**: markyoga@best.com

**Airport Information**: Fly into Denpasar International Airport. The recommended ticketing agent for this tour is Linda Yaxley, 800/956-1993. Although travel expense to and from Bali is not included in the tour, participants are encouraged to make their travel arrangements in consultation with Mark Horner.

**How to Get There**: Participants will be greeted and picked up by the Laughing Duck Tours hosts.

**Teacher Background**: Mark Horner is the codirector of the Yoga and Movement

Center in Walnut Creek, California, where he teaches weekly yoga classes. Mark has been practicing yoga and meditation for more than 15 years. He has trained in both the Iyengar and Ashtanga Vinyasa styles of yoga. His background includes eight years of experience as a certified rolfer and consultant. Mark is especially interested in exploring and sharing with others the purifying effects of yoga, which help to awaken our inherent ease, well-being, happiness, and freedom.

**Style of Yoga**: Iyengar and Ashtanga yoga. Classes are dynamic and challenging, with humor and clear instruction.

**Philosophy of Teacher**: "I strive to create a gentle, supportive yoga environment with clear guidance, humor, and passion."

**Student Criteria**: All levels are welcome.

**Disability Access**: No access

**What to Bring**: Yoga mat, blanket, and strap. Also bring rain gear, mosquito repellent, a sweater and long pants for cooler climate in mountains, Teva-type sandals or light hiking boots for river hikes, a flashlight, sunscreen, and sun hat. Men need to bring a white shirt with collar (short sleeves are okay) for temple ceremonies.

**Yoga Room Size and Description**: Two rooms are used for yoga during the tour. One, in Ubud, is a spacious room with hardwood floors and views of a rice field. The other site is at a newly built mountain retreat center, which allows for much privacy and silence.

**Number of Participants Possible**: 20

**Accommodations**: During the first part of the trip participants stay in an small family-run hotel in Ubud. Set among coconut and clove trees, the hotel overlooks the gorge of the Wos River. Rooms have private baths with tub/shower and hot water. Construction is "Balinese style"—lots of carvings and grass roofs. The other hotel participants stay in is built in a valley in Sideman on the edge of a river, surrounded by rice fields and overlooked by Bali's largest volcano. Guests stay in villas (triple occupancy) and cottages (double occupancy). Each has a tub/shower with hot water. There is a swimming pool and a hot tub.

**Meals**: Two vegetarian (Balinese cuisine) meals are provided each day.

**Fee**: $1,795 per person includes 13 days and 12 nights in Bali, accommodations, two vegetarian meals daily, yoga instruction, Balinese arts studies, cultural lectures, dance performances, group tours, and scheduled transportation. International airfare is not included.

**Credit Cards**: Not accepted

**Sample Daily Schedule**:

| | |
|---|---|
| 7:30–9:30 a.m. | Yoga class |
| 9:30 | Breakfast |
| 10:30 | Cultural tours and activities |
| 4:30–6:30 p.m. | Yoga class |
| 6:30 | Dinner |
| 8:00 | Evening activities |

**Other Activities**: This tour offers lots of opportunities to interact with the Balinese people. There will be visits to local artists, lessons in gamelan music at the local *banjar* community hall, classes in Balinese cooking, Balinese dance performances, and guided walks through villages and rice fields. The group will take advantage of opportunities to participate in colorful temple festivals or accept invitations to weddings, tooth fillings, cremations, or other family ceremonies. The program remains as flexible as possible for such activities.

**Guest Comment**: *"Jean and William as tour guides were extraordinary because of their attention to detail and their generosity in sharing the cultural aspects of Bali. As a group we felt well taken care of. The first place we stayed at outside of Ubud was a dream. It was beautiful, lush, perfect for yoga on the patio, where we practiced as the sun came up and practiced again as the sun went down."*
Darril Tighe—Oakland, California

**Summary**: Twice-daily yoga classes with Mark Horner offer a unique opportunity to deepen your yoga practice during this two-week study in Bali. Participants stay in two locations—a family run hotel in Ubud and a hotel near the village of Sideman, where yoga is interspersed with insight and exploration into Balinese lifestyle, rituals, and culture. Laughing Duck Tours of Bali helps facilitate this unique vacation tour.

# YASODHARA ASHRAM
# KOOTENAY BAY, BRITISH COLUMBIA, CANADA

## YEAR-ROUND

Yasodhara Ashram was established in 1963 by Swami Radha, a western woman who traveled to Rishikesh, India, in 1955 to meet her teacher, Swami Sivananda, and returned to found the first yoga ashram in Canada. Yasodhara Ashram is situated on 120 acres of forest on a large mountain lake in southeastern British Columbia. The setting is quite beautiful and includes small paths and walkways leading through the woods and the garden and along the lakeshore. The main meeting facility is referred to as the Mandala House. The Temple of Light is another facility used specifically for meditation. An eight-sided dome with windows on every side and a simple oil lamp in the center, the temple is dedicated to the Light in all religions. The atmosphere throughout the ashram is peaceful, gentle, and clean.

**Address**: Yasodhara Ashram
Box 9
Kootenay Bay, BC
V0B 1X0
Canada
**Phone**: 800/661-8711
**Fax**: 250/227-9494
**E-mail**: yashram@netidea.com
**Web site**: www.yasodhara.org

**Airport Information**: Daily connector flights from the international airports in both Vancouver and Calgary come to Castlegar. The airport limousine will bring you to Nelson, and a local bus will bring you to the ferry at Balfour. The ashram staff will pick you up at the ferry landing at Kootenay Bay.

**How to Get There**: The ashram is about 10 hours by car from Vancouver, seven hours from Calgary, and four hours from Spokane, Washington.

**Teacher Background**: Teachers are all certified by Yasodhara Ashram and offer the teachings of Swami Radha.

**Style of Yoga**: All branches of yoga are offered: Kundalini, Karma, Raja, Hatha, and Bhakti. Specifically, the Hidden Language Hatha yoga, which is a reflective, symbolic approach to the poses. Kundalini yoga is offered as the study of mind and consciousness. Dream yoga is offered as a way to connect with different levels of mind, and Mantra and prayer dance are used as devotional tools.

**Philosophy of Teachers**: "We teach from our own experience and from a basis of self-study. We draw on the innate Light and intelligence of the students."

**Student Criteria**: A desire to learn about themselves and then to apply what has been learned to their lives.

**Disability Access**: There is one room available for disabled persons for residential programs.

**What to Bring**: Casual clothing, seasonal outdoor wear, and loose clothing for

Hatha. An alarm clock and a flashlight are useful. In the winter waterproof footwear and jackets are needed. In the summer it can be hot during the days and cool in the evenings. Slippers are nice for indoors.

**Yoga Room Size and Description**: There are two spacious classrooms (2,400 square feet) with wooden floors and floor-to-ceiling windows overlooking the lake and mountains. The temple has a nourishing round space for meditation.

**Number of Participants Possible**: As many as 25 to 30 can be in a Hatha class, but usual numbers are 10 to 15.

**Accommodations**: Guests are accommodated in two beautiful cedar lodges that offer spectacular views of the mountains, lake, and forest. Rooms are usually shared with one other person, although single rooms are sometimes available upon request.

**Meals**: Three meals are served a day, and each meal has a vegetarian component. Fish, poultry, and meat are served several times a week for nonvegetarians. In the summer meals include organic fruits and vegetables from the ashram garden and orchards, and year-round the ashram uses its own dairy products and eggs. People usually eat in silence.

**Fee**: Ten-day packages are $650 (U.S.) and include classes and room and board. Otherwise, retreat guests pay $60 per day for two hours of instruction and room and board. Different programs have different prices. Call for a catalog. If available, a private room may be reserved at an additional cost. All rates include dinner on the evening of your registration and breakfast on the day following completion of your course.

**Credit Cards**: Visa and Mastercard

**Sample Daily Schedule**:

| | |
|---|---|
| 7:00–8:45 a.m. | Chanting in temple or Hatha yoga |
| 9:00–9:30 | Breakfast |
| 10:00–12:30 p.m. | Class |
| 12:30–2:30 | Lunch |
| 2:30–6:00 | Class |
| 6:00 | Dinner |
| 8:00–9:00 | Satsang (evening meditation in temple) |

**Other Activities**: Wonderful opportunities exist for walking and hiking, swimming in the lake during the summer, enjoying the pebble beach, and cross-country skiing in the winter. There is a library for reading, and guests have access to prayer rooms for private meditation practices.

**Guest Comment**: *"The Yasodhara Ashram is an incredible haven, especially for women. The Spirit of Divine Mother is all around—in the beautiful natural surroundings, in the teachings of Swami Radha, and through the female instructors. It's a place of integrity for working on personal issues and growth, balanced with support from the staff and enough space to be independent as well."*

Beverly Malouf—
San Francisco, California

**Summary**: Open year-round, Yasodhara Ashram offers programs and retreats that vary in length from two days to three months. One of the most popular programs is a package of classes called Ten Days of Yoga. A safe and sacred place started by Swami Radha, a woman who was one the pioneers in bringing yoga to the West, Yasodhara Ashram nurtures inward self-discovery through all branches of yoga and special workshops using dance, art, and music to create a bridge between Eastern and Western approaches. The setting embraces a quality of calmness, cleanliness, and devotion to spiritual practices.

# SALT SPRING CENTRE
# SALT SPRING ISLAND, BRITISH COLUMBIA, CANADA

*Salt Spring Centre Yoga Retreats*

## MARCH–OCTOBER

Salt Spring Centre is a community designed to support the creative and healing arts within the framework of spiritual growth and discovery. The center sits in the heart of 69 acres of cedar forest, wild meadows, organic gardens, and orchard on beautiful Salt Spring Island. The center's residents make up the Dharma Sara Satsang Society, a community based on selfless service and Ashtanga yoga's eight-fold path. The inspiration for this community is yoga master Baba Hari Dass, who visits Salt Spring Centre once a year as the honored guest at their annual Ashtanga Yoga Retreat.

A large refurnished country farmhouse built in 1911 serves as the main gathering place for programs. Oak floors, stained-glass windows, and a sunny dining area make this place warm and homey. On the grounds there is a wood-fired sauna, a greenhouse, and a school. This private rural setting offers a supportive atmosphere for relaxation, reflection, and learning.

Various retreats are offered March through October, including yoga and Ayurveda weekends, Relax and Renew with Yoga for Women weekends, Spa and Spirit vacations, the annual Ashtanga Yoga Retreat with Baba Hari Dass, and a weeklong yoga intensive with Angela Farmer and Victor van Kooten. (Please call for specific dates and program fees.)

**Address**: Salt Spring Centre
355 Blackburn Rd.
Salt Spring Island, BC
V8B 2B8
Canada
**Phone**: 250/537-2326
**Fax**: 250/537-2311
**E-mail**: ssc@saltspring.com
**Web site**: www.retreatsonline.com/can
/goto/saltsprings.htm

**Airport Information**: Victoria International airport is close by.

**How to Get There**: Salt Spring Island is in the Strait of Georgia just off Vancouver Island's southeastern coast. Salt Spring staff will pick people up for their programs. Salt Spring Island is easily accessible from Vancouver and Seattle by both air and car ferry. There is a picturesque half-hour ferry ride available from Victoria, British Columbia.

**Teacher Background**: Various staff members of Salt Spring Centre take turns leading yoga postures and meditation classes and assisting in teaching the various courses.

**Style of Yoga**: Ashtanga yoga as taught by Baba Hari Dass, including methods of body/mind purification, asanas, pranayama, *mudra* (energy-raising techniques), and meditation. Visiting teachers offer other styles (call for descriptions).

Salt Spring Centre

*Salt Spring Centre*

**Philosophy of Teachers**: "Programs offered are designed to support the creative and healing arts within the framework of spiritual growth and discovery. The foundations of yoga and selfless service are the foundations of our lives. We try to live what is taught."

**Student Criteria**: All are welcome.

**Disability Access**: No access

**What to Bring**: Yoga mat and loose, comfortable clothing. There are no yoga props at the center. If you are used to working with props, you may want to bring a strap, block, or blanket.

**Yoga Room Size and Description**: The yoga room is 1,500 square feet and has a wood floor and carpeting that can be rolled up. A beautiful stained-glass window accents one wall. An altar sits to one side. Wood fire heats the asana room, and at times the fire is reflected in the wood floor. The room has a view toward Belcher Mountain.

**Number of Participants Possible**: 35

**Accommodations**: Guests sleep in the main house upstairs. Rooms are warm and comfortable, with quilts and subdued lighting. Each room has a special view. In the summer there are some campsites available, as is a wooden yurt space that sleeps five.

**Meals**: Three vegan and vegetarian meals are served daily. During the Ashtanga yoga retreat with Baba Hari Das there are two meals per day. A large organic garden provides much of the food.

**Fee**: Rates vary with programs. Weekend programs hosted by the center and other organizations range from $200 to $350 (Canadian) depending on the program.

**Credit Cards**: Not accepted

**Sample Daily Schedule:**

| | |
|---|---|
| 7:00–8:00 a.m. | Meditation |
| 8:00–9:30 | Yoga asanas |
| 9:30–10:00 | Light breakfast |
| 11:00–12:30 p.m. | Yoga asanas |
| 12:30–3:00 | Lunch and free time |
| 3:00–5:00 | Yoga asanas |
| 5:30–7:00 | Dinner |
| 7:00–9:00 | Evening program |

**Other Activities:** Great hiking trails, nature walks, beachcombing, and kayaking. There is a wood-fired sauna on the property. Nearby is Blackburn Lake, where guests enjoy swimming. Salt Spring Centre is close to the town of Ganges, where there are wonderful shops, restaurants, and an arts-and-crafts fair each Saturday.

**Services:** The Salt Spring Health Collective offers healing therapies, including herbal steam baths, Swedish massage, reflexology, and fragrant flower facials that are specially available during the Yoga for Women weekends.

**Guest Comment:** *"My weekend stay at Salt Spring Centre left me feeling a much greater peace and calm. The staff are warm-hearted and helpful, the organic vegetarian fare is bountiful and tasty, and the center itself, with surrounding garden, pastures, and forest, is delightfully comfy."*
Leslie Campbell—Victoria, B.C., Canada

**Summary:** Salt Spring Centre, in the heart of Salt Spring Island, lies in a meadowland sheltered by mountains and forests and has lakes nearby. This quiet retreat center has the feeling of a nature reserve—eagles soar and deer roam freely. The community is inspired by the teachings of Baba Hari Dass, which are based on Ashtanga yoga and the practice of selfless service.

# KING VIEW FARM
# KING TOWNSHIP, ONTARIO, CANADA

*Yoga Retreat with Esther Myers*

## JUNE
### FOUR DAYS, THREE NIGHTS

King View Farm is a country retreat located on 86 acres of scenic rolling hills, organic farmland, maple trees, cedar bushes, and marked walking trails. The land has been lovingly nourished and chemical-free for more than 20 years. Bountiful herb gardens provide moments of quiet and meditation. King View Farm is also a spiritual community operated by the Society of Emissaries of Divine Light. The community's 20 residents appreciate life's sanctity and pursue personal growth and learning. Various growth and learning retreats are held at King View Farm, including Esther Myers's annual yoga retreats.

**Address**: Esther Myers's Yoga Studio
390 Dupont St.
Toronto, Ontario
M5R 1V9
Canada
**Phone**: 416/944-0838
**Fax**: 416/944-9151

**Airport Information**: Fly into Toronto. A ride can be arranged to King View Farm if needed.

**How to Get There**: King View Farm is 45 minutes north of Toronto, north of King City, and west of Aurora, Ontario.

**Teacher Background**: Esther Myers began practicing yoga in London, England in 1972. She was certified by the B. K. S. Iyengar Institute in 1976. She then returned to Toronto and began teaching. In 1984 Esther began studying with Vanda Scaravelli, author of *Awakening the Spine*, who had developed her own method of yoga practice. From Vanda's method and teaching, Esther gained a

deepening sense of self-acceptance, compassion, security, and joy. She is the author of two books: *The Ground, the Breath, and the Spine* and *Yoga and You.*

**Style of Yoga**: Scaravelli method, which supports individuals in adapting postures to their own needs and utilizing love and acceptance as the essence of the work.

**Philosophy of Teacher**: "Focus on breath awareness and allow postures to unfold organically with the breath."

**Student Criteria**: All levels of experience are welcome.

**Disability Access**: No access

**What to Bring**: Yoga mat, strap, and blanket; comfortable, casual clothes; swimsuit; walking shoes; and personal toiletries.

**Yoga Room Size and Description**: Two rooms are used for yoga. One is referred to as the chapel and is a 22' x 56' carpeted room with windows that open out to green lawns and give the room lots of natural light. The other room is called the reception room and is 24' x 24' with wood floors and windows. Sometimes yoga is practiced on the lawn.

**Number of Participants Possible:** 25

**Accommodations:** Guests sleep on the second floor of the main house, which offers apartments with three or four rooms and a private bath. Or guests are placed in rooms that share a hall bathroom. Both queen-size beds and single beds are available.

**Meals:** Three vegetarian meals, with chicken and fish options, are served daily. The farm's own organically grown vegetables are served in season. Their freshly baked bread is served year-round. Special diets can be accommodated. Meals are served buffet-style in a warm and spacious dining room.

**Fee:** $400 per person includes three nights' stay at King View Farm, three meals daily, morning breathing classes, and daily yoga classes with Esther.

**Credit Cards:** Visa

**Sample Daily Schedule:**

| | |
|---|---|
| 7:30–8:30 a.m. | Morning breathing practices |
| 8:30 | Breakfast |
| 9:45–12:15 p.m. | Yoga class |
| 12:30–1:30 | Lunch |
| 1:30–4:15 | Free time |
| 4:15–5:45 | Yoga class |
| 6:00 | Dinner |

**Other Activities:** The area offers wonderful hiking trails that wind through scenic woods and groves. The gardens are lovely to browse through and send fresh herbal fragrances to all who walk by. There are many farm animals on the property to enjoy: horses, cows, ducks, and geese. The retreat has an above-ground swimming pool, a hot tub, and sauna available for guest use.

**Services:** Shiatsu and reflexology are available by appointment.

**Guest Comment:** *"My introduction to King View Farm was through yoga retreat workshops. The farm offers great accommodations in a very simple way, with much thought given to maintaining balance with the natural environment. Excellent and wholesome meals are prepared from mostly fresh ingredients grown on land that has been organic for several years. The farm offers a peaceful respite from daily activites— walking and nature trails surrounding the area. I, like many others, enjoyed my stay and look forward to opportunities to be there."*

Sybil Wilkinson —
Toronto, Ontario, Canada

**Summary:** King View Farm is an intentional spiritual community staffed by people who are dedicated to translating spirit into daily living. The community opens its home and facilities as a loving place for workshops and retreats. Yoga teacher Esther Myers offers annual yoga retreats at this spiritually focused and healing sanctuary. The property offers marked trails that wind through sugar maples and enchanted cedar groves. Food is freshly made from organic produce grown on land that has been nourished for more than 20 years.

# SIVANANDA ASHRAM YOGA CAMP
# VAL-MORIN, QUÉBEC, CANADA

## YEAR-ROUND

The Sivananda Ashram Yoga Camp sits on 250 forested acres of Canada's Laurentian Mountains. Abundant wildlife, tended gardens, secluded shrines, and the magnificent native forest offer an ideal atmosphere for the practice of yoga and meditation. Facilities include a new ecologically built straw-bale lodge and a beautiful temple near the highest place in the ashram.

The yoga camp was founded in 1962 and is one of five ashrams founded by Swami Vishnu Devananda to carry on the teachings of his master, Swami Sivananda of Rishikesh. The center offers year-round programs providing guests with the opportunity to participate fully in the ashram routine, experiencing both its joys and its challenges. The daily program is based on classical yogic teachings passed down through the ages from guru to disciple.

**Address**: Sivananda Ashram Yoga Camp
673 8th Ave.
Val-Morin, Québec
J0T 2R0
Canada
**Phone**: 819/322-3226
**Fax**: 819/322-5876
**E-mail**: HQ@sivananda.org
**Web site**: www.sivananda.org

**Airport Information**: International, U.S., and Canadian flights land at Dorval Airport in Montréal. Bus service is available from the main bus terminal in Montréal to Val-Morin.

**How to Get There**: The yoga camp is located in Val-Morin, Québec, approximately one hour by car from the city of Montréal.

**Teacher Background**: Classes are taught by ashram staff on a rotating basis. All teachers have been trained in the Sivananda yogic teachings and philosophy.

**Style of Yoga**: Classical yoga, including a synthesis of Raja, Hatha, Karma, and Bhakti yoga. There is a strong emphasis on breathing. Each class includes 12 basic postures and their variations to give a comprehensive class that is both relaxing and meditative. Devotional practices such as silent meditation, chanting, prayers, and Sanskrit verses help cultivate the teachings.

**Philosophy of Teachers**: Vedanta philosophy, exploring the nature of self and truth. Five basic principles of health: proper exercise, breathing, relaxation, diet, positive thinking, and meditation.

**Student Criteria**: The only criteria is a sincere desire to participate in the program.

**Disability Access**: Yes, full access

**What to Bring**: Light cotton clothing for yoga classes, toiletries and personal items, shawl and sweater for cool evenings, a swimsuit for the sauna and swimming pool, and yoga mat (may be rented).

**Yoga Room Size and Description**: During the winter, classes are often held in the main room of the lodge (30 maximum), which has large windows overlooking the valley. During the summer there are several platforms available for outdoor classes as well as larger asana rooms.

**Number of Participants Possible**: The number of guests at the ashram varies with the season. In the summer there may be as many as 250 residents from all corners of the world.

**Accommodations**: There are two buildings with guest rooms: a new ecologically built straw-bale lodge with comfortable shared rooms (each with a private bathroom) and an older building with smaller rooms and separate bathrooms. A number of rustic cabins are also available, and camping is welcome for those who bring their own tents.

**Meals**: The yogic vegetarian diet consists of pure, simple, natural foods with the least negative impact on the environment and least pain to other beings. Some of the vegetables and herbs are grown in the ashram gardens, while other produce is obtained locally in season. Meals are lacto-vegetarian but do not use garlic, onions, vinegar, or eggs. Drinking water comes from an 80-foot-deep artesian well. Herbal teas are always available.

**Fee**: $45 (U.S. dollars) per person per night for a shared room, $285 per person per week for a shared room, $30 per person per night for tent space, and $170 per person per week for tent space.

**Credit Cards**: Visa and American Express

**Sample Daily Schedule**:

| | |
|---|---|
| 5:30 a.m. | Wake-up bell |
| 6:00 | Morning satsang |
| 8:00 | Asana-pranayama class |
| 10:00 | Brunch |
| 11:00 | Karma yoga |
| noon | Free time |
| 2:00 p.m. | Special workshops |
| 4:00 | Asanas and pranayama |
| 6:00 | Supper |
| 8:00 | Evening satsang |

Satsang includes silent meditation, chanting, readings, discussion, and prayers to remember the divine in all aspects of our lives.

**Other Activities**: A swimming pool (used during the summer) and a sauna are available for guests. You can hike, snowshoe, or cross-country ski on the camp's numerous forest trails. Local activities include canoeing, cycling, and lake swimming in summer and fall and downhill skiing and skating in the winter.

**Guest Comment**: *"Because I have benefited from many summer vacations at the Sivananda Yoga Camp in Val-Morin, I know that whatever stress or negativity you bring with you transcends to a feeling of exhilaration, high energy, and blissful peace. Those who come from every corner of the world express in many languages the phrase: 'This is Prana City—It does not get better than this!'"*

Ruby Blue — Washington, D.C.

**Summary**: This Sivananda Ashram Yoga Camp is situated on acres of beautiful forest land. Opportunities for enjoying outdoor activities are abundant here, while the main focus is on maintaining spiritual purity and purpose in accordance with the yogic teachings of Swami Sivananda and Swami Vishnu Devananda. Families are welcome: a monthlong children's yoga camp takes place in July, and there is a special family week in August.

SEE PHOTOS, PAGE 147.

# SIVANANDA ASHRAM YOGA RETREAT
# PARADISE ISLAND, BAHAMAS, CARIBBEAN

## YEAR-ROUND

The Sivananda Ashram Yoga Retreat on Paradise Island is located on four acres of tropical white-sand beach next to clear ocean water. The retreat is built around a semi-enclosed outdoor meditation temple. This yoga retreat is a place to relax, exercise, learn, and meditate. The programs of the ashram are based on Swami Vishu Devananda's five points for a holistic evolution of body, mind, and soul: proper exercise, proper breathing, proper relaxation, proper diet, and positive thinking and meditation. During special times throughout the year, such as Christmas, Thanksgiving, and Easter, the yoga retreat offers specialized programs on the themes of peace, health, parapsychology, and spiritual practices. Special guests are invited to enhance the retreat with lectures, workshops and classes. (Call for program descriptions.) Families with children are welcome.

**Address**: Sivananda Ashram Yoga Retreat
P.O. Box N7550
Nassau, Bahamas
**Phone**: 242/363-2902
**Fax**: 242/363-3783
**E-mail**: nassau@sivananda.org
**Web site**: www.sivananda .org

**Airport Information**: Fly into Nassau. The retreat is accessible by boat only, as it is located on Paradise Island. Guests call the retreat from the airport after clearing customs. Take a taxi to the Sugar-Reef (Mermaid Dock), where you will be taken by boat to the retreat.

**How to Get There**: The Sivananda Ashram Yoga Retreat is just across the bay from Nassau on Paradise Island.

**Teacher Background**: Classes are taught by ashram staff on a rotating basis. All staff teachers have been trained in the Sivananada yogic teachings and philosophy.

**Style of Yoga**: Classical yoga, which includes a synthesis of Raja, Hatha, Karma, and Bhakti yoga. Classes are taught by ashram staff and follow the teachings set by Swami Sivananda. Twelve main asana positions are used. Devotional practices such as silent meditation followed by mantra chanting in Sanskrit are used daily to help cultivate the teachings.

**Philosophy of Teachers**: "Vendanta philosophy, exploring the nature of self and truth. Five basic principles of health: proper exercise, breathing, relaxation, diet, positive thinking and meditation. Discipline can provide physical, psychological, and spiritual balance and harmony."

**Student Criteria**: No experience necessary. All guests must participate in the daily schedule.

**Disability Access**: No access

**What to Bring**: Yoga mat (rentals available), meditation shawl, casual, comfortable clothing, slip-on sandals, rain gear, swimsuit, beach towel, sunscreen, snorkeling equipment if desired, flashlight, toiletries; campers bring their own tent, towels, and blanket.

**Yoga Room Size and Description:** Three outdoor wooden platforms are used for yoga—bay side, oceanside, and garden—as are two indoor facilities.

**Number of Participants Possible:** 200

**Accommodations:** Guests stay in beach huts, cabins, dormitories, or tents. These simple lodgings include semi-private rooms overlooking the ocean or comfortable cabins clustered around an oriental-style footbridge. All accommodations are simple, small, and without air-conditioning or private bathrooms. Guests who wish to camp should bring their own tents and request tent space before arriving.

**Meals:** Two lacto-vegetarian meals are served buffet-style daily—brunch and dinner. Meals are prepared according to yogic dietary principles. The menu does not include meat, fish, fowl, eggs, garlic, onions, tea, or coffee.

**Fee:** A private room costs $85 per day; a semi-private room with ocean view, $70; a semi-private room, $60; dormitory, $55; and tent space, $50. December 20 to January 4 and April 4 to 19 prices increase $10 per day. Children under 12 stay for half price.

**Credit Cards:** All major credit cards are accepted.

**Sample Daily Schedule:**

| | |
|---|---|
| 5:30 a.m. | Wake up |
| 6:00 | Meditation, chanting, lecture |
| 8:00 | Separate Hatha yoga classes, for beginners and intermediate students |
| 10:00 | Brunch |
| noon | Workshop (optional) |
| 4:00 p.m. | Hatha yoga class |
| 6:00 | Dinner |
| 8:00 | Meditation and evening program |
| 10:00 | Lights out and silence observed |

The evening program includes spiritual music and art performances and world-renowned speakers and lecturers on topics of spirituality and holistic healing. Attendance at the two daily meditations and asana classes is mandatory.

**Other Activities:** Walking, hiking, reading, relaxing on the beach, swimming in the ocean, snorkeling, and local and island excursions.

**Guest Comment:** *"My experience at the Sivananda Ashram Yoga Retreat has been one of relaxation, rejuvenation, friendship, and spiritual upliftment. It has been a wonderful place to learn about new and esoteric subjects and have a lot of fun at the same time. There is simply no better place for me to recharge myself and get prepared for new challenges in life."* Alan Ginsberg—Boston, Massachusetts

**Summary:** This yoga ashram on Paradise Island invites students to experience a thorough, step-by-step yoga program that embraces the teachings of Swami Sivananda and Swami Visnu Devananda. Each day begins with the serenity of early meditation. The clear sea air and radiant dawn help aid the yoga practices in stilling the mind. The environment of this ashram, with its pristine beach, offers a special sanctuary of peace and beauty for in-depth yoga study in the warmth of the Caribbean.

SEE PHOTOS, PAGE 148.

# TRUION
# TORTOLA, BRITISH VIRGIN ISLANDS, CARIBBEAN

*Restorative Yoga Retreat for Women with Patricia Brown*

### FEBRUARY AND MARCH
#### NINE-DAY RETREATS

This retreat takes place on Tortola, one of the Caribbean Virgin Islands. It is a mountainous island created by volcanic activity many years ago. The mountainous edges fall into the sea, creating a dramatic topography. The ocean water is blue-green and a comfortable temperature for swimming and snorkeling. The area is sparsely populated.

Up a dirt road and nestled in gardens of tropical flowers, Truion, the private residence where this retreat is held, is a classic island home with open-air terraces and views of the sea from every room. It is set on five private acres, and there are no other homes in sight. Views are spectacular; you can watch the sunrise and the sunset from the property. An idyllic crescent beach is a five-minute walk down a dirt path. Yoga teacher Patricia Brown offers two nine-day Restorative Yoga Retreats for Women in this private home on the west end of Tortola.

**Address**: Women's Restorative Retreats
P.O. Box 448
Camden, ME 04843
**Phone**: 207/236-6412

**Airport Informatjion**: Fly into either St. Thomas or Tortola airports.

**How to Get There**: From St. Thomas take a ferry to Tortola, where you will arrive one mile from the retreat location. All island transportation is provided.

**Teacher Background**: Patricia Brown has been teaching yoga for more than 18 years. She received her nursing diploma from Yale New Haven Hospital and has developed her method of Hatha yoga from a synthesis of the many forms of yoga, movement, and breath work she has studied. She is a practitioner of Vipassana meditation and is a student of Ayurvedic medicine.

**Style of Yoga**: Patricia offers a meditative approach to yoga, blending conscious breathing with clear and sensitive guidance. She encourages students to follow their own way of finding peace and stillness in the body through the practice of yoga. Her style is a blend of Iyengar, Desikachar with meditative approach, and a strong emphasis on the breath.

**Philosophy of Teacher**: "To provide students with clear, sensitive guidance while making space for their own understanding of finding peace and stillness."

**Student Criteria**: This retreat is for women only. All levels of yoga experience are welcome.

**Disability Access**: No access

**What to Bring**: Yoga mat and two blankets, sunscreen, sun hat, bath towel, journal, light summer clothing, swimsuit, and walking sandals or shoes.

**Yoga Room Size and Description**: Yoga is practiced in an outdoor covered terrace that overlooks the Caribbean from a hilltop. The room is 35' x 16'.

**Number of Participants Possible**: 9

**Accommodations**: Participants stay in a Caribbean-style stucco home, set high in a remote part of the island. The home is simple yet elegant. Rooms are single and double occupancy with a shared bath between two rooms. One single with a private bath is available. Views look out to the sea.

**Meals**: Three vegetarian meals are served daily: a hearty breakfast, light lunch, and full dinner. Local island produce is included. Meals are prepared by a professional whole-foods chef and teacher of vegetarian cooking. The group enjoys outdoor dining on covered terraces.

**Fee**: $1,250 to $1,400 per person includes nine days' accommodations, three vegetarian meals daily, and all yoga classes with Patricia.

**Credit Cards**: Not accepted

**Sample Daily Schedule**:

| | |
|---|---|
| 7:00–8:30 a.m. | Yoga focusing on the classic asanas |
| 8:45 | Breakfast |
| 11:30–12:15 p.m. | Midday meditation |
| 12:15 | Lunch |
| 4:30–5:30 | Restorative poses and breathing |
| 6:00 | Dinner |
| 8:00 | Evening meditation |

Silence is practiced each evening beginning after meditation and until the morning yoga class. Three to four days of silence are held during the middle of the retreat.

**Other Activities**: The area offers wonderful dirt-road walks over hillsides and through sparsely settled island communities. All walks provide either access to the water or have fabulous views from high points. People also enjoy swimming and snorkeling in the warm Caribbean ocean.

**Services**: Japanese-style acupressure massage is available at an additional fee.

**Guest Comment**: *"I am so grateful to Patricia Brown for the beauty, peace, and healing that she helped bring into my life. For me the Tortola retreat was perfect."*
Heather Ravenscroft—Camden, Maine

**Summary**: This Caribbean island retreat offers a supportive environment for women who know they need silence, rest, and renewal amid the beauty of the natural world. Participants stay in a simple yet elegant private home that is surrounded by gardens of tropical flowers and gorgeous vistas. Yoga teacher Patricia Brown finds this quiet island to be a nurturing atmosphere that allows for a deepening yoga practice, meditation, and personal rejuvenation.

# CORAL SEAS CLIFF HOTEL
# NEGRIL, JAMAICA, CARIBBEAN

*Yoga in Jamaica with Barbara Benagh and John Schumacher*

## FEBRUARY
### ONE OR TWO WEEKS

Negril is renowned as a small, relaxed resort on the beautiful Caribbean island of Jamaica. Its spectacular coastline includes a world-famous seven-mile beach. Negril is a vibrant place, brought alive by the Jamaican people, their reggae music, dancing, and the sultry climate that invites a leisurely way of life.

For more than 15 years John Schumacher and Barbara Benagh have welcomed yoga students to join them for one or two weeks of yoga in Negril. They rent a small, newly built hotel and offer their yoga course there. The hotel sits right on the cliff side of the sea and offers diving into 30-foot-deep warm Caribbean water. There are several ladders for those who prefer to climb down into the sea for a refreshing dip. There is also a swimming pool on the hotel grounds, and guests can use a private beach. Participants enjoy the colorful setting, mingling with the locals, excellent food, music and dancing, and swimming in the Caribbean Sea.

**Address**: The Yoga Studio—Negril Yoga Vacation
Attention: Barbara Benagh
74 Joy St.
Boston, MA 02114
**Phone**: 617/523-7138
**Fax**: 617/734-7280
**E-mail**: yoga@world.std.com

**Airport Information**: Fly into Montego Bay Airport.

**How to Get There**: Transportation is provided to Negril (about two hours away).

**Teacher Background**: Barbara Benagh offers an eclectic style of yoga that reflects her personal practice and study with many teachers, most notably Angela Farmer, for more than two decades. Through the vivid use of image and metaphor Barbara encourages students to approach asanas from deep within, allowing poses to emerge naturally and with a sense of inner substance. She uses a combination of flowing asana sequences and passive traction, utilizing the breath as the guide for all movement. Her asanas are challenging yet taught in the softest way possible so that students learn the easiest ways to accomplish difficult or challenging poses. Inner awareness and consciousness are encouraged.

John Schumacher is a longtime pupil of B. K. S. Iyengar. He has studied in India with B. K. S. Iyengar on numerous occasions and is a certified Iyengar teacher. John incorporates clarity, humor, and directness in his teaching, which helps guide his students toward experiencing the richness and vitality that is possible through the practice of yoga.

**Style of Yoga**: Eclectic Iyengar

**Philosophy of Teachers**: "Diverse interpretations of Hatha yoga can, in combination, create a yoga practice that gives rise to inspiration and self-expression."

**Student Criteria**: Intermediate or advanced levels—students must have yoga experience.

**Disability Access**: No access

**What to Bring**: Yoga mat, two blankets, strap or belt for yoga, comfortable clothes for warm tropical weather, sunscreen, sun hat, swimsuit, and good walking shoes.

**Yoga Room Size and Description**: Yoga is practiced in a covered, open-air room. The room is about 1,500 square feet, and students have a great view of the Caribbean.

**Number of Participants Possible**: 30

**Accommodations**: Most students stay at the Coral Seas Cliff Hotel, where the yoga classes are held. Each room has two double beds and a private bath. Each room also has a balcony facing the ocean. Daily maid serve is included.

**Meals**: Tea and coffee are offered before morning class. A large vegetarian brunch buffet is served every morning after class. Saturday dinner is also included in the workshop fee. Other meals are at your own expense. Local restaurants offer a wide range of cuisine, including vegetarian and fresh seafood.

**Fee**: $950 per person for one week and $1,900 per person for two weeks. Includes hotel lodging (double occupancy), daily brunch, one dinner, all yoga classes with Barbara and John, and transportation to and from Montego Bay Airport. Private rooms are available at additional cost. The yoga course only is $450 weekly.

**Credit Cards**: Not accepted

**Sample Daily Schedule**:

| | |
|---|---|
| 8:00–10:00 a.m. | Yoga class |
| 10:00 | Brunch |
| 11:00–4:00 p.m. | Free time for outings, personal relaxation, group activities |
| 4:00–5:30 | Yoga class, ending with sunset |
| 6:00 | Dinner and evening activities |

**Other Activities**: The warm Caribbean Sea offers swimming, snorkeling, scuba diving, sailing, windsurfing, sea kayaking, and sunset cruises. People also enjoy walking, horseback riding, mountain biking, and sightseeing. Negril offers an abundance of reggae music and dancing on beaches and in local hotels and clubs.

**Guest Comment**: *"When I was in Negril I found myself busting out of old concepts and beliefs, and I was invited to connect to core rhythms in nature through the yoga, and the gentle cycles in the movement of the ocean, clouds, and Jamaican life. Who could resist this?"*
Connie Harris—Kittery Point, Maine

**Summary**: This Caribbean vacation offers experienced yoga students the opportunity to explore two distinctly different approaches to yoga in depth. Yoga teachers Barbara Benagh and John Schumacher combine their teaching skills to create a yoga practice that gives rise to inspiration and self-expression. Participants enjoy twice-daily yoga and the exotic rhythm of Jamaica, which allows for a relaxed and vibrant lifestyle experience. White-sand beaches, live music, dancing, delicious food, and the beautiful Caribbean Sea make Negril a great place to unwind and restore the soul.

# MARINER'S INN
# NEGRIL, JAMAICA, CARIBBEAN

*Yoga Adventure in Negril, Jamaica,*
*with Tara Stiles and Virginia Callaghan*

## NOVEMBER
### ONE WEEK

A phrase heard often in Jamaica is "ya mon," accompanied with a vibrant smile and often a slapping of hands between companions. It is an affirmation of life, a broad, bright yes! Yoga teacher Tara Stiles, along with cofacilitator Virginia Callaghan, brings groups to the small town of Negril for a wintertime Jamaican yoga retreat. Negril offers beautiful beaches on the warm Caribbean Sea, tall trees, exquisite tropical flowers, and a friendly community of people whose vibrancy comes through their musical speech, posture, dance, and hospitality.

Participants stay in the Mariner's Inn, a locally owned and operated resort set in a lush, tropical garden with on-site dining, a swimming pool, and a Jacuzzi. Coleader Virginia Callaghan, who has traveled to Jamaica more than 10 times, utilizes her familiarity with the culture to coach and guide participants in the customs of the Jamaican people. Morning yoga and sunset tai chi are practiced on the beach daily. Participants also enjoy playing in tropical waterfalls, dancing to live reggae music on the beach, swimming in the ocean, and making heartfelt connections with the people of the local community.

**Address**: Jamaican Adventure
2526 27th St.
Sacramento, CA 95818
**Phone**: 916/454-5526 or 916/443-7682

**Airport Information**: Fly into Montego Bay Airport.

**How to Get There**: Ground transportation is provided to Negril (which is two hours away) by private minivan.

**Teacher Background**: Tara Stiles began reading yoga philosophy and practicing Hatha yoga at the age of 15. A year later she learned Transcendental Meditation and has since studied many different approaches to physical and spiritual integration. She

has been practicing yoga for more than 20 years.

Virginia Callaghan is an established community organizer, professional fundraising consultant to nonprofit agencies, and one of Jamaica's inspired ambassadors. Virginia has been to Jamaica more than 10 times and enjoys introducing the Jamaican culture to travelers by educating them and integrating them into the local community lifestyle.

**Style of Yoga**: Tara's classes blend classical and contemporary practices. Tara was originally trained in Sivananda and Vedanta yoga and has since studied other styles, including the Iyengar method. She has developed her own unique, eclectic style of teaching inspired by her own 20 years of regular personal practice, principles, poses of the Iyengar method, and breath-release techniques.

**Philosophy of Teachers**: "Yoga is a means for exploring the somatic and spiritual realms and for self-care in the context of physical, emotional, and spiritual health."

**Student Criteria**: All levels are welcome.

**Disability Access**: No access

**What to Bring**: Yoga mat; casual, comfortable clothes for warm, tropical weather; sunscreen; sun hat; swimsuit; good walking shoes; and an open attitude and willingness to make significant connections with the Jamaican people.

**Yoga Room Size and Description**: Yoga is practiced outdoors on the sand and in an open-sided, covered, patio-type room.

**Number of Participants Possible**: 12

**Accommodations**: Participants stay in the Mariner's Inn in Negril. Rooms are simple and have ceiling fans, high ceilings, kitchenettes, and verandas with ocean views. Guests sleep two to a room in single beds. A private room is available.

**Meals**: A buffet brunch is provided each day after morning yoga class. The brunch consists of tropical fruit, vegetarian side dishes, and fresh fish. Other meals are at your own expense. Local eating establishments where the group interacts with the Jamaican people are recommended.

**Fee**: $900 per person includes one week's lodging (double occupancy) at the Mariner's Inn, ground transportation, cultural introduction and guidance by Virginia, daily brunch, and daily yoga with Tara. Gratuities are not included.

**Credit Cards**: Not accepted

**Sample Daily Schedule**:

| | |
|---|---|
| 7:30–8:00 a.m. | Morning meditation/Chi Kung |
| 8:00–9:45 | Yoga class |
| 10:00 | Brunch |

Free time for outings, personal relaxation, or group activities

| | |
|---|---|
| 5:00 p.m. | Sunset tai chi |
| 7:00 | Dinner and evening activities |

**Other Activities**: Jamaica offers an abundance of popular reggae music and dancing. The warm Caribbean Sea offers swimming, snorkeling, scuba diving, sailing, and sunset cruises. There is a beautiful waterfall nearby where people play on rope swings, dive under the waterfall, and swim in the lagoon.

**Guest Comment**: *"The essence of Tara's yoga teaching is moving into a greater sense of connectedness with the creator/universe, and Jamaica was a perfect setting for me to experience that. The soothing sea, the warming sun, the vibrant colors, the genuineness of the Jamaican people all served to give me a wonderful, enriching, total yoga experience."*
Alice Howell—Sacramento, California

**Summary**: This vacation offers spiritual rejuvenation through the practice of meditation, yoga, and tai chi in the beautiful Caribbean combined with the opportunity to sample the color, music, and magic of the Jamaican culture and land. Virgina Callaghan and Tara Stiles inspire participants to make significant connections with the local people. Participants stay in Negril, a small town with a building code that does not permit any buildings taller than the tallest palm tree. Negril is known for its joyful music and dancing, displayed each night along the beaches.

# BAYVIEW VILLAS
# CULEBRA, PUERTO RICO, CARIBBEAN

*Power Yoga Retreat with Beryl Bender Birch and Thom Birch*

## FEBRUARY AND MARCH
### ONE WEEK

The small island of Culebra, known as the Spanish Virgin Island, is seven miles long and three miles wide. It is a place of undeveloped beauty. There are no major hotels, casinos, fast-food chains, or nightclubs. Beryl Bender Birch and Thom Birch find this quiet, tropical paradise to be a wonderful location for a yoga vacation. Participants stay in private villas with magnificent, unobstructed views of the sea. The island offers beautiful virgin coral reefs and fabulous snorkeling and swimming in protected coves. Temperatures hover in the mid 80s and refreshing tradewinds help keep things cool. Numerous dazzling white-sand beaches surround Culebra and its off-shore islands and bays.

Culebra is officially part of Puerto Rico, so visitors are within a commonwealth of the United States. Passports are unnecessary, and the currency is U.S. dollars. Culebra has approximately 3,000 residents, and most will return a smile or an *holá*. The official language is Spanish, though a majority of the people speak English. With small-town values, the island offers warm hospitality and the experience of simple living.

**Address**: Beryl Bender Birch and Thom Birch
325 East 41st St., #203
New York, NY 10017
**Phone**: 212/661-2895
**Fax**: 516/329-5221
**E-mail**: yoga@power-yoga.com
**Web site**: www.power-yoga.com

**Airport Information**: Fly into Culebra airport. Fly from San Juan on Isla Nena Airlines or Flamenco Air. Do not fly from San Juan to Culebra on Carib Air, as this airline can be unreliable. Another option is to call Culebra Air Charters, which takes up to five people for $250 (one way) on fairly new planes.

**How to Get There**: Culebra is 17 miles east of the big island of Puerto Rico,

halfway between Puerto Rico and the island of St. Thomas.

**Teacher Background**: Beryl Bender Birch and Thom Birch have been offering yoga vacations internationally since 1985. They are both students of Krishnamacharya and Patanjali, author of the *Yoga Sutras*. Beryl has been teaching yoga for more than 25 years, and Thom has been teaching for more than 15 years.

**Style of Yoga**: Ashtanga or Power yoga. Beryl Bender Birch first coined the term *Power yoga* as a user-friendly word for the Western mind when describing Ashtanga yoga. Power yoga is a strong practice that utilizes strength and heat in the body. Beryl and Thom teach Power yoga in a way that is tailored to each individual's needs and abilities.

**Philosophy of Teacher**: "We are classical teachers of Patanjali's yoga, or Ashtanga yoga—the eight-limbed path."

**Student Criteria**: Students of all ages and abilities are welcome.

**Disability Access**: No access

**What to Bring**: Yoga mat, sunscreen, mosquito repellent, clothes for warm weather (75 to 80 degrees during the day), and a sweater or long-sleeved shirt for evenings. Tropical rains are common, so bring a lightweight rain jacket. Bring a pair of running shoes and sandals or thongs.

**Yoga Room Size and Description**: Yoga is practiced in an open-air covered deck. The deck has a wood floor and beautiful views of the ocean. Yoga is done in the morning as the sun rises and everything is quiet and still.

**Number of Participants Possible**: 20 to 25

**Accommodations**: Participants stay in private villas that are spacious, light, and comfortable. They generally have wood floors, ceiling fans, screens, Caribbean-style furniture, fully equipped kitchens, and modern appliances. Different villas are used every year, depending upon the number of participants. Bedrooms have queen and twin beds. Bathrooms are private. All villas have ocean views.

**Meals**: Two vegetarian meals a day are served: a huge brunch and dinner. All meals are cooked by a gourmet chef who uses only natural, organic foods.

**Fee**: $1,500 per person includes two yoga classes per day, evening programs, meals, and accommodations for one week.

**Credit Cards**: Not accepted

**Sample Daily Schedule**:

| | |
|---|---|
| 7:00 a.m. | Meditation and breathing |
| 8:00 | Yoga practice |
| 11:00 | Brunch |
| Free time (hiking, swimming, biking, relaxing on the beach, reading) | |
| 3:30 p.m. | Afternoon lecture |
| 6:30 | Dinner |
| 8:00 | Evening program |

**Other Activities**: Snorkeling, scuba diving, sea kayaking, swimming, beach walking, bird-watching, biking, and lots of fabulous hiking to remote beaches. Participants are allowed to use rental cars for exploring the island. There are only four small gift shops and one health food store on the entire island. This is not a place for lots of shopping. One of the main hangout spots is a small bar called Dingy Dock, where locals gather for afternoon drinks on the harbor.

**Guest Comment**: *"The Birch's yoga vacation was an extraordinary experience in rejuvenating the mind, body, and spirit. The island of Culebra provided an unspoiled tropical setting ideally suited to a great yogic experience. This beautiful setting will nourish your soul, and the Birch's vegetarian chef, Darlene, will nourish your body."* Dee Silvers—Bryn Mawr, Pennsylvania

**Summary**: Culebra is an unspoiled treasure of the Caribbean. Approximately one-third of its 7,000 acres are designated as wildlife reserves. With miles of empty white-sand beaches that are the protected habitat of giant sea turtles, this lovely vacation spot is a peaceful place to experience Power yoga with Thom and Beryl Birch. This yoga retreat offers a truly unhurried pace on an island where roosters and horses have the right-of-way and cars travel on traffic-free roads at 20 miles per hour. The local people are warm and friendly, and the land is undeveloped and beautiful.

# MAHO BAY CAMPGROUNDS
# ST. JOHN, U.S. VIRGIN ISLANDS, CARIBBEAN

### *Yoga with Arthur Kilmurray*

## MARCH
### ONE OR TWO WEEKS

Maho Bay Camps is based on the concept that environmental sensitivity, human comfort, and responsible consumption not only are compatible but can also enhance your vacation experience. Tent cottages, hidden among the trees and connected by elevated wooden walkways, are hand-constructed to avoid soil erosion, which endangers the beach and fragile coral. The camp is set on a hillside overlooking Maho Bay, with gorgeous views of the Caribbean and other islands.

St. John is the smallest of the three major U.S. Virgin Islands and provides a beautiful setting for yoga teacher Arthur Kilmurray's retreat, "Embodying the Elements." Participants come for one or two weeks to enjoy yoga, breathing, and meditation in this natural environment.

**Address**: Mystic River Yoga
c/o Arthur Kilmurray
196 Boston Ave.
Medford, MA 02155
**Phone**: 781/396-0808
**Fax**: 781/396-0808
**E-mail**: yogarthur@aol.com

**Airport Information**: Fly into St. Thomas Airport.

**How to Get There**: From the airport take a taxi to Red Hook Ferry (30 to 45 minutes). Then take the ferry from Red Hook, St. Thomas, to Cruz Bay, St. John (20 minutes). Take a taxi at the ferry dock (ask for Frett's taxi) from Cruz Bay to Maho Bay Campground (30 minutes).

**Teacher Background**: Arthur Kilmurray has more than 20 years experience teaching Iyengar yoga. He draws upon his experience with Bonnie Cohen's body/mind centering as well as his own Buddhist studies to bring a unique approach to the strength and detail of B. K. S. Iyengar's yoga.

**Style of Yoga**: Iyengar Hatha yoga

**Philosophy of Teacher**: "To integrate our way of being with the earth and cosmos through mindful posture and breath work."

**Student Criteria**: Students need at least one year of yoga experience for the beginning-level week and three or more years of yoga experience for the intermediate-level week.

**Disability Access**: No access

**What to Bring**: Yoga mat, blanket, and other useful props. There is no porter service at Maho, so pack light. Dress is casual on the island. Sometimes luggage is delayed in transit, so carry by hand all essentials: swimsuit, shorts, T-shirts, flashlight, beach towel, bug repellent, toiletries (including soap), and any medication you might need. A sweater or light jacket may be needed on occasion.

**Yoga Room Size and Description**: Yoga is practiced on an outdoor pavilion on a hill overlooking Maho Bay. The room holds 20 people comfortably.

**Number of Participants Possible**: 20

**Accommodations**: Participants stay in roomy tent-cottages (double occupancy), which are built on 16-square-foot platforms and are nearly hidden by lush foliage. Translucent fabric on wood frames provides shelter while screens and terraces allow you to take advantage of the cooling trade winds. Bed linens, blankets, towels, cooking and eating utensils are all provided, as are a propane stove and ice cooler. Every tent cottage has its own private deck. Hillside views of the Caribbean waters can be seen from many of the dwellings. Barbecue areas and fresh water are available along the walkways. Maho's centrally located bathhouses are equipped with modern low-flush toilets and pull-chain showers connected to a recycling system to irrigate the surrounding vegetation.

**Meals**: Meals are at your own expense. An outdoor restaurant serves a wide variety of healthy meals for breakfast and dinner every day (this includes at least one vegetarian entree). The Maho Bay store is stocked with produce, breads, canned foods, frozen foods, dairy products, juices, soft drinks, beer, and wine. Each cabin is equipped with a stove and cooking utensils.

**Fee**: $975 per person per week includes a double-occupancy room in a Maho Bay tent-cottage, two daily yoga classes with Arthur, and morning meditation sessions.

**Credit Cards**: Not accepted

**Sample Daily Schedule**:

| | |
|---|---|
| 6:10–7:00 a.m. | Morning meditation |
| 7:00–9:00 | Yoga asanas |
| 9:15–10:00 | Breakfast |
| 10:00–4:00 p.m. | Free time |
| 4:00–5:30 | Yoga asanas |
| 5:30–2:30 | Dinner |
| 7:30 | Evening programs (optional) |

**Other Activities**: The area offers fabulous snorkeling, including a nighttime snorkling opportunity, scuba diving, sailing, boating, fishing, windsurfing, kayaking, hiking, national park tours, island tours, swimming, and relaxing on the beach.

**Guest Comment**: *"The annual Mystic River Yoga vacations have been a wonderful opportunity to deepen my yoga practice in a setting of remarkable natural beauty. Arthur's teaching embodies a deep connection to the natural world, and Maho Bay is an exceptional place in which to explore that connection."*

Trude Kleinshmidt—
Newton, Massachusetts

**Summary**: This Caribbean yoga vacation on St. John is held in a lovely, low key environment that offers glorified camping. Yoga teacher Arthur Kilmurray teaches yoga as a vehicle for embodying the spiritual connectedness of our selves with Mother Earth and the living cosmos. Two weeks are offered: one for students with at least one year of experience and the second for students with three or more years of yoga experience.

# PAPILLOTE WILDERNESS RETREAT
# WINDWARD ISLANDS, CARIBBEAN

*Yoga Retreat with Inez Stein*

## APRIL
### ONE WEEK

The Papillote Wilderness Retreat, near the Morne Trois Pitons National Park and Trafalgar Falls, is a small, secluded inn at the top of a sun-filled valley in the middle of a nature sanctuary. It boasts beautiful flower gardens, pristine rainforest, natural hot springs, a variety of exotic birds, and cascading waterfalls.

Dominica is called the nature island of the Caribbean. As you take the transinsular route from the airport, the sweeping mountain and coastline vistas will be the start of your decompression into island time. Mountain vistas, fields of dasheen (a local tuber), and banana groves gently compete for your attention as you climb into the mist of the rainforest. Called the largest plant laboratory in the world by the Smithsonian, Dominica offers nature lovers, hikers, adventurers, and divers an enjoyable vacation. Large tracts of conservation land have been set aside as national parks and forests. Rain forests provide an opportunity to observe a dazzling abundance of plant and bird life. Orchids, bromeliads, and tree ferns abound.

**Address**: In the Moment Yoga & Adventure Vacations
63 Cherrywood Dr.
Norwood, MA 02062-5502
**Phone**: 800/548-7651
**Fax**: 781/769-9341
**E-mail**: tours@conejo.com
**Web site**: www.conejo.com

**Airport Information**: Papillote is approximately 45 minutes from Melville Hall Airport (where American Eagle flights arrive). Transportation to and from Melville Hall Airport is provided.

**How to Get There**: The commonwealth of Dominica, not to be confused with the Dominican Republic, is part of the Windward Island and is located between Guadeloupe and Martinique.

**Teacher Background**: Inez Stein is a certified Kripalu teacher with continuing training with Iyengar master teacher Patricia Walden. She has been teaching for more than six years and is the director of In the Moment Wellness Center in Norwood, Massachusetts.

**Style of Yoga**: Kripalu with Iyengar influence. Inez places emphasis on the meditative aspects of yoga that lead to self-awareness. She is attentive to detail in yoga poses and sensitive to each individual's capacities.

**Philosophy of Teacher**: "Yoga is a spiritual practice, bringing us back to the present moment. I stress being mindful of the body, listening to the body's needs and not pushing or straining."

**Student Criteria**: All levels are welcome.

**Disability Access**: No access

**What to Bring**: Yoga mat (if you have one), loose, comfortable clothing, water bottles, and hiking boots and backpacks if you plan to hike.

**Yoga Room Size and Description**: Yoga is practiced in a large, open-air dining room or veranda.

**Number of Participants Possible**: 18

**Accommodations**: The Rain Forest Lodge rooms are simple and have twin beds (double or triple occupancy); local quilts and artwork complement the spectacular views. The cottage suites are similarly equipped and have vaulted ceilings and optional kitchenettes. There are no telephones or radios in the rooms. All rooms have private baths. Wooden shutters take the place of window panes, but no stagnant pools mean virtually no mosquitoes. Elevation replaces the need for air conditioning.

**Meals**: The optional meal plan for the week includes daily breakfast and dinner served at the Rain Forest Restaurant, which is an open-air dining room on a hill. There are other restaurants available in the town of Roseau, which is 10 or 15 minutes away.

**Fee**: $440 per person per week for a cottage suite (double occupancy). $365 per person per week for a room in the lodge (double occupancy). Call for single, triple, or quadruple occupancy price rates. Tuition for yoga and meditation classes is $140 per person per week. The optional meal plan is $240 per person for the week. All other meals, additional activities, and tours are at an additional cost. Call for specific prices.

**Credit Cards**: Not accepted

**Sample Daily Schedule**:
| | |
|---|---|
| 5:30–6:00 a.m. | Meditation |
| 6:25–7:30 | Yoga |
| 7:30–9:00 | Breakfast |

Afternoon: Optional planned adventures, such as snorkeling at Champagne Bay, a beach trip to Point Baptiste Beach, or a visit to Victorian Falls.

| | |
|---|---|
| 4:45–5:15 p.m. | Pranayama |
| 5:15–5:45 | Meditation |
| 6:00–7:15 | Yoga |
| 7:30–8:30 | Dinner |

**Other Activities**: Many exotic birds and plants live in the rain forest. Hiking trails are not clearly marked, so local guides are recommended. Guides not only take you to your destination but also are knowledgeable about the flora and fauna of the area and the history of Dominica.

**Guest Comment**: *"Papillote is as close to nirvana as we have found. At night we go to sleep to the trill of tree frogs and rushing water. During the day we are overwhelmed by the colors and textures of Papillote's garden. After spending time hiking, there is nothing to compare to soaking in one of Papillote's natural hot springs, watching butterflies, hummingbirds, and countless other fauna move among the flora of the rain forest with, perhaps, a rainbow overhead."*
Jim Breslauer—Lowell, Massachusetts

**Summary**: This retreat, located in the middle of a rain forest, is surrounded by lush foliage and beautiful birds. The week includes planned afternoon adventures, with meditation and yoga starting and ending each day. Three hot mineral pools at the retreat are comforting and relaxing after a day of hiking and exploration.

# NOSARA RETREAT
# NICOYA PENINSULA, GUANACASTE, COSTA RICA

## YEAR-ROUND

Nosara Retreat is located on the Pacific coast of Costa Rica overlooking four miles of pristine white beach—excellent for swimming, boogie boarding, surfing, and shelling. Founded and directed by Amba and Don Stapleton, Nosara Retreat is a haven for renewal through yoga and nature. Surrounded by tropical forest and alive with the jungle sounds of monkeys, colorful birds, and coatimundis, the retreat offers yoga instruction along with nature excursions to create a relaxing and rejuvenating vacation. Only 12 guests are accepted at a time, so instruction and services are personalized and meet each person's needs. Nosara also offers yogassage retreats for couples—a special combination of massage and yoga.

**Address:** Nosara Retreat
c/o Don and Amba Stapleton
Interlink 979, P.O. Box 02-5635
Miami, Florida 33102
**Phone:** 888/803-0580
**Fax:** 506/682-0072
**E-mail:** yogacr@sol.racsa.co.cr
**Web site:** www.nosara.com

**Airport Information:** Fly to San José or Liberia international airports in Costa Rica. There is a commuter flight from San José to Nosara twice a day (7:00 a.m. and 1:20 p.m.), or you can take a taxi. Nosara is only a two-hour drive from Liberia Airport.

**How to Get There:** Nosara Retreat is located on the Pacific coast of Costa Rica, about five hours from San José.

**Teacher Background:** Amba Camp Stapelton has more than 20 years of experience in Hatha yoga. Her training is in Kripalu and Ashtanga yoga. She taught at the Kripalu Center for Health and Yoga for six years and then taught in Los Angeles until she came to Costa Rica.

Don Stapelton, Ph.D., pioneered the development of the yoga curriculum at the Kripalu Center in Massachusetts. He has more than 25 years experience in the practice of yoga as a fundamental discipline for self-discovery. His approach to yoga draws from his training in Iyengar and Kripalu yoga as well as Feldenkrais, the Alexander technique, and Pilates.

**Style of Yoga:** Nosara yoga is interdisciplinary yoga. Don and Amba honor the wisdom of all yoga traditions and structure learning environments as is appropriate for the interests and life stage of the student.

**Philosophy of Teachers:** "When placed in natural surroundings, the mind and body can heal themselves."

**Student Criteria:** All levels are welcome.

**Disability Access:** No access

**What to Bring:** Pack lightly. Bring a few sets of exercise clothes, beach sandals, walking shoes, water bottle carrying case, swimsuit, and casual clothing.

**Yoga Room Size and Description**: Yoga is practiced in a covered, open-air pavilion with a hardwood sprung floor and beautiful arches. The monkeys often visit the trees surrounding the pavilion to "join in" the yoga class. The pavilion is equipped with ropes and yoga props.

**Number of Participants Possible**: 12

**Accommodations**: Two standard rooms downstairs feature full bath, two single beds, fans, and a closet. Upstairs, three deluxe suites overlook the Pacific Ocean and the pool area. These suites have French doors that open onto the veranda and either one or two double beds, fans, closets, and luxurious bathrooms that include Roman tubs for soaking.

**Meals**: Vegetarian Costa Rican cuisine is served. The main meal is lunch. Breakfast, dinner, and snacks are offered as well. Fruits and vegetables fresh from local growers are served in season. Fresh herbs come from the garden. Dinners are served by candlelight.

**Fee**: $245 per person per night for a deluxe shared room, $320 per person per night for a deluxe private room, and $200 per person per night for a shared standard room. Inquire about special rates for groups. Price includes accommodations; all vegetarian meals, snacks, and fresh vegetable and fruit juices throughout the day; guided nature walks; two hours of yoga instruction daily; and transfers from Nosara Airport.

**Credit Cards**: Visa

**Sample Daily Schedule**:

| | |
|---|---|
| 6:30 a.m. | Tea and coffee |
| 7:00 | Morning hike |
| 9:00 | Breakfast |
| 10:45 | Yoga |

| | |
|---|---|
| 12:45 p.m. | Lunch |

Afternoon excursions, personal services, or rest.

| | |
|---|---|
| 5:30 | Sunset beach meditation |
| 7:00 | Dinner |

**Other Activities**: Nosara Retreat is surrounded by a natural wildlife preserve. Bring binoculars and catch glimpses of colorful exotic birds. Nosara Beach is one of the few places where sea turtles can be observed emerging from the ocean to lay their eggs in the warm sand. The area offers jungle tours, horseback riding, kayaking, canoeing, beach walks, swimming in the ocean or the freshwater swimming pool, a waterfall hike, and excursions to other sights in Costa Rica, such as rain forests and volcanoes.

**Services**: Swedish massage, Thai massage, deep tissue massage, yogassage, physical therapy, nutritional counseling, manicures, and pedicures are available.

**Guest Comment**: *"The Nosara Retreat is an oasis of peace and simplicity. The jungle setting, the magnificent beaches, the friendly people, and especially Don and Amba Stapleton's expert yoga instruction all combine to make Nosara an extraordinary experience. I look forward to going back!"*

Andrew K. Franklin—
Old Greenwich, Connecticut

**Summary**: Nosara Retreat invites guests to experience yoga in an environment that brings people as close as possible to nature. This rich Costa Rican ecosystem offers a variety of wildlife-discovery opportunities, exploration, and adventure. The philosophy at Nosara Retreat is to live in harmony with the wisdom of the planet as reflected in our own bodies. By attuning to and caring for our bodies through yoga, we cultivate respect for

# PURA VIDA RETREAT CENTER
# SAN JOSÉ, COSTA RICA

## YEAR-ROUND

Pura Vida, meaning pure life, is located on a 12-acre private estate of tropical splendor atop a mountain in Costa Rica's Alajuela province. The retreat property, at 5,200 feet, is surrounded by coffee plantations and is only 20 minutes from San José's airport. Pura Vida Retreat Center offers a variety of accommodations amid enchanted gardens, fountains, pools, waterfalls, flowers, ornamental trees, fruit trees, and colorful birds. The whole estate commands views of the surrounding volcanoes Irazu, Barva, and Poas as well as of the central valley in which San José, the capital, sits. Vacations that include yoga, meditation, hiking, and eco-adventure tours are offered year-round. Pura Vida is managed by resident yoga teachers Paul Gould and Jennifer Fox. All programs have a spiritual, holistic approach to individual and group needs and include daily yoga classes. Specialty yoga retreats with various guest yoga teachers are offered as well. (Please e-mail for schedule information.)

**Address**: Pura Vida Retreat Center U.S.
P.O. Box 3029
San Rafael, CA 94912
**Phone**: 888/767-7375
**Fax**: 415/457-3535
**E-mail**: reservations@puravidaspa.com
**Web site**: www.puravidaspa.com

**Airport Information**: Fly into San Jose International Airport in Costa Rica. Pura Vida is 20 minutes away.

**How to Get There**: Transportation is provided for guests on a weekly basis. Call for details.

**Teacher Background**: Jennifer Fox, a certified Iyengar yoga teacher, has been teaching yoga for more than 16 years. Former owner of the Mill Valley Yoga Studio, she is a graduate of the San Francisco Iyengar Institute and has trained with the Iyengars in India and with senior teachers of many yoga methods throughout the United States.

Paul Gold, a former commodity futures trader and land developer, traded in his business careers to become a personal trainer with a degree in Fitness Training. He is now an avid meditator and yoga teacher who specializes in back care.

Both Jenni and Paul have studied Astanga, Viniyoga, and Integrative Yoga Therapy, and they are students of Zen Buddist meditation and Engaged Mindfulness Training.

**Style of Yoga**: Iyengar-based yoga with an emphasis on the inward journey. Guest teachers offer various styles—call for information.

**Philosophy of Teachers**: "Our goal is to communicate yoga in a joyful, down-to-earth manner in order to help students of all levels experience its many benefits to body, mind, and spirit."

**Student Criteria**: All levels are welcome.

**Disability Access**: Yes

**What to Bring**: Casual, comfortable clothes, alarm clock, swimsuit, beach towel, waterproof sandals or "surf shoes," sunscreen, sun hat, and water bottle. Pura Vida's year-round daytime temperature averages 73 degrees Fahrenheit. Nights are mild, and there is no need for air conditioning or supplemental heat.

**Yoga Room Size and Description**: Yoga is practiced in a 2,500-square-foot yoga studio fully equipped with a rope wall and props. The room has soothing fountains nearby.

**Number of Participants Possible**: 40

**Accommodations**: Pura Vida offers a variety of housing options. A private pagoda (deluxe) has a living room, fireplace, kitchenette, Jacuzzi, king-size bed, deck, and private bath. A Japanese Tea House has a living room, kitchenette, king-size bed, deck, and private bath. Casa Tica Bungalow features two bedrooms (single or double beds), semiprivate bath, kitchenette, living room, Jacuzzi, and deck. Several tent chalets, which are fully furnished outdoor tenthouses, have two beds (single or double) and shared baths in close proximity. A guest room in the main house, with a private entrance, queen-size bed, and bath, is also available.

**Meals**: Three meals a day are offered. Meals are mostly vegetarian, with some fish dishes included.

**Fee**: Weeklong programs run from $599 to $1,300 per person and include lodging, meals, classes, excursions, and transfers.

**Credit Cards**: Most credit cards are accepted, although there is a 7 percent surcharge in Costa Rica.

**Sample Daily Schedule**:

| 6:30 a.m. | Yoga class |
| 8:00 | Breakfast |

Free time for excusions (white-water rafting, hiking, eco-touring)

| 5:00 p.m. | Yoga class |
| 6:30 | Dinner |
| 8:30 | Meditation |

**Other Activites**: There are many choices for day trips: rain forests, volcanoes, cloud forests, river rafting, and any of Costa Rica's beautiful beaches. The area offers wonderful hiking, exploration, and bird-watching. Shopping in San José or in the nearby towns is also a pleasant experience.

**Services**: Massage is available.

**Guest Comment**: *"Green, lush views . . . hikes in the coffee fields . . . the raft trip . . . I was fortunate to see Poas on a clear day, and it was like nothing I had ever seen. Yoga sessions were excellent. Most intense classes I have attended. Wonderful private instruction. I will return! Beautiful, relaxing, friendly, and fun."* Noelle Colome — Los Angeles, California

**Summary**: This Coast Rican retreat center offers a beautiful, tropical environment for yoga, rest, and renewal as well as eco-adventure and education. Yoga teachers Paul Gold and Jennifer Fox invite guests to immerse themselves in the good life for which the center is named: good food, good friends, feel-good yoga, meditation, and fitness — all with a spiritual and holistic approach. Various guest yoga teachers offer retreats at Pura Vida. (E-mail for schedule information.)

SEE PHOTOS, PAGE 149.

# VILLA RAYMONDE
# BRITTANY, FRANCE

*Woman's Yoga Retreat with Rory C. Capalupa*

## SEPTEMBER
### ONE WEEK

Brittany, the Celtic region of France, is the land of druids and magic. The area is rich in history, heather-topped cliffs, and small, sandy beaches. Yoga teacher Rory C. Capalupa lived in France at one time and now goes back every year to offer a women's yoga retreat at a private villa in Brittany, located only one and one-half miles from the beach. The retreat is intimate and personalized, with room for only six to nine participants. Surrounding areas of interest include Pont-Aven, "the city of artistes"; Quimper, a picturesque eleventh-century town know as "the most Celtic of all Breton cities"; and Carnac, the site of the famous field of menhirs (prehistoric obelisks). Although referred to as the French Retreat, classes are taught in English.

**Address**: Laughing Wolf Yoga/Healing Centre
c/o Rory C. Capalupa
413 Crawford Ave.
Syracuse, NY 13224
**Phone**: 315/446-7994
**Fax**: 315/446-7994

**Airport Information**: Fly from Paris to Lorient Airport, which is 30 minutes from the retreat. Transportation to and from the retreat is provided.

**How to Get There**: By train take TGV (speed train) to Quimperlé, 10 minutes from the retreat.

**Teacher Background**: Rory C. Capalupa has been a seriously playful student of Hatha yoga for 25 years. While living in France she studied Hatha yoga under Andre Van Lysbeth. In New York City she has studied with Lindsey Clennell (Iyengar) and Beryl Bender Birch (Ashtanga). In 1994

Rory founded the Laughing Wolf Yoga/Healing Centre in Syracuse, New York.

**Style of Yoga**: Hatha, Iyengar, and Ashtanga. Rory combines the science of bio-mechanical alignment, the art of inner body awareness, and the celebration of the heart in her practice and teaching.

**Philosophy of Teacher**: "To develop loving kindness (*metta*) toward self and others."

**Student Criteria**: All levels of yoga experience are welcome.

**Disability Access**: No access

**What to Bring**: Yoga mat, blanket, beach towel, swimsuit, sweater, light jacket, rain gear, and hiking shoes. Also bring a good curiosity, a love of nature and beauty, and a healthy appetite.

**Yoga Room Size and Description:** Two spaces are used for yoga classes. Yoga is practiced in a bright, light-filled room that is 18' x 24' and has an oak floor. A large covered veranda overlooking the beautiful gardens is also used.

**Number of Participants Possible:** 69

**Accommodations:** Participants stay in a private villa surrounded by lush gardens. Rooms are comfortable and semi-private. Each room has two single beds, ceramic-tile floors, and windows looking out onto the gardens. Rooms also look out on a large pond, which is home to playful ducks and lovely floating water lilies. Guests share a hall bathroom. The villa is stucco and has ceramic roof tiles. The entire property is enclosed and very private.

**Meals:** Three French vegetarian meals are served daily and include fresh local produce and ingredients. Brittany is known for its crepes, cider, and dairy products. Special diets are accommodated, if possible.

**Fee:** $711 per person includes seven days', six nights' lodging in a private French villa, three vegetarian meals daily, and all yoga classes with Rory.

**Credit Cards:** Not accepted

**Sample Daily Schedule:**

| | |
|---|---|
| 7:00–7:30 a.m. | Breakfast |
| 9:15–11:15 | Chanting, yoga asanas and meditation |
| 12:30–1:30 p.m. | Lunch |
| 1:30–3:30 | Free time (optional day trips to local sites and towns) |
| 3:30–5:30 | Afternoon yoga session |
| 6:00–7:00 | Dinner |

Some of the evenings are free, while others will include group discussions/satsangs.

**Other Activities:** There are wonderful biking and hiking trails to explore. The hiking terrain is mostly hilly. Bikes are available for rent. The Atlantic Ocean offers warm water for swimming. The beaches are located in coves surrounded by gorgeous cliffs and heather-covered dunes. Cafés are five minutes by car. Visiting nearby French towns and historic sites is appealing to many visitors.

**Guest Comment:** *"Rory's approach is very friendly, caring, precise in instructions, and spiritual. Her knowledge of yoga is immense. She takes time to understand each person's body and what's going on, how to better it mentally, physically, and spiritually. During the retreat there was a nice balance of instruction, guidance, and free time. The accommodations were excellent. Rory knows France well and is a helpful tourist guide, too."*

Regina Whiteside—
Syracuse, New York

**Summary:** This retreat for women only is offered in a quaint French villa near the sea. Yoga teacher Rory Capalupa lived in France at one time and offers a wealth of knowledge of French culture and yoga. There is room for only six to nine participants at this retreat, which keeps classes small and intimate and allows for plenty of individual attention.

# THE YOGA HALL
# MOLIVOS, LÉSVOS, GREECE

*Yoga Course with Angela Farmer and Victor van Kooten*

### MAY AND JUNE
#### ONE, TWO, OR THREE WEEKS

Molivos, a small fishing village on the north coast of Lésvos, is built on the side of a hill, crowned with an ancient castle, and overlooks the fishing harbor on the Aegean Sea. For more than 20 years Angela Farmer and Victor van Kooten have been offering three-week yoga courses in this quaint Greek village. Yoga classes are conducted in the Yoga Hall on the northwest end of the island. The surrounding rugged hill country is perfect for exploration, walks, and hikes. Three miles northeast of Molivos are the pebble beaches of Eftalou, which feature a natural spring and views of the Turkish coast on the horizon to the north and east. This trip is a pilgrimage in that participants are required to find their own lodging once they arrive on the island, which can be challenging if you don't speak Greek. An independent and adventuresome spirit is helpful.

**Address**: Angela and Victor Yoga Holiday c/o Patricia Schneider
139 E. Davis St.
Yellow Springs, OH 45387-1815
**Phone**: 937/767-7727
**Fax**: 937/767-7366

**Airport Information**: Fly from Athens to Mitilíni (the port of arrival) on Lésvos. For European students there are charter flights available from many cities direct to Mitilíni. There is also a sea route: you can take an overnight ferry from Piraeus (the harbor in Athens) to Mitilíni.

**How to Get There**: To reach Molivos from Mitilíni take a local bus or hire a taxi. If you carry your yoga mat, fellow yoga students may spot you and share a taxi with you. Negotiate with the driver at the start! Molivos is 200 miles northeast of Athens and a few miles from the coast of Turkey.

**Teacher Background**: Angela Farmer and Victor van Kooten are internationally renowned yoga teachers, each with more than 30 years of experience. For many years they studied separately with B. K. S. Iyengar in India, becoming quite accomplished in the Iyengar method. Each of them moved away from that system to create a more internal and meditative approach to yoga. They have worked together for more than 15 years, influencing many leading teachers in the West today with their unique and supportive "inner body" work.

**Style of Yoga**: Angela and Victor teach yoga that utilizes the deep internal flow of energy they call the "inner body" rather than the muscles. Instead of focusing on external alignment, they guide their students to an internal awareness and movement. To them asanas are "maps" or tools to help explore how energy moves inside us. Their practice is explorative and empowering, leading to each individual's own development and practice.

**Philosophy of Teachers:** "We guide our students toward the abundant richness that the internal world provides."

**Student Criteria:** An interest in self-development. All levels are welcome.

**Disability Access:** No access

**What to Bring:** Yoga mat and a blanket. In May Molivos can get one or two rainy and cool days, so bring some warm clothes along with casual beach and yoga attire, swimsuit, towel, sunscreen, and toiletries.

**Yoga Room Size and Description:** Yoga Hall is in the village of Molinos, a few hundred yards from the sea. The hall accommodates 35 students. It has a wooden floor, wall straps, a pelvic swing, a back bender, and a headstand bench. There is also a changing room with two bathrooms.

**Number of Participants Possible:** 35

**Accommodations:** Participants are on their own in finding a place to stay. Molivos provides many alternatives: hotels, guest houses, rooms in local houses, and apartments. Most rooms range between $5 and $10 a night and are simple and clean, and some include private showers and cooking facilities. You should arrive two or three days before the yoga course begins to get situated. You can book a hotel for one or two nights and then look around for something that suits your needs. Please call for a list of nearby hotels and rooms used by previous students.

**Meals:** Meals are at your own expense. A good variety of groceries, fresh fruits, and vegetables are available in local stores. There are also hotel restaurants and Greek taverns, coffee bars, and bakeries. If you have special dietary needs you should bring what you require with you.

**Fee:** $950 per person for three weeks of yoga instruction, $700 for two weeks, and $400 for one week. This does not include room, meals, or travel expenses.

**Credit Cards:** Not accepted

**Sample Daily Schedule:**

| | |
|---|---|
| Morning: | Three-hour asana and movement class |
| Free time | |
| Late afternoon: | One-and-one-half-hour breathing and sitting (meditation) class |

**Other Activities:** Explore this picturesque island, which is home to many artists, poets, writers, and others with creative alternative lifestyles. Enjoy swimming, water sports, good walking in the surrounding hills, and a natural hot spring on a beach five kilometers away.

**Guest Comment:** *"The trip transformed me more than any other in my life. Maybe it was the sweet village of Molivos, crowned with an old castle and surrounded by the Aegean Sea. Maybe it was the chance to spend three weeks far away from familiarity . . . exploring, expressing, and unwinding. And most certainly it was Angela and Victor and their remarkable yoga. I returned home inspired, restored, and revitalized with a belly full of life again. I'd recommend this workshop to anyone interested in a more internal approach to yoga, to anyone who yearns to breathe and live and move from inside out."*
Claudia Cummins — Mansfield, Ohio

**Summary:** Angela Farmer and Victor van Kooten are known for their internal style of yoga, which draws on the rich well of energy deep inside. This Greek intensive offers one, two, or three weeks of yoga classes while surrounded by the beauty of the Aegean Sea. Participants arrange their own housing and meals, so a pilgrimage spirit is recommended.

# SIVANANDA YOGA VEDANTA DHANWANTHARI ASHRAM KERALA, INDIA

## YEAR-ROUND

The Sivananda Yoga Vedanta Dhanwanthari Ashram is located on 12 acres in the quiet foothills of Kerala's Western Ghats. This tropical area offers the natural beauty of the Neyyar Dam Lake and its surrounding coconut palms and flower-filled views. The ashram provides a disciplined classical yoga program designed to instill a deep awareness of the spiritual essence of life. Yoga vacations begin on the first and fifteenth of every month and last for two weeks. Classes are based on the teachings of Swami Sivananda and Swami Vishnu Devananda. By closely observing the lifestyles and needs of people in both the East and West, Swami Visnu Devananda synthesized the ancient wisdom of yoga into five basic principles that can be easily incorporated into your own pattern of living. The ashram incorporates these principles into daily routines to provide the foundation for a long and healthy life of peace and fulfillment.

**Address**: Sivananda Yoga Vedanta Dhanwanthari Ashram
Neyyar Dam P.O.
Tjhiruvananthapuram Dist., Kerala, India 695 576
**Phone**: 011-91-471-290-493
**Fax**: 011-91-471-290-493/451 776
**E-mail**: YogaIndia@sivananda.org
**Web site**: www.sivananda.org/locations/ashrams/neyyardam/ndam.htm

**Airport Information**: There are daily flights direct from Bombay (Mumbai), New Delhi, and Madras (Chennai) to Trivandrum. From the airport you may catch a taxi directly to the ashram (40 kilometers).

**How to Get There**: The Kerala Express (train), which departs Delhi at 11:30 each day, will bring you into Trivandrum Central, where you will find the bus stand opposite the train station. There is regular bus service to Neyyar Dam (28 kilometers). If you need assistance in Trivandrum please contact the Sivanan-

da Yoga Vedanta Centre, 37/1929, West Fort, Airport Road, Trivandrum. Phone: 011-91-471-450-942.

**Teacher Background**: Classes are taught by members of the ashram staff on a rotating basis. All teachers have been trained in the Siva-nanda yogic teachings and philosophy.

**Style of Yoga**: Classical yoga, which includes a synthesis of Raja (which includes Hatha), Jnana, Karma, and Bhakti yoga. Classes are taught by ashram staff and follow teachings set by Swami Sivananda. Twelve main asanas are used. Devotional practices, such as silent meditation followed by mantra chanting in Sanskrit, are used daily to help cultivate the teachings.

**Philosophy of Teachers**: "Vendanta philosophy, exploring the nature of self and truth. Five basic principles of health: proper exercise, proper breathing, proper relaxation, proper diet, positive thinking, and meditation. Discipline can provide physical, psychological, and spiritual balance and harmony."

**Student Criteria:** No experience necessary. All guests must participate in the daily schedule.

**Disability Access:** No access

**What to Bring:** Light cotton clothing for asanas, toiletries and personal items, a shawl for cool evenings, yoga mat or pad, towels, a sleeping bag or sheets, and a mosquito net during November to May.

**Yoga Room Size and Description:** Yoga is practiced beneath palm trees on the shore of a quiet lake.

**Number of Participants Possible:** 200

**Accommodations:** The Kailash building has 10 double rooms with private bathrooms and a balcony. All rooms are simple and have picturesque views of the valley below. Dormitory accommodations provide sleeping space for 25 people together with shared bathrooms. There are some lovely huts available; each contains two to three beds and shared bathrooms. Camping space is also available.

**Meals:** Pure, South India, buffet-style vegetarian meals are served daily at brunch and dinnertime. Meals are prepared according to yogic dietary principles. Meat, fish, fowl, eggs, garlic, onions, tea, and coffee are not served.

**Fee:** $300 per person for Kailash rooms, $250 per person for double rooms, and $200 per person for dormitory or tenting space. During low season (June to October) deduct $50. Rates include lodging, meals, and the full yoga program for two weeks. Special cultural programs, teacher trainings, and children's camp have additional fees.

**Credit Cards:** Not accepted

**Sample Daily Schedule:**

| | |
|---|---|
| 6:00 a.m. | Meditation, *kirtan*, lecture |
| 7:30 | Tea time |
| 8:00 | Asana and pranayama class |
| 10:00 | Brunch |
| 11:00 | Karma yoga (one hour) |
| 2:00 p.m. | Afternoon talk |
| 4:00 | Asana and pranayama class |
| 6:00 | Dinner |
| 8:00 | Meditation, *kirtan*, lecture |
| 10:00 | Lights out (silence observed) |

**Other Activities:** There is a wildlife sanctuary near the ashram, which allows for wonderful hiking and walking. There is a hot tub available for use. Weekly jungle excursions to a waterfall are available, as are excursions to nearby places of cultural and religious interest.

**Guest Comment:** *"The Sivananda Ashram in Neyyar Dam, Kerala, South India, is fairly unique insofar as it provides a traditional setting where foreigners as well as Indians can practice and study Yoga under the guidance of English-speaking teachers. I spent nearly two months there and loved every aspect: the opportunity to practice yoga in its broadest sense in such a positive atmosphere, the stunning scenery, the peace and quiet, and of course the amazing food. Meditation at dawn as the pinks and oranges of the lightening sky reflect off the still waters of the lake is an incredible way to begin a day of spiritual practice. I can't wait to go back."*
Robin Catto — London, England

**Summary:** Students from all over the world come to this ashram to immerse themselves in Sivananda's teachings in the country where yoga has its roots. This ashram also offers two pilgrimages yearly (February and September), one through North India and one through South India, where participants visit and experience sacred temples and holy places.

SEE PHOTOS, PAGE 150.

# THE BEACH HOUSE AND MAN OF ARAN COTTAGE INISHMORE, IRELAND

*Yoga with Kevin Gardiner on the Aran Islands*

## MAY AND JUNE
### ONE WEEK

Inishmore is the largest of the Aran Islands. The landscape, carved by ice, wind, and sea, is remote. Ancient tombs, stone forts, holy wells, and endless stone walls delicately shape the environment. Yoga teacher Kevin Gardiner offers a weeklong yoga vacation on this Irish island. Lodging is at local bed-and-breakfasts in Kilmurvey, a small community about three miles from the ferry docks where you can sometimes catch a glimpse of the dolphins dancing in Galway Bay. The island is a botanist's paradise, with hundreds of unusual varieties of wildflowers. The sun sets this time of year around 10:00 p.m., and the long dusk lingers in the sky until almost midnight.

**Address**: Kevin Gardiner
301 East 61st St., #2D
New York, NY 10021
**Phone**: 212/755-6324
**Fax**: 212/755-6324

**Airport Information**: Arrive at Shannon Airport.

**How to Get There**: There is a convenient bus to Galway (Bus Eireann); the trip takes about two hours. Once in Galway, head for the Island Ferries office. The bus to the ferry leaves from there one and one-half hours before ferry departure. Ferry departure times are 11:00 a.m., 2:00 p.m., and 7:00 p.m. The Island Ferry phone number is 011-353-568-903-56176. The ferry leaves from Rossaveal and docks at Kilronain Pier on Inishmore. From there you catch a small van or a horse-drawn two-wheeler and head out to Kilmurvey and "Man of Aran Cottage."

**Teacher Background**: Kevin Gardiner

has been a yoga practitioner since 1970 and is a core faculty member of the Iyengar Institute of New York. He is a Certified Instructor in the Iyengar method and has made extended trips to India to study with the Iyengars.

**Style of Yoga**: Iyengar. Kevin's instruction is precise and detailed. His demonstration is graceful and dynamic.

**Philosophy of Teacher**: "I see yoga as an art and a science. My philosophy about yoga comes in part from my teacher, B. K. S. Iyengar, who tells his students that enthusiasm brings concentration; concentration brings precision; precision brings freedom."

**Student Criteria**: Approximately one year of experience with Iyengar yoga is required.

**Disability Access**: No access

**What to Bring**: Yoga mat, three blankets,

two belts, wooden blocks, rain gear, and rugged shoes.

**Yoga Room Size and Description:** Yoga is practiced in a beautiful room with hardwood floors located on the second floor of the International School of Irish. The room is spacious and has French-style windows that open out onto wide vistas of both sides of the island. Downstairs there is a huge space that is actually a racquetball court, also with hardwood floors, and enough space for 40-plus students.

**Number of Participants Possible:** 40

**Accommodations:** Most participants stay in a bed-and-breakfast beach house. This is a new four-star guest house. It sits on the southern end of Kilmurvey Beach. Each room has a private bathroom. Rooms are double occupancy. Single occupancy is available at additional cost. If there is a large group, other B&Bs on the island are also used. Each B&B offers clean, comfortable rooms with nice environments and warm, friendly hosts.

**Meals:** Delicious Irish breakfasts are served at the bed-and-breakfast. Lunches and evening meals are served at the famous Man of Aran Cottage, a local inn built in the 1930s. All the food there is homecooked: organic salads complete with edible flowers, fresh-baked breads, scones, soups, quiches, vegetables, and fresh catch-of-the-day fish. Desserts include freshly baked strawberry and rhubarb pies. An assortment of Irish cheeses is also served.

**Fee:** $950 per person includes six days and nights, double occupancy, three meals, and 30 hours of yoga, as well as day trips and evening programs.

**Credit Cards:** Not accepted

**Sample Daily Schedule:**

| | |
|---|---|
| 7:30–8:00 a.m. | Breakfast |
| 8:30–11:30 | Yoga class |
| noon | Lunch |
| 1:00–4:30 p.m. | Day trips |
| 5:00–7:00 | Yoga class |
| 7:30 | Dinner |
| 9:30 | Evening program |

**Other Activities:** One day the group can take a boat to Inishmaan, a smaller Aran Island. Another day an organized trip is available to Black Fort, on the other end of the island.

**Guest Comment:** *"The Aran Island of Inishmore was a wonderful place for a yoga retreat. The accommodations were comfortable, the food from our host's organic garden delicious, and the setting simply stunning. Kevin Gardiner's strong connection to the barren, windswept landscape provided a wonderful context in which to experience yoga. The structure of the ancient stone forts and walls, the power of the ocean, and the gentle quality of the islanders contributed to an important learning experience in my yoga practice."*
Sharon Smith — New York, New York

**Summary:** Yoga teacher Kevin Gardiner offers six days of yoga on the Aran Island of Inishmore. This ancient Irish landscape rises from the sea 20 miles off the coast of Clare. Classes are held at the International School of Irish; guests stay at cozy bed-and-breakfasts. Kevin provides sophisticated Iyengar yoga instruction with plenty of individual attention and feedback to students. His love and enthusiasm for Ireland's landscape and culture is contagious.

SEE PHOTOS, PAGE 151.

# KILLARY LODGE
# LEENANE, COUNTY GALWAY, IRELAND

*Iyengar Yoga Retreat with Kevin Gardiner*

## MAY
## ONE WEEK

Kevin Gardiner offers two consecutive yoga vacation opportunities in Ireland. The first is seven days of yoga held at Killary Lodge in Connemara's wilderness.

Killary Lodge is a comfortable conference center located on 200 acres of land on the shores of Killary Fjord. Built in 1852, it has been renovated to the highest standards. The facility offers a spacious setting with sauna facilities, tennis court, archery, boat moorings, and a private beach. The surrounding wilderness is mesmerizing and pristine. Canoes, bikes, and hiking trails are available. Guests can take a day trip to the island of Inishboffin and climb up Ireland's holy mountain, Croagh Patrick. The entire area is rich in prehistoric and early Christian ruins.

**Address**: Kevin Gardiner
301 East 61st St., #2D
New York, NY 10021
**Phone**: 212/755-6324
**Fax**: 212/755-6324

**Airport Information**: Shannon Airport is preferable to Dublin. Ann Sullivan at Hill & Dale Travel, 718/797-2300, ext. 0, is handling travel arrangements. Coordinating group arrival is preferred so that a van can be waiting to take participants to Killary.

**How to Get There**: If you make your own travel arrangements, Bus Eireann departs regularly from Shannon to Galway. Or you can drive from Shannon to Galway town to Clifton, through Kylemore Abby toward Leenan, where you will see the turn to Killary Lodge on your left. Allow three hours to make the trip.

**Teacher Background**: Kevin Gardiner has been a yoga practitioner since 1970

and is a core faculty member of the Iyengar Institute of New York. He is a Certified Instructor in the Iyengar method and has made extended trips to India to study with the Iyengars.

**Style of Yoga**: Iyengar. Kevin's instruction is precise and detailed. His demonstration is graceful and dynamic.

**Philosophy of Teacher**: "I see yoga as an art and a science. My philosophy about yoga comes in part from my teacher, B. K. S. Iyengar, who tells his students that enthusiasm brings concentration; concentration brings precision; precision brings freedom."

**Student Criteria**: Approximately one year of experience with Iyengar yoga is required.

**Disability Access**: No access

**What to Bring**: Yoga mat, three blankets,

two belts, wooden blocks, rain gear and rugged shoes.

**Yoga Room Size and Description**: The room used for yoga at Killary Lodge is approximately 30' x 20' and has hard-wood floors, large recessed window sills, plenty of light, and two full walls for yoga. The room has large sturdy tables and cushioned metal chairs that are moved aside unless needed.

**Number of Participants Possible**: 20

**Accommodations**: Killary Lodge has 20 rooms available, and they are a mixture of doubles, twins, and singles. All have bathrooms ensuite and telephones. As a matter of policy there are no televisions. The lodge owners encourage the art of conversation and reading as much better alternatives.

**Meals**: The kitchen at Killary Lodge concentrates on good, wholesome cuisine, locally sourced when possible, with fresh fish and chicken options. Vegetarians are accommodated, as are other special diets. Lunches are packed for day trips, if needed; otherwise they are buffet-style. Breakfast and dinners are plentiful.

**Fee**: $1,100 per person includes seven days in a double-occupancy room, three meals daily, and more than 30 hours of yoga instruction. Evening programs, day trips, and group transportation to and from the airport are also included.

**Credit Cards**: Not accepted

**Sample Daily Schedule**:

| 7:00 a.m. | Breakfast |
| 8:00–11:00 | Yoga class |
| noon | Lunch |
| 1:00–4:00 p.m. | Day trips, free time |
| 5:00–7:00 | Yoga class |
| 7:30 | Dinner |
| 8:45 | Evening program |

**Other Activities**: One afternoon the group will take a boat trip to Inishboffin (Isle of the White Cow) to explore the site of the seventh-century monastic ruins of St. Coleman. Another day the group has the opportunity to climb Mount Croagh Patrick, known as "the Holy Mountain of Ireland." The climb rewards people with views of the 365 islands of Clew Bay and the mountains of Galway and Mayo Counties.

**Guest Comment**: *"Serendipity can be defined as an assumed gift for finding valuable and agreeable things not sought for. The gift was a week of yoga exercises, stretching every part of my body under the brilliant, intense, and careful guidance of Kevin Gardiner in faraway Galway, Ireland. Not sought for but overwhelming was the never-to-be-forgotten experience of being surrounded by deep beauty, serenity, and mystery. The sea and mountains merged to form the world's deepest fjords. The sun and moon flooded our views at a fine inn. Now I better understand Irish folklore along with the Irish love of poetry, literature, and drama. Yoga and Ireland are perfectly matched. The trip was a pure experience—like breathing in light and expelling darkness, as their poets say."*
Laura Odell—New York, New York

**Summary**: Yoga teacher Kevin Gardiner offers seven days of Iyengar yoga in Connemara's wilderness. Participants enjoy day trips to the island of Inishboffin and a climb up Ireland's holy mountain Croagh Patrick. Killary Lodge is a comfortable conference center with high-standard accommodations and delicious cuisine. In the evenings local storytellers, musicians, and experts on Celtic mythology share their arts and insights.

# ANANDA ASSISI
## ASSISI, ITALY

## YEAR-ROUND
## (EXCEPT TWO WEEKS EACH JANUARY)

Assisi has often been called the spiritual heart of Italy. Ananda Assisi, a spiritual retreat center founded by Swami Kriyananda (J. Donald Walters), a direct disciple of Paramhansa Yogananda, for the purpose of realizing the higher self, sits on about 60 acres in the foothills of Umbria. Guests are lodged in country-style houses that are a 15-minute walk from the main activity center—a three-story historic building that was at one time a traveler's inn. Now called Il Rifugio (the refuge), this lovely inn was built out of rose-colored ancient stones from Assisi. The second floor, where meals are served, has arched windows that look out to the countryside and surrounding hills of Umbria. Incredible sunsets are enjoyed at dinnertime. Also on the property is an impressive duomo called the Temple of Light, which has high ceilings, cobalt-blue tiled floors, and a crystal cupola. In the springtime gorgeous red poppies fill the surrounding meadows.

**Address**: Ananda Assisi
Casella Postale 48,
06088 Santa Maria degli Angeli (PG)
Italy
**Phone**: 011-390-742-813620
**Fax**: 011-390-742-813536
**E-mail**: ananda@cline.it
**Web site**: www.ananda.org/Assisi

**Airport Information**: Fly into Rome, Florence, or Perugia. Assisi is three hours from Rome and Florence and one hour from Perugia, by train or highway.

**How to Get There**: Ananda is located 16 kilometers (15 minutes) from the town of Assisi, Italy. From the Assisi train station, take a taxi directly to Ananda. A taxi will be reserved for you at a reduced rate if you inform Ananda of your arrival time.

**Teacher Background**: Trained staff members of Ananda Assisi take turns leading daily energization, yoga postures, and meditation sessions and assist in teaching the various courses offered.

**Style of Yoga**: "Ananda Yoga for Higher Awareness" integrates the practices of yoga postures, breathing exercises (pranayama), energy-control techniques, affirmation, and meditation. All teachers at Ananda Assisi live according to and share the teachings of Paramhansa Yogananda and Swami Kriyananda.

**Philosophy of Teachers**: "We follow Yogananda's teachings, practicing Karma yoga, Bhakti yoga, Gyana yoga, and Raja yoga with special emphasis on meditation. Hatha yoga serves as a preparation for body and mind for meditation and contacting higher consciousness."

**Student Criteria**: All levels are welcome.

**Disability Access**: Yes

Ananda Assisi

*Ananda Assisi*

**What to Bring**: Warm, comfortable clothes for yoga, shawl, alarm clock, flashlight, slippers, walking shoes, warm sweater, coat (in winter), scarf, gloves, and rain gear.

**Yoga Room Size and Description**: Yoga is practiced in the Temple of Light, an exotic cobalt-blue-tiled duomo with eight carved beams, an altar, a sound system, and a terrace. The temple is topped with a lotus-shaped crystal cupola, which creates a lens that focuses spiritual energy.

**Number of Participants Possible**: 45

**Accommodations**: Most rooms are doubles with or without bath. There are also a few single rooms and rooms with four or five beds and shared bathrooms. All rooms have windows looking out at the countryside.

**Meals**: Three vegetarian meals are served daily. Food that is organically grown is used as much as possible, including vegeta-bles from Ananda's own gardens. Dairy-free and wheat-free dishes are available.

**Fee**: Ranges from $45 per night per person in the dormitory-style rooms to $60 per night per person in a double-occupancy room with bath (higher prices for single rooms). Costs include lodging, meals, classes and activites.

**Credit Cards**: Not accepted

**Sample Daily Schedule**:

| | |
|---|---|
| 7:00–8:30 a.m. | Energization, Hatha yoga, chanting and meditation |
| 8:30 | Breakfast in silence |
| 9:00 | Karma yoga |
| 11:00 | Lesson on some aspect of Yogananda's teachings |
| 12:30 p.m. | Lunch |
| 4:00 | Hatha yoga |
| 5:30 | Classes on meditation techniques |
| 6:30 | Dinner in silence |
| 7:30 | Evening program |

Ananda Assisi

*Ananda Assisi*

**Other Activities**: Every week a guided tour is offered to holy shrines in and around Assisi, where Saint Francis and Saint Claire spent their lives in prayer, meditation, and service. In addition to Assisi, there are several other charming medieval towns in the vicinity to explore. Monte Subasio, near Ananda Assisi, is the mountain on which Saint Francis built his hermitage, L'Eremo delle Carceri. You can hike to this sacred place and to the top of the mountain, where you'll find spectacular views.

**Guest Comment**: *"I went to the Ananda Assisi retreat with few expectations, as I had been a world traveler a few years back when I worked for an airline. What a joyful surprise it was for me—certainly unlike any place I had visited before in Europe. Just meditating and praying in the places built or sanctified by Saint Francis, Saint Claire, and other very highly advanced souls is an amazing experience. The countryside and the medieval town of Assisi are beautiful beyond description. Ananda's sweet, nourishing hospitality, its magnificent new Temple of Light, the staff, the food, doing yoga with people from many countries in several languages— all of it adds up to a life-changing experience. I hope with all my heart to return again someday!"* Jane Simpson—Nevada City, California

**Summary**: This year-round retreat center (closed only two weeks each January) offers classes on spiritual teachings, Hatha yoga, and above all the opportunity to experience life in a spiritual community. Participants share meditation, mealtimes, and other activities with the more than 50 staff members of all nationalities who live according to Paramhansa Yogananda's ideals and yogic teachings.

SEE PHOTOS, PAGE 152.

# CENTRO D'OMPIO
# PETTENASCO, ITALY

*Yoga retreat with Lauren Lo Presto*

## JUNE AND OCTOBER
### ONE WEEK

Centro d'Ompio is a nonprofit cultural center located in the Lake Country of northern Italy's Piedmont region, in the foothills of the Alps. It lies just beneath the peak of Monte Crabbia on a sunny terrace in the village of Pettenasco, which overlooks Lago d'Orta. It includes two guest houses (restored farmhouse villas), various studios and meeting rooms, a swimming pool, a sauna, sweat lodges, hiking trails, and a gourmet kitchen. The center covers an area of 100,000 square meters, including gardens, terraces, a chestnut forest, and meadows, all connected with hiking trails. Yoga teacher Luciana Lo Presto uses this cultural center for her annual yoga vacation, incorporating her two passions: Italy and yoga.

**Address**: Yoga Trips
c/o Luciana Lo Presto
P.O. Box 242
Santa Cruz, CA 95061
**Phone**: 831/421-YOGA (9642)
**E-mail**: yogaplanet@aol.com
**Web site**: www.yogatrips.com

**Airport Information**: Centro d'Ompio is northwest of Milan's two airports: a one-hour drive from Malpensa and a two-hour drive from Linate.

**How to Get There**: Centro d'Ompio is a two-hour train ride from the central train station in downtown Milan (approximately $25 one way). The center is 70 kilometers from the Swiss border and west of Lago Maggiore. By car, it is three to four hours from Berne, Lucerne, and Zürich, Switzerland.

**Teacher Background**: Luciana developed her techniques from 20 years of study in body therapies ranging from Iyengar, Ash-tanga, and Bikram yoga to Continuum Movement and Graham (modern dance) technique. She believes in the self-healing mechanisms inherent in each of us to integrate body, mind, and spirit. She embodies her work as a sensual art of self-expression and as a connection to the higher self.

**Style of Yoga**: Vinyasa

**Philosophy of Teacher**: "Yoga helps to align the visible, outer body with the inner, less-tangible world within. I teach ways to integrate yoga into our daily lives. My philosophy is to live yoga all the time, not just while on the mat."

**Student Criteria**: All levels welcome.

**Disability Access**: No access

**What to Bring**: Comfortable clothes for yoga and hiking, jacket, flashlight, swimsuit, sunglasses, sunscreen, and a journal. Yoga props are provided.

**Yoga Room Size and Description**: A free-standing octagonal wooden pavilion with floor heating and large windows is used for yoga. Two other meeting rooms are also available, one with an open fireplace and the other in a private villa.

**Number of Participants Possible**: 25

**Accommodations**: The main building accommodates 50 people in 18 rooms, some with private bathrooms. There is also a private villa on the property that accommodates 23 people in seven bedrooms. The villa is secluded yet close to all the other facilities and services.

**Meals**: The gourmet kitchen offers three daily meals of Italian vegetarian food (including eggs and dairy products). Special diets can be accommodated. Organically grown food is used as much as possible.

**Fee**: Depending on type of accommodations, $795 to $1,050.

**Credit Cards**: Not accepted. Travelers checks, U.S. dollars, or Italian lire are accepted.

**Sample Daily Schedule**:

| | |
|---|---|
| 7:30–8:30 a.m. | Pranayama (optional) |
| 8:30–9:30 | Breakfast |
| 10:00–1:00 p.m. | Asana practice—a Hatha practice based on the fundamentals of Iyengar, Ashtanga, and Bikram. |
| 1:30–2:30 | Lunch |
| Free time | Afternoon trips planned to Orta and Isola San Giulio, the waterfalls, and Lago Maggiore. One afternoon is reserved for a foot-massage class. |
| 7:30–9:00 | Dinner |

**Other Activities**: The center has a 25 x 10 meter swimming pool, a sauna, and hiking trails. The waterfalls of Alpe Selviana are a 90-minute hike from the center and feature rock pools washed out over thousands of years. The nearby village of Orta, with its narrow streets and medieval villas, boasts a piazza opening onto the lake for which it is named. The village of Orta is free of motor traffic and is a perfect place to visit cafés and open markets. You can also take the short boat ride to the secluded Isola San Giulio, which rises from the center of the lake. The tiny island makes a delightful waking tour on which to view its twelfth-century Romanesque basilica, frescoes from the fifteenth to eighteenth centuries, and other 300-year-old palazzi.

**Services**: Massage and Ayurvedic treatments are available for an additional fee.

**Guest Comment**: *"My experience at Centro d'Ompio in the lake district of northern Italy was one of the best experiences of my life. The atmosphere of being in a secluded area of fresh air night and day, with the nearby lake and hiking trails, just charmed my socks off! To complete this idyllic picture we started each day with yoga sessions and ended each day with delicious food, camaraderie, and music. It satisfied my urge to travel in Europe and to do something positive for my body and spirit."*

Lillian Strang—
Half Moon Bay, California

**Summary**: This yoga vacation takes you to a lovely cultural retreat center surrounded by several historic Italian villages. Centro d'Ompio is an international gathering place that offers a peaceful environment with unspoiled nature and a mild climate. Yoga teacher Luciana Lo Presto leads participants through a challenging three-hour yoga session each day. Afternoons are free for hiking, relaxing by the pool, receiving a massage, or touring Italian villages.

# HOTEL CABO SAN LUCAS RESORT
# CABO SAN LUCAS, BAJA CALIFORNIA, MEXICO

*Iyengar Yoga with Elise Miller and Julie Lawrence*

## APRIL
## ONE WEEK

Hotel Cabo San Lucas, located on a 2,500-acre estate between the towns of Cabo San Lucas and San Jose, is one of Baja's most beautiful resorts. Though the hotel is in the desert, the surrounding landscape is lush, and you'll have views of the gorgeous Chileno Bay. In this ideal spot for a yoga, with air-conditioned accommodations that are designed to ensure privacy, teachers Elise Miller and Julie Lawrence hold an annual retreat for both beginner and intermediate yoga students. The all-inclusive hotel offers the perfect blend of safe swimming, beaches, and warm sunny days. A dramatic cliff-side dining area looks down hundreds of feet to the azure blue ocean, excellent for whale and dolphin watching. Chileno Bay is a wonderful snorkeling and scuba diving spot, with hundreds of tropical fish swimming in the tranquil waters and acres of undisturbed multicolored coral beds.

**Address**: Iyengar Yoga Retreat
c/o Elise Miller
P.O. Box 60746
Palo Alto, CA 94306
**Phone**: 650/493-1254
**Fax**: 650/857-0935

**Address**: Julie Lawrence
600 S.W. 10th Ave., Suite 406
Portland, OR 97205
**Phone**: 503/227-5524

**Airport Information**: San Jose/Cabo San Lucas Airport. From the airport Hotel Cabo San Lucas is a 30-minute cab ride.

**How to Get There**: The hotel is located on historic Chileno Bay between Cabo San Lucas and San Jose at the tip of the Baja Peninsula on Mexico's far west coast.

**Teacher Background**: Elise Miller, M.A. in Therapeutic Recreation, is a senior certified Iyengar yoga teacher who has been teaching throughout the United States and internationally for 26 years. She has studied numerous times in India with B. K. S. Iyengar and teaches special workshops on back care and scoliosis.

Julie Lawrence, Director of the Julie Lawrence Center in Portland, Oregon, is a certified Iyengar yoga teacher who has been teaching throughout the United States and internationally for 22 years. She has studied numerous times in India with B. K. S. Iyengar and is known nationwide for her audio tapes *Yoga for Health and Relaxation*.

**Style of Yoga**: Iyengar yoga

**Philosophy of Teacher**: "To provide the teaching of yoga in a safe environment with precise instruction and the ability to handle special needs."

**Student Criteria**: A willingness to play and to learn.

**Disability Access**: Limited access

**What to Bring**: A yoga mat, two blankets, and a belt and block if needed. Casual beach wear, swimsuit, clothes for yoga, sunscreen, sun hat, and a beach towel.

**Yoga Room Size and Description**: The room used for yoga is a large square room with hardwood floors and lots of windows and light. Some of the classes are held outside on terraces with the sound of the ocean in the background.

**Number of Participants Possible**: 40

**Accommodations**: The hotel rooms are designed in traditional Mexican style. Each room is spacious and air-conditioned and has its own private terrace. Participants share double occupancy in a studio, suite, or villa. Single occupancy is available at added cost.

**Meals**: Delicious fresh food is presented three times a day by the hotel's bilingual staff. Meals include all kinds of fresh fruits, vegetables, Mexican cuisine, and tasty local delicacies from the sea. Crystal-clear spring water assures a carefree and healthy retreat.

**Fee**: $1,325 per person includes yoga classes, three meals daily, and double occupancy in studio accommodations with ocean view. The cost for a single room is $495 extra. Suites are also available for $220 extra. Suites contain two rooms and can accommodate one person.

**Credit Cards**: Not accepted

**Sample Daily Schedule**:
7:30– 9:30 a.m.   Yoga class

| | |
|---|---|
| 9:30–10:30 | Breakfast |
| 12:30–2:30 p.m. | Lunch |
| 4:00–6:00 | Yoga class |
| 7:00 | Dinner |

**Other Activities**: Swimming, snorkeling, and scuba diving in Chileno Bay. Chileno Bay has acres of undisturbed coral beds and hundreds of tropical fish. Swim the hotel's waterfall-fed three-tiered freshwater pool with beautiful hand-painted mosaics of dancing dolphins, mermaids, turtles, and tropical fish. Other activities include whale watching, tennis, sailing, parasailing, kayaking, horseback riding, windsurfing, or taking a long walk on the beach.

**Services**: Massage is available for group participants at $50 an hour.

**Guest Comment**: *"This retreat is an external trip to a beautiful and inspiring location and an internal trip to a landscape of emotional and sometimes spiritual terrain. Our instructors were fabulous. They both bring that wonderful balance of working us hard physically while explaining the teachings on an intellectual/spiritual level as well. They set a tone of respect, joy, dedication, and peace."*
Joan Tabb—Mountain View, California

**Summary**: This beach resort yoga vacation taught by Elise Miller and Julie Lawrence offers two beginning and two intermediate yoga classes each day as well as ample time for rest or to partake in the many outdoor activities available in this warm ocean climate. Participants stay in a luxurious hotel overlooking Chileno Bay. Enjoy warm sunny days and glorious nights serenaded by mariachi musicians.

# RANCHO LA PUERTA
# TECATE, BAJA CALIFORNIA, MEXICO

*Yoga Specialty Weeks*

www.rancholapuerta.com    760-744-4222

## JUNE, JULY, AUGUST, SEPTEMBER, AND DECEMBER
### WEEKLONG RETREATS

For those who want to experience a yoga vacation at a resort/spa atmosphere, Rancho La Puerta is the place to go. Set in a valley at the foot of the sacred Mount Kuchumaa, the ranch is designed in the style of a Mexican village, with beautifully landscaped gardens and brick and tile villas that can accommodate up to 150 guests. During six weeks of every year the ranch invites several prominent yoga teachers to offer a specific yoga specialty week, which is an addition to Rancho La Puerta's usual fitness activities. (Please call for schedule of yoga specialty teachers.)

The ranch is known as the world's first fitness spa. The resort was built on 300 acres of unspoiled rolling countryside at an altitude of 1,800 feet. It offers an ideal year-round climate, with beautiful sunny days accompanied by a pleasant prevailing breeze. In addition to a fully equipped yoga room, the ranch has three outdoor swimming pools, five whirlpool-jet therapy pools, three saunas, six lighted tennis courts, six aerobic gyms, weight-training equipment, and a volleyball court. There are separate women's and men's health centers for massage, herbal wraps, and other spa services, including private Jacuzzis and steam rooms. Guests arrive on Saturday for a minimum seven-day stay, which permits them to follow a progressive program, each day's classes increasing in intensity.

**Address**: Rancho La Puerta
Tecate, Baja California
Mexico
**Phone**: 011-52-654-1155; in the U.S.: 760/744-4222, 800/43-7565
**Fax**: 011-52-654-1108
**Web site**: www.rancholapuerta.com

**Airport Information**: Fly into the San Diego (California) Airport. Four buses take guests to Rancho La Puerta on Saturdays only, departing the airport at 8:00 a.m., 10:00 a.m., 12:15 p.m. and 2:45 p.m.

**How to Get There**: Forty miles southeast of San Diego, California, and three miles from the Tecate border gate, the Ranch is approximately a three-hour drive from Los Angeles.

**Teacher Background**: The teachers who come to Rancho La Puerta have a variety of backgrounds, many in Iyengar or Ashtanga yoga. Please call with questions regarding the different specialty weeks that are offered.

**Style of Yoga**: Mostly Iyengar for the specialty yoga weeks, with some Ashtanga.

**Philosophy of Teachers**: "We encourage a holistic approach to movement, breathing, and mental focus. Hatha yoga practice helps harmonize the body, mind, and spirit, and brings balance, harmony, and well-being."

**Student Criteria**: All levels are welcome.

**Disability Access**: Yes, full access

**What to Bring**: Exercise and yoga clothes, casual wear, swimsuit, personal toiletries, hiking boots with good tread.

**Yoga Room Size and Description**: The yoga room is spacious (50' x 60') and has floor-to-ceiling windows/sliding doors that open out to the vineyard, gardens, and mountain scenery. The room has a rope wall and a full range of yoga props, including blocks, belts, mats, and blankets.

**Number of Participants Possible**: 60

**Accommodations**: Single-level studio ranchera rooms, one-bedroom haciendas and villa studios, and two-bedroom villa suites are available; all have private baths. All are built in traditional Mexican style of locally fired bricks and quarried stone. Each cottage is tucked into its own garden and is decorated with painted tiles, hand-woven cloth, and unique Mexican crafts. All but the Studio Ranchera rooms have fireplaces and a living/dining area.

**Meals**: The diet at Rancho La Puerta is lacto-ovo vegetarian, with fresh fish served twice weekly, plenty of greens, legumes, whole grains, and other fiber. Food is raised in organic gardens on the property.

**Fee**: Cost is $1,500 to $2,200 per person per week depending on the type of accommodations chosen.

**Credit Cards**: Visa

**Sample Daily Schedule**:
6:00–6:45 a.m.   Yoga three mornings

| | |
|---|---|
| | each week |
| 6:30 | Mountain hike |
| 8:00 | Breakfast |
| 9:00 | Stretching |
| 10:00 | Yoga fundamentals class |
| 11:00–12:30 | Yoga specialty class |
| 12:30 p.m. | Lunch |
| 1:00 | Nutrition lecture |
| 2:00 | Tai chi |
| 3:00–4:30 | Yoga specialty class |
| 6:00 | Dinner |
| 8:00 | Evening program |

**Other Activities**: Wonderful hiking in the mountains and lowlands. There are 60 classes offered each week, including aerobics, step, weight training, water exercise, walking, nutrition, African dance, tai chi, yoga, and more. There are three swimming pools, six tennis courts, Jacuzzis, saunas, and steam baths.

**Services**: Facials, herbal wraps, massages, and other spa services are available. There is also a full-scale salon for hairstyling, manicures, and pedicures.

**Guest Comment**: *"The yoga week at Rancho La Puerta was incredible. It was my introduction to yoga, and it was fantastic. The teacher was excellent."*
Karen Wagstaffe — Burlingame, California

**Summary**: Rancho La Puerta lies at the foot of Mount Kuchamaa, home to hawks, quail, hummingbirds, coyotes, and countless cottontails. This spacious resort offers yoga specialty weeks in combination with its usual weekly programs, which include morning hikes, spa treatments, aerobics, weight training, and other mind/body activities. The staff is cheerful and caring, and the facilities are lovely and have a Mexican-style elegance. This is the place to experience a combination yoga and spa vacation.

# PLAYA LA ROPA
# ZIHUATANEJO, GUERRERO, MEXICO

*Iyengar Yoga Intensive with Gayna Uransky*

## FEBRUARY AND MARCH
### ONE WEEK

For the past 12 winters, Gayna Uransky has been offering yoga intensives in Zihuatanejo on the Pacific Coast of Mexico. A jewel-like bay provides the focal point for this Mexican fishing village. Four beaches on the bay each have their own character. Playa La Ropa, where the yoga intensive is held, is one of the loveliest beaches, with three-quarters of a mile of clean, white sand. The water is warm, without sharks or riptides. Temperatures average 86 degrees Fahrenheit during the day and 68 degrees during the evenings. Participants stay in their choice of beachfront hotels and drift off to sleep each night with the sound of the surf drawing all their tension away.

**Address**: Gayna Uransky
220 Harmony Ln.
Garberville, CA 95542
**Phone**: 707/923-9363
**Fax**: 707/923-5010
**E-mail**: woodsky@humboldt.net,
gaynauransky@hotmail.com
**Web site**: www.humboldt.net/~woodsky

**Airport Information**: Fly directly into Zihuatanejo Airport, Mexico.

**How to Get There**: Playa La Ropa is a 30-minute flight from Mexico City or a three-hour drive (150 miles) from Acapulco (paved highway).

**Teacher Background**: Gayna Uransky, M.Ed., is a certified Iyengar yoga instructor and has been teaching yoga since 1971. She studied with the Iyengars in Pune, India, and also with Pattabhi Jois in Mysore, India. Gayna teaches yoga throughout the U.S. and Mexico and is the resident yoga teacher at Heartwood Institute in Garberville, California.

**Style of Yoga**: Iyengar. The Iyengar approach emphasizes precise alignment and balance as well as increasing your body's range of motion through conscious extension. Attention is paid to your endurance and abilities.

**Philosophy of Teacher**: "I encourage students to explore challenges that they are capable of. Yoga allows for continued expansion."

**Student Criteria**: Intermediate level, with background in Iyengar yoga. The workout is on a fairly advanced level, but with help from assistants it works for all.

**Disability Access**: No access

**What to Bring**: Yoga mat, belt, blanket, and block or book. Casual, comfortable clothes, swimsuit, sunscreen, beach towel, and sweater for cool evenings.

**Yoga Room Size and Description**: Yoga is practiced on a large, shaded patio with a lovely view of Zihuatanejo Bay.

**Number of Participants Possible**: 24

**Accommodations**: Most participants stay in Hotel Catalina, situated on Playa La Ropa, a lovely white-sand beach. Hotel Catalina offers breeze-cooled oceanfront rooms with queen and single beds and bay-view terraces. Purified ice and drinking water are supplied by the hotel. Some retreat participants choose to stay in less-expensive hotels nearby.

**Meals**: Meals are at your own expense. There are a variety of open-air thatched-roof restaurants providing wonderful Mexican dishes. While rice and beans are popular with vegetarians, seafood provides a fresh option for many. Coconut water is a definite plus. Fresh juices and smoothies made with tropical fruits abound. The Mexican market offers a sense of adventure.

**Fees**: Tuition for the one-week yoga intensive is $450 per person. Rooms at Hotel Catalina (double occupancy) range from $70 to $150 per day per room. Price depends on type and size of room. Less-expensive hotels can be found in the nearby area.

**Credit Cards**: Not accepted

**Sample Daily Schedule**:

| | |
|---|---|
| 7:00–8:00 a.m. | Optional half-hour of pranayama and half-hour of meditation |
| 8:00–10:00 | Yoga asanas |
| Free time to eat, swim, explore, relax | |
| 4:30–6:00 p.m. | Yoga asanas, either inversions or restorative poses |

**Other Activities**: The land-locked bay is safe for swimming, and the water is warm. Windsurfing, sailing, parasailing, snorkeling, scuba diving, deep-sea fishing, kayaking, and body surfing are all at your disposal. Shopping is an experience, whether it is for a 50-cent foot-long papaya, fine silver, or ethnic crafts. Hiking, painting, biking, horseback riding, reading, meeting the local artisans—there are plenty of choices to make.

**Guest Comment**: *"Zihuatanejo is one of the most beautiful places I have ever visited. Yoga is taught on an open patio overlooking the Pacific by an excellent teacher who knows when to push you harder and also supports and respects the individual abilities of each student. Gayna is a wonderful teacher. The most difficult part was leaving."*
Peg Sjogren—Ashland, Oregon

**Summary**: Gayna Uransky offers a week of Iyengar yoga, relaxation, sun, the gentle ocean, warm tropical breezes, and a taste of Mexico in Zihuatanejo. Guests stay in their choice of beachfront hotels. The many restaurants in this small coastal town serve fabulous local as well as international cuisine. Seafood is a specialty. Some places will even cook your catch for dinner. The gentle waves of the bay are perfect for swimming and body surfing. White sand beaches, warm waters, palm tress and refreshing sea breezes make this tropical paradise an ideal setting for a yoga vacation.

SEE PHOTOS, PAGE 153.

# HOTEL NA BALAM
# ISLA MUJERES, QUINTANA ROO, MEXICO

*Seasonal Yoga Retreats*

## YEAR-ROUND

The Hotel Na Balam on Isla Mujeres, a tiny island encircled by white coral and sand beaches and the turquoise waters of the Caribbean, hosts several yoga retreats each year (see schedule below). Isla Mujeres (island of women) is only five miles long by one and one-half miles wide. The streets are made of stone, and the *zocolo*, or town plaza, is often the center of evening activities. For a small island there can be lots of tourists, and local shops with handcrafted Mexican goods are plentiful. At the south end of the island is Garrafon National Park, an internationally renowned snorkeling area.

Hotel Na Balam lies on Playa Norte (North Beach), where you can enjoy swimming in the protected placid waters. The hotel, a compound of small buildings, is set in spacious tropical gardens with hammocks and chairs set out for reading, talking, or dozing off. There is also a swimming pool. A beachfront snack bar offers juice and yogurt-based drinks as well as a palapa bar happy hour, during which magnificent sunsets can often be seen.

**Address**: Hotel Na Balam
**Attention**: Judith Fernandez
Calle Zazil-Ha No. 118, Playa Norte,
Isla Mujeres, Q. Roo, Mexico C.P.77400
**Phone**: 011-52-987-702-79
**Fax**: 011-52-987-704-46
**E-mail**: nabalam@cancun.rce.com.mx

**Airport Information**: Fly into Cancun Airport.

**How to Get There**: The hotel staff often picks up yoga groups at the airport. There is a 20-minute ride to Puerto Juarez, where you take a 15-minute ferry ride to Isla Mujeres and then a short taxi ride to the hotel.

**Disability Access**: Yes

**What to Bring**: Clothes for yoga, swimsuit, beach towel, rain jacket, sweater, walking shoes, hat or sun visor, sunscreen, clothes for warm tropical weather. Hair dryers are not provided; bring one if you want one (no adapter needed).

**Yoga Room Size and Description**: Hotel Na Balam has two palapa-roofed structures built especially for yoga. One is an upstairs palapa next to the pool that has open views but is sheltered by a thatch roof. This yoga palapa has a wood floor. Yoga mats and blankets are provided. The other yoga palapa is by the beach at the edge of the compound. It has a thatch roof and a tile floor.

**Accommodations**: All of the rooms (31 total) have an ocean view, are spacious, and come with a sitting area and a private patio or balcony. Each room has two queen-size beds, a private bath, ceiling fans, screens, and air-conditioning.

Each room also has a large sink and vanity area plus a bathroom and shower as well as a large closet with a lockable safe inside. The rooms are decorated with Mexican art and green plants.

**Meals**: Three gourmet vegetarian meals are served daily, plus complimentary fruit and fruit juices for yoga groups. The hotel's Zazil-Ha restaurant features exotic cuisine with Mayan and Mexican dishes, catch-of-the-day fish dishes, homemade bread, soups, and fresh tropical fruits and juices. Special diets can usually be accommodated with advance notice.

**Other Activities**: Part of the Great Maya Reef lies just off the island's southern end, where snorkelers can enjoy El Garrafon National Park and dive around Manchones Reef. To the north is Isla Contoy, a national wildlife reserve with numerous species of birds, animals, and plants. Boating and scooter-riding around the island are available. Visits to the mainland to see the ancient Mayan cities of Tulum, Coba, and Chichen Itza are easily arranged one-day adventures.

**Summary**: Hotel Na Balam is nestled in a lush tropical garden setting. It is cool and shady in contrast to the hot, sunny beach just a few feet away. Various yoga teachers offer yoga retreats on this small island not far from Cancun. The staff is friendly and speaks English. The beach offers spectacular sunsets.

SEE PHOTOS, PAGE 154.

## CALENDAR OF YOGA RETREATS AT HOTEL NA BALAM:

### JANUARY AND FEBRUARY
ONE WEEK EACH MONTH

**Yoga Teacher**: Maryann Parker
**Address**: 4517 Moorland Ave.
Minneapolis, MN 55424
**Phone**: 612/927-9380
**Fax**: 612/922-5762

**Teacher Background**: Maryann's background includes Himalayan Institute, Iyengar (she studied one month at the Iyengar Institute in India), and Kripalu yoga studies. She has more than 18 years of teaching experience and has been leading yoga retreats for six years.

**Style of Yoga**: Her classes include breathing, posture work, and relaxation.

**Philosophy of Teacher**: "Internal awareness and the joy of doing yoga are emphasized in my teaching."

**Student Criteria**: All levels of experience are welcome.

**Number of Participants Possible**: 18

**Fee**: $1,400 per person includes room for the week, three meals daily, and four hours of yoga per day.

**Credit Cards**: Not accepted

**Sample Daily Schedule**:
| | |
|---|---|
| 8:00 a.m. | Breakfast |
| 9:30–noon | Yoga |
| noon | Lunch |
| Free time | |
| 4:30–6:00 p.m. | Restorative yoga |
| Enjoy sunset on the beach | |
| 7:00 | Dinner |
| Evening program | |

**Guest Comment**: *"What a fabulous vacation. Na Balam is beautiful beaches, blue water, wonderful food, and serene spaces. Maryann brings a fearless and nurturing spirit that fosters a camaraderie within the group and encourages each person to exceed his or her physical and mental limitations to make great strides in their yoga practice. Her teaching style* *is disciplined and rigorous yet constructive, affirming and kind. I returned home feeling stronger physically than ever before and spiritually renewed."*

Laurie Krivitz — Bloomington, Minnesota

## FEBRUARY AND DECEMBER
### ONE WEEK EACH MONTH

**Yoga Teacher**: Valerie Butler
**Address**: P.O. Box 151
Milford, NH 03055
**Phone**: 603/673-5595

**Teacher Background**: Valerie Butler is a certified Integrative Yoga Therapist with a masters degree in psychotherapy. A mother of eight, Valerie has been studying yoga and meditation for more than 20 years. She has also studied Feldenkrais movement therapy, which she incorporates into her classes.

**Style of Yoga**: Valerie's approach to yoga is a gentle one, encouraging each individual to explore capabilities and strengths. The emphasis is on developing awareness on all levels and refining that awareness beyond the yoga practice, bringing clarity to everyday situations, improving the quality of life.

**Philosophy of Teacher**: "Yoga views each individual as whole . . . body, mind, and spirit . . . evolving toward greater wholeness."

**Student Criteria**: No experience in yoga or meditation is needed.

**Number of Participants Possible**: 10

**Fee**: The December retreat is $600 per person, all-inclusive (seven nights' accommodations, three meals, two yoga sessions daily). The February (high season) retreat is $700 per person, all-inclusive.

**Credit Cards**: Not accepted

**Sample Daily Schedule**:
Sunrise meditation followed by light stretching.

| | |
|---|---|
| 7:30 a.m. | Breakfast |

Free time (usually spent on the beach)

| | |
|---|---|
| 11:30 | Late-morning yoga class |
| 1:00 p.m. | Lunch |

Free time (exploring island, boating, shopping excursions)

| | |
|---|---|
| 5:30 | Late-afternoon yoga class |
| 7:00 | Dinner |
| 9:30 | Evening meditation |

**Guest Comment**: *"Valerie Butler's yoga and meditation retreat at Hotel Na Balam is a trip to paradise for the body and soul. Gourmet meals are prepared with the freshest tropical fruits and veggies and served under rustling palm trees. Rooms overlook the aqua-blue Caribbean. Swimming in 83-degree crystal-clear water. We even did some yoga and meditation sessions on the beach! I highly recommend the side trip."*

Ellen Zibailo —
Westminster, Massachusetts

## MARCH
### ONE WEEK

**Yoga Teacher**: Gayle Dielman
**Address**: P.O. Box 26133
116 Sherbrook St.
Winnipeg, MB R30 4K9
Canada
**Phone**: 204/783-0029
**Fax**: 204/783-8313
**E-mail**: 2nirvana@escape.ca

**Teacher Background**: Gayle Asha Dielman is a certified trainer of Kripalu yoga teachers. She has been a fitness professional for more than 15 years and has a background in music and dance. She is the founder of Westminster Yoga Center in Winnipeg, Canada. For the last three years she has been studying Maya yoga under the tutelage of Elder Hunbatz Men.

**Style of Yoga**: Gayle teaches a combination of Kripalu, Chakra, Maya, and Power yoga. Maya yoga, or "yok'ha," practices utilize the sun's energy to enliven the seven sacred centers within the body, thereby making cosmic consciousness possible.

**Philosophy of Teacher**: "Yoga is about transformation of self in body, mind, and spirit. My approach is geared toward self-knowledge and self-empowerment."

**Student Criteria**: Students should have at least six months' experience studying yoga.

**Number of Participants Possible**: 30

**Fee**: $650 per person (double occupancy)

includes seven nights' accommodations at Hotel Na Balam, all meals and snacks, and all yoga classes.

**Credit Cards**: Not accepted

**Sample Daily Schedule**:
7:00–9:00 a.m.    Moderate yoga
Free time
4:30–6:00 p.m.    Gentle yoga and
                  meditation
Note: A tour of sacred Mayan pyramid sites led by Gayle and Elder Hunbatz Men is available on the weekend prior to this retreat for an additional fee.

**Guest Comment**: *"The setting, the people, and the yoga were ideal. I could not have asked for more! I returned home feeling refreshed and renewed. This feeling seems to last for weeks after."*

Cathy Spack
—Winnipeg, Manitoba

# RIO CALIENTE HOT SPRINGS SPA
# LA PRIMAVERA, JALISCO, MEXICO

## *Seasonal Yoga Retreats*

Beyond the tiny village of La Primavera, in the subtropical forest of a Sierra Madre mountain valley, flows a hot mineral-water river channeled into the warm mineral pools of Rio Caliente Hot Springs Spa. This volcanic water has been used for curative purposes for thousands of years. The land was once a spiritual center for the Huichol Indians (the healing people) and now is the home of this spa, which offers overnight accommodations, spa treatments, yoga, hiking, and wonderful vegetarian food. In addition to their own program, Rio Caliente hosts various healers, teachers, and groups—including yoga groups.

**Address**: Rio Caliente Hot Springs Spa
U.S. Contact: Marian Lewis
Spa Vacation LTD
P.O. Box 897
Millbrae, CA 94030
**Phone**: 650/615-9543
**Fax**: 650/615-0601
**E-mail**: RioCal@aol.com
**Web site**: www.netpac.com/provenance/vol2/no1/travel/riomex96.html

**Airport Information**: Fly into Guadalajara, Mexico. Airport taxis are available to Rio Caliente.

**How to Get There**: Rio Caliente Hot Springs Spa is located in a national forest in the Primavera Valley 25 miles outside of Guadalajara.

**Disability Access**: No access

**What to Bring**: Loose, comfortable, casual clothes, swimsuit, hiking boots, water bottle, sunscreen, and personal toiletries.

**Yoga Room Size and Description**: The yoga room is 40' x 22'. It is an airy room with three walls of large windows and one wall that is a ceiling-to-floor mirror. The room is located in a quiet area of the spa.

**Accommodations**: Fifty guest rooms occupy both an upper level, where the dining room is, and a lower level, by the pools and steam room. Each cottage has a private bath/shower, single or double beds, and a fireplace. The rooms are simple, clean, and decorated with native crafts. Windows look onto the spa and surrounding valley.

**Meals**: Three vegetarian meals are served daily in an "all you can eat" buffet. Meals include grains, complex carbohydrates, and low-fat foods that include fresh fruits and vegetables, optional dairy products, and fresh homemade bread and muffins. Drinking water is purified.

**Other Activities**: The spa offers a variety of hiking opportunities, horseback riding, swimming, a sauna, mineral baths, and plenty of time for relaxation in the sun or shade. Transportation to nearby sightseeing opportunities is available; this includes shopping tours to Guadalajara, Talquepaque, Tonala, Chapala, and Tequila.

**Services**: There is a treatment room at the spa that features massage, facials, and mud wraps.

**Summary**: This lovely spa is surrounded by the Primavera National Forest of aromatic Moctezuma trees. Offering a simple, peaceful setting for yoga groups, the spa invites guests to relax in warm mineral baths, the steam room, and cozy red brick and adobe cottages. The Rio Caliente "hot river" winds horseshoe-like around the spa, which is perched at 5,500 feet. Guests enjoy a casual, relaxed atmosphere that caters to rest and rejuvenation.

SEE PHOTOS, PAGE 155.

# CALENDAR OF YOGA RETREATS AT RIO CALIENTE HOT SPRINGS SPA:

## FEBRUARY AND MARCH
### ONE WEEK
*Yoga and Shamanism Retreat*

**Yoga Teachers**: Jyoti Crystal and Dr. Jason Martin
**Address**: Starseed c/o Jyoti Crystal
211 Glenridge Ave.
Montclair, NJ 07042
**Phone**: 973/783-1036
**Fax**: 973/783-5028
**E-Mail**: starseed@aol.com
**Web site**: www.starseedonline.com

**Teacher Background**: Jyoti Crystal studied in India with B. K. S. Iyengar and for 20 years with senior Iyengar teachers. Jyoti is a Phoenix Rising yoga therapist and has acquired considerable experience in and knowledge of Ashtanga. Her most recent interest has been the study of Viniyoga with Mark Whitwell. Jyoti applies the principles of shamanism in her teachings and has developed a unique and passionate style of teaching. She is currently writing a book on shamanic yoga.
    Jason Martin, Ph.D., is a playwright, and his academic area of specialization is the Arthurian legends. He has been trained in yoga by Jyoti, and has studied with various senior Iyengar teachers as well as with Mark Whitwell.

**Style of Yoga**: Therapeutic yoga, including Ashtanga, Iyengar, restorative, and shamanic yoga.

**Philosophy of Teachers**: "To produce a supportive and healing environment while providing the highest quality of teaching to allow students to grow on all levels of consciousness."

**Student Criteria**: All levels are welcome.

**Number of Participants Possible**: 25

**Fee**: $1,650 per person includes accommodations for one week at Rio Caliente (double occupancy); three vegetarian meals daily, full use of the hot springs, pool, and sauna; hiking and all yoga/shamanism classes with Jyoti Crystal and Dr. Jason Martin.

**Credit Cards**: Visa and Mastercard

**Sample Daily Schedule**:
8:00–9:30 a.m.    Yoga class
5:00–6:00 p.m.    Yoga class
8:00–9:30    Shamanic journey or meditation

**Guest Comment**: *"The weeklong yoga retreat at Rio Caliente is pure joy for both body and spirit. After a week of doing yoga twice a*

Rio Caliente Hot Springs Spa

*Yoga and shamanism with Starseed teachers Jyoti Crystal (standing center) and Jason Martin (seated right). Photo taken at Rio Caliente Spa.*

day and enjoying the benefits of life at the spa, I felt as if my bones had melted and my body was filled with pure energy. Best of all, I was part of a tribe of wonderful people. We shared energy and ideas in a safe, nurturing community. There is no better way to rest and renew."

Linda Pasquale—
Egg Harbor, New Jersey

## NOVEMBER AND DECEMBER
### ONE WEEK
*Yoga and Creative Watercolor Retreat*

**Yoga Teachers**: Annalisa Cunningham and Marianna Love
**Address**: P.O. Box 3363
Chico, CA 95927
**Phone**: 530/343-9944
**Fax**: 530/343-9944
**E-mail**: RioAnalisa@ aol.com

**Teacher Background**: Marianna Love,

MFCC, artist and watercolor teacher, has been offering watercolor, creativity and intuition, yoga, and relaxation training courses for the past 20 years. In her private psychotherapy practice, Marianna specializes in holistic wellness using creative visualization and emotional clearing. Marianna teaches the basics of watercolor by helping her students to claim the artist within, allowing creativity to flow, and to use techniques in an intuitive playful process.

Annalisa Cunningham, M.A. Counseling, has been offering yoga classes and retreats since 1985. She has certification in the Ananda Yoga Teacher Training and White Lotus Teacher Training and as an Integrative Yoga Therapist.

**Style of Yoga**: Gentle Hatha yoga practiced in an atmosphere of acceptance and calmness. Annalisa combines yoga postures, focused breath awareness, positive affirmations, massage, and healing visualizations to invite participants to open their hearts as well as their bodies.

**Philosophy of Teachers:** "We believe there is a creative artist and healer within each person. We share techniques in watercolor and yoga as ways to listen to and follow the wisdom of the heart."

**Student Criteria:** Students of all levels and nonparticipating spouses and partners are welcome.

**Number of Participants Possible:** 20

**Fee:** $1,550 per person includes accommodations for one week (double occupancy); three meals daily; full use of the hot springs, pool, and sauna; hiking; daily yoga classes with Annalisa; and daily watercolor instruction with Marianna. Art supplies will be provided. Subtract $50 if you bring your own art supplies.

**Credit Cards:** Not accepted

**Sample Daily Schedule:**

| | |
|---|---|
| 7:30–9:00 a.m. | Yoga class |
| 9:00 | Breakfast |
| 10:00 | Hiking |
| 1:00 p.m. | Lunch |
| 2:00–4:00 | Watercolor class |
| 4:00–6:00 | Free time for hiking, soaking in the springs, and massage |
| 6:30 | Dinner |
| 8:30 | Evening toning, visualization, and meditation |

**Guest Comment:** *"This has been the best experience of my life. The combination of yoga and self-expression with watercolor in such a relaxed atmosphere was healing. I had arrived feeling very stressed out and left feeling peaceful and renewed."*

Lisa Daniels—
Dallas, Texas

# MAR DE JADE
# LAS VARAS, NAYARIT, MEXICO

## *Yoga Retreat with Barbara Luboff*

## FEBRUARY
### ONE WEEK

Mar de Jade (Sea of Jade) is a simple and rustic resort located on a beautiful beach on the Pacific Coast of Mexico. This small, intimate hotel is situated in a jungle setting at the end of a beautiful bay with most rooms facing the sea. Nearby palm-covered beaches offer sparsely populated stretches of sand for walking, horseback riding, and relaxation. The small bay is called Chacala. At the other end of the bay there is a small fishing village with a few hundred residents and one or two small grocery stores. Several palapa restaurants are scattered along the beach. Yoga teacher Barbara Luboff holds her annual yoga retreats in this unspoiled natural setting.

**Address**: Mar de Jade c/o Barbara Luboff c/o Mail Boxes Etc.
1900 Fox Dr., Suite 84-189
McAllen, TX 78504
**Phone**: 011-52-415-20241
**E-mail**: luboff@unisono.net.mx
**Web site**: www.mardejade.com

**Airport Information:** Fly into Puerto Vallarta, Mexico. Someone from Mar de Jade will usually pick up people at the airport for a fee. Taxis are available as well.

**How to Get There:** Mar de Jade is one and one-half hours from Puerto Vallarta, on the ocean. The nearest town of any size is Las Varas, which is about six miles away. To get to Mar de Jade, turn off the main highway at Las Varas onto a dirt road that winds through lovely farmland and coconut plantations.

**Teacher Background:** Barbara Luboff has been a student of yoga for more than 30 years and has studied many different forms, including Iyengar, Ashtanga, and others.

**Style of Yoga:** Flowing Ashtanga style. Although Barbara takes yoga very seriously, she teaches with humor and lightness. She likes to see students grow in all aspects of their practice and challenges people to go beyond what they think are their limits.

**Philosophy of Teacher:** "I feel that yoga should be approached with an open mind, with joy, and with love."

**Student Criteria**: All levels of yoga experience are welcome.

**Disability Access:** No access

**What to Bring:** Yoga mat, towels, leotards and loose clothing for yoga (depending on temperature), swimsuits, sunscreen, sun hat, beach sandals, and walking shoes.

**Yoga Room Size and Description:** The yoga room is on the second floor of the main building and is quite beautiful. It has hardwood floors, ceiling fans, and huge windows that overlook the ocean and from which you can watch the sunset. The room is about 1,000 square feet.

**Number of Participants Possible**: 35

**Accommodations**: Mar de Jade offers a variety of room options, from private suites to small, rustic rooms. The majority of rooms are in a two-story building, sleep four (in single beds), and have one bath. Hot water is available all the time. The rooms are simple, clean, and comfortable and have fans and porches. In another building there are three rustic rooms with thatched roofs that do not have private baths but do have a nice shared bath facility nearby. There are also two separate suites in an adobe building: one has a king-size bed, and the other has two double beds (ideal for couples). In addition, there are two simple but beautiful apartments with two bedrooms (double beds), a bath, a kitchen, and a dining room in each.

**Meals**: Three meals a day are provided and include a wide variety of vegetables, fruits, soups, salads, fish, and chicken dishes, plus desserts. Tea and coffee are always available. Sodas and beers are extra. Special diets are accommodated if possible. The dining area is a porch with palapa roof that provides a shaded outdoor setting for enjoying meals while facing the sea.

**Fee**: $600 per person includes six nights' lodging at Mar de Jade, three meals a day, and all yoga classes with Barbara. Transportation, laundry, horse and boat rides are at your own expense.

**Credit Cards**: Not accepted

**Sample Daily Schedule**:

| | |
|---|---|
| 7:00–8:00 a.m. | Morning meditation |
| 8:00–9:30 | Gentle beginning-to-intermediate yoga class |
| 9:30 | Breakfast |
| 10:30–1:30 p.m. | Free time |
| 1:30–3:00 | Lunch |
| 3:00–5:00 | Free time |
| 5:00–6:45 | Intermediate yoga class |
| 7:00 | Dinner |

Evening dancing, games, reading and relaxation

**Other Activities**: Ocean swimming on both heavy-surf and no-surf beaches, sea kayaking, boat rides, snorkeling, horseback riding, beach walks, and hiking.

**Guest Comment**: *"This yoga retreat was a wonderful and full experience, from the professional manner in which the week was conducted to the relaxed atmosphere that surrounded us all. The rooms were clean and comfortable. The food was absolutely fantastic and prepared with great care. The staff of the Mar de Jade were always ready to help our every need. There were two scheduled yoga classes per day, and Barbara gave participants options to do the level of practice and number of hours they wanted. The rest of the day was free for touring, hiking, swimming, resting and reading. Many of us took our sketch pads or watercolors and painted the local sights. It truly was an oasis—a beautiful, intimate hotel on the end of a beautiful bay."*

Aurora Renee Roy—
Naramata, British Columbia, Canada

**Summary**: Mar de Jade (Sea of Jade) is a rustic hotel situated on 10 coconut-palm-covered acres at the end of a lovely bay. Two deserted beaches with good snorkeling are within walking distance. Yoga teacher Barbara Luboff, who has made her home in Mexico, offers weeklong yoga retreats at this remote, peaceful setting.

# OJO DE AGUA
# PUERTO MORELOS, QUINTANA ROO, MEXICO

### *Mayan Goddess Yoga Retreat with*
### *Annalisa Cunningham and Sandra Dayton*

### JANUARY
### ONE WEEK

Isla Mujeres and Cozumel, two islands off the coast of the Yucatán Peninsula, have sacred sites to which ancient Mayan women from Mesoamerica traveled in canoes to perform ceremonies to honor the "Great Mother Goddess Ixchel." Women came to the shores of Puerto Morelos to prepare themselves for their pilgrimage.

This retreat takes participants on a similar pilgrimage and celebrates in song, dance, and yoga the reawakening of the feminine aspect of God. Participants will spend a day before the journey at the Botanical Garden gathering medicinal plants for purification and cleansing and preparing Huipiles (Mayan dresses) for ceremonial costume. Participants stay at Ojo de Agua (Eye of the Water) in Puerto Morelos, which offers rooms right on the beach with ocean views. Each day begins with sunrise yoga and ends with sunset meditation in a palapa looking out to the sea.

**Address**: Annalisa Cunningham
P.O. Box 3363
Chico, CA 95927
**Phone**: 530/343-9944
**Fax**: 530/343-9944
**E-mail**: RioAnalisa@aol.com

**Airport Information**: Fly into Cancun Airport. Puerto Morelos is 20 minutes south of the airport. Taxi service or buses are available from the airport.

**How to Get There**: Puerto Morelos is a small, unassuming fishing village situated on the Gulf of Mexico in Quintana Roo.

**Teacher Background**: Sandra Dayton, the Goddess Journey hostess, has lived in Mexico for many years. She is co-founder of a local nonprofit organization, Lu'um K'aa nab, and has made a commitment to help the local people conserve their environment, culture, and tradition through intelligent tourism.

Annalisa Cunningham, M.A. Counseling, has been offering yoga classes and retreats since 1985. She has certification in the Ananda Yoga Teacher Training and the White Lotus Teacher Training and as an Integrative Yoga Therapist.

**Style of Yoga**: Vinyasa sun salutations (flowing movement) combined with gentle Hatha yoga postures, focused breath awareness, prayer, and meditation. Emphasis is placed upon trusting inner guidance and moving with ease.

**Philosophy of Teachers**: "We share ceremony, yoga, and ritual to unite women in gratitude to the divine feminine. We honor the environment, Mayan women, and their traditions."

**Student Criteria**: All are welcome.

**Disability Access**: No access

**What to Bring**: Yoga mat; comfortable, casual clothes; comfortable shoes with flat, thin soles for dancing; good travel bag to carry to ceremonies; swimsuit; towel; sunscreen; sun hat; insect repellent; Dramamine (if needed); and musical instruments such as flutes, bells, tambourines, drums, and guitars.

**Yoga Room Size and Description**: Yoga is practiced in a palapa facing the ocean. The palapa is 12 x 5 meters and has a tile floor.

**Number of Participants Possible**: 20

**Accommodations**: Rooms are double occupancy with two double beds and a private bath. Rooms face the ocean.

**Meals**: Daily breakfast is included, as are two lunches (during the day trips) and two dinners. Other meals are at your own expense. There is a restaurant on the premises, and several others are within walking distance.

**Fee**: $777 per person includes lodging, breakfast every morning, and daily yoga classes with Annalisa. Transportation to and from Botanical Gardens, Isla Mujeres, and Cozumel is included, as are the Huipiles (dresses), ceremonial dance instruction, purification practices, two lunches, and two dinners.

**Credit Cards**: Not accepted

**Sample Daily Schedule**:

| | |
|---|---|
| 6:30–7:30 a.m. | Sunrise meditation |
| 7:30–9:00 | Yoga class |
| 9:30 | Breakfast |
| 11:00 | Day trip to either the Botanical Gardens for ceremony preparation, a Mayan jungle community, or ceremonial sites on Isla Mujeres and Cozumel |
| 6:00 p.m. | Return to Puerto Morelos |
| 7:30 | Yoga and meditation followed by celebration of the Moon Goddess, sharing, music, song, dance, and conversation. |

**Other Activities**: The world's second largest reef, just 200 yards offshore, is inviting to those who enjoy scuba diving or snorkeling. The Mayan ruins of Tulum and Coba are 60 to 90 minutes away; the magnificent Chichen Itza is approximately three to four hours away. You can also enjoy bird-watching on the beach.

**Guest Comment**: *"This retreat was special in so many ways. Fifteen people joined together for daily yoga each morning as part of the Goddess Journey. Each day we learned more about the Mayan people, respect for the land, the importance of ceremony (song, dance, drumming, flowers, copals, herbs), gratitude, humility, and the feminine aspect of the Divine. For me, the opening of my heart to embrace the divine feminine has opened a void and allowed me to fill each day with a new richness, a new wholeness, a sense of feeling more complete."*
Laurel O'Gorman — Roseville, Minnesota

**Summary**: This Mayan Goddess yoga retreat takes participants on daylong journeys to the islands of Isla Mujeres and Cozumel for the performance of sacred ceremonies designed to unite women for the reemergence of self-empowerment and healing of the feminine aspect of God. Yoga begins each day, and evenings are spent in celebration of the Moon Goddess, sharing music, song, dance, and conversation.

# VILLAS SHANTI
# PUERTO MORELOS, QUINTANA ROO, MEXICO

*Seasonal Yoga Retreats*

## YEAR-ROUND

Villas Shanti means "village of peace," and that's just what this yoga retreat center offers. Located on the Gulf of Mexico just 20 minutes south of Cancun's airport in the small fishing village of Puerto Morelos, Villas Shanti hosts several yoga vacations each year. Owners Jack and Jean Loew are wonderfully accommodating and obviously enjoy sharing their facility with the groups who arrive there. I have had the pleasure of experiencing Villas Shanti both as a yoga workshop participant and as a workshop leader. The setting is ideal for yoga and relaxation and is a great base for those who want to do some sightseeing or exploring, or for those who simply want time for introspection, rest, and quiet.

**Address**: Villas Shanti
c/o Jack and Jean Loew
P.O. Box 789, Cancun, Q.R. Mexico
(Dec–May); or
P.O. Box 464, Glen, NH 03838-0464
(May–Dec)
**Phone**: 011-52-987-100401; in the U.S.:
603/383-6501
**Fax**: 011-52-987-100401
**E-mail**: vshanti@cancun.com.mx; or
vshanti@ncia.net
**Web site**: www.villasshanti.com

**Airport Information**: Fly into Cancun
Airport. Puerto Morelos is 20 minutes
south of the airport. Taxi service is available from the airport.

**How to Get There**: Puerto Morelos is a
small fishing village situated on the Gulf
of Mexico in Quintana Roo.

**Disability Access**: Yes

**What to Bring**: Sweater, sweatshirt,
socks (mornings and evenings can be

cool), beach towel, mosquito repellent,
sunscreen, sun hat, walking shoes, and
comfortable clothes for yoga. Yoga mats
and Mexican blankets are provided, as
are straps and a few blocks.

**Yoga Room Size and Description**:
Yoga classes are held in a screened,
thatched-roof 1,350-square-foot facility.
The yoga room has fans and a sound
system. Mats, blankets, blocks, and
chairs are provided.

**Accommodations**: Located across the
street from the beach, Villas Shanti is a
Mediterranean-style complex with an
enclosed courtyard and pool. Eight apartments surround the courtyard, which
offers lounge chairs, a barbeque grill, and
an icebox with an endless supply of bottled drinks. Each apartment provides comfortable living space for two. Apartments
are air-conditioned and have a kitchenette,
a modern bath with shower, and a private
balcony. Downstairs apartments have two
single beds, and upstairs apartments have

one double and one single bed. Daily maid service and bottled water are provided. In addition there is a two-bedroom villa available for families or groups. The villa has two queen-size beds in each bedroom, two full baths upstairs, and a downstairs kitchen, dining area, full bath and living room with a hideaway double bed. Adjacent to the villa is a palapa strung with hammocks for afternoon naps.

**Meals**: Catered meals are offered by reservation only. Individual teachers choose what they want for their group. Most groups have a welcome dinner and farewell dinner. Some groups provide a brunch each day after yoga class. Meals fit the dietary needs of the participants. Sampling local restaurants is a fun part of the experience here, and because each apartment has a kitchenette, leftovers make great meals.

**Other Activities**: The world's second largest reef, just 200 yards offshore, is inviting to those who are interested in scuba diving or snorkeling. The Mayan ruins of Tulum and Coba are 60 to 90 minutes away; the magnificent Chichen Itza is approximately three to four hours away. A local tour can take you into the jungle to meet a Mayan family and to visit a botanical garden. Do some bird-watching or relax on the white-sand beaches.

**Summary**: A peaceful retreat across the street from the beach, Villas Shanti is a delightful setting for yoga groups. Apartments open onto a courtyard that surrounds a pool and patio area and serves as a nice gathering place. The yoga room is airy and spacious, offering a serene feeling and privacy. The average temperature is 85 degrees Fahrenheit, and at night you can enjoy cool ocean breezes and a beautiful starry sky. Participants enjoy the safe, friendly, informal atmosphere that owners Jack and Jean Loew provide. Puerto Morelos is a tranquil village, adding to the restful ambience of Villas Shanti.

SEE PHOTOS, PAGE 156.

## CALENDAR OF YOGA RETREATS AT VILLAS SHANTI:

### JANUARY
### ONE WEEK

**Yoga Teacher**: Annalisa Cunningham
**Address**: P.O. Box 3363
Chico, CA 95927
**Phone**: 530/343-9944
**Fax**: 530/343-9944
**E-mail**: RioAnalisa@aol.com

**Teacher Background**: Annalisa is certified in the Ananda Yoga Teacher Training and the White Lotus Teacher Training, and as an Integrative Yoga Therapist.

**Style of Yoga**: Gentle Hatha yoga practiced in an atmosphere of acceptance and calmness. Annalisa combines yoga postures, focused breath awareness, visualization, and meditation and places an emphasis on mind/body healing.

**Philosophy of Teacher**: "It takes willingness, patience, and acceptance to practice yoga. Our bodies have their own rate of opening and surrender. Our inner wisdom will guide us if we pay attention. Accepting where we are now, while patiently continuing to practice, brings healing to the body, mind, and spirit."

**Student Criteria**: Students of all levels and nonparticipating spouses and partners are welcome.

**Number of Participants Possible**: 20

**Meals**: A welcome dinner is catered for the group (authentic Yucatecan food). All other meals will be at your own expense.

**Fee**: $725 per person includes accommodations for one week at Villas Shanti (double occupancy), all yoga classes, and welcome dinner.

**Credit Cards**: Not accepted

**Sample Daily Schedule**:
7:30–9:30 a.m.    Morning yoga class
On some afternoons we meet again at 4:00 p.m. for restorative yoga and meditation. Other days we meet together in the evening for healing imagery, visualization, ritual, and meditation before bedtime.

**Guest Comment**: *"The Yucatán is wonderful as well as beautiful. Villas Shanti is 25 steps from the ocean (I counted) and still unspoiled. I'm not a morning person, but yoga with Annalisa is worth getting up for. Her approach is gentle, encouraging, and yet challenging at the same time. My abilites improved during the week. I loved the day trips to the Mayan ruins and exploring local beaches. Returning each evening for meditation was a gift. The week was peaceful, healing, and fun."*
Lorraine Van Elswyk—Chico, California

~

# JANUARY
## ONE WEEK

**Yoga Teacher**: Kristin Chirhart and Lee Sverkerson
**Address**: B. K. S. Iyengar Yoga Center
2736 Lyndale Ave. S
Minneapolis, MN 55408
**Phone**: 612/872-8708
**Fax**: 612/872-1893
**E-mail**: chirh001@tc.umn.edu

**Teacher Background**: Kristin Chirhart has been practicing Iyengar Yoga since 1979. She is certified and has made several trips to Pune, India, to study with B. K. S., Geeta, and Prashant Iyengar.

Lee Sverkerson has been practicing Iyengar yoga since 1981. He has been teaching since 1988 and is certified by and studies regularly with B. K. S., Geeta, and Prashant Iyengar.

Both Kristin and Lee teach full-time at the B. K. S. Iyengar Yoga Center in Minneapolis, Minnesota.

**Style of Yoga**: Iyengar method.

**Philosophy of Teachers**: "Our philosophy is based on the classical yoga of Patanjali as commented on and developed by B. K. S. Iyengar."

**Student Criteria**: At least six months study of Iyengar yoga.

**What to Bring**: Yoga mat and belt. Other props are provided.

**Number of Participants Possible**: 30

**Meals**: A welcome dinner is catered for the group. All other meals will be at your own expense.

**Fee**: $655 per person includes accommodations for one week at Villas Shanti (double occupancy), all yoga classes, and a welcome dinner.

**Credit Cards**: Not accepted

**Sample Daily Schedule**:
7:00–9:00 a.m.    Yoga asana class
5:00–6:00 p.m.    Pranayama class or other presentation
6:00–8:00         Yoga asana class

**Guest Comment**:
*"Classes are demanding, but I gained a new insight into yoga, and my own daily practice will never be the same. It was there that I stopped being afraid of back bends. Under the guidance of Kristin and Lee, it was possible to*

find new levels of confidence and insight into the practice of yoga."

Ruth Murphy — St. Paul, Minnesota

## FEBRUARY
### ONE WEEK

**Yoga Teacher**: Amanda McMaine Smith
**Address**: 154 Redwood Dr.
Richmond, KY 40475
**Phone**: 606/624-0413
**Fax**: 702/831-7711

**Teacher Background**: Amanda studied the Iyengar method for 10 years and further enriched her learning through the teachings of Angela Farmer. Amanda focuses on the asanas from deep within her body, allowing them to unfold gradually. Her teaching style, with use of vivid imagery, is clear and distinctive, and she encourages students to move with respect to their own natural rhythms.

**Style of Yoga**: Hatha yoga. Amanda teaches a breath-initiated form of movement with an emphasis on accessing the subtle yet powerful flows of energy of the inner body.

**Philosophy of Teacher**: "The essence of yoga is to awaken our own true nature and to experience a connection with something far greater than ourselves."

**Student Criteria**: Students of all levels and nonparticipating spouses and partners are welcome.

**Number of Participants Possible**: 30

**Meals**: There will be an early dinner (authentic Yucatecan food) in the courtyard on the first night of the workshop. All other meals will be at your own expense.

**Fee**: $700 per person includes accommodations for one week at Villas Shanti

(double occupancy), all yoga classes, and one arrival dinner.

**Credit Cards**: Not accepted

**Sample Daily Schedule**:
Morning yoga class two and one-half hours
Evening yoga class one and one-half hours

**Guest Comment**: *"I have had the privilege of experiencing Amanda's workshops at Villas Shanti for the past two years. The first year was so nourishing I invited my husband to join me the following year. As a result we were both able to grow personally and together. Amanda is a master teacher able to work with students at all levels and help them fulfill their potential both physically and emotionally."*

Nancy Stewart Hindman — Richmond, Kentucky

## FEBRUARY
### ONE OR TWO WEEKS

**Yoga Teachers**: William Prottengier and Gabriel Halpern
**Address**: The Minneapolis Yoga Workshop
c/o William Prottengeier
810 West 31st St.
Minneapolis, MN 55408-2803
**Phone**: 312/915-0750 (Gabriel)
**Fax**: 312/915-0750
**E-mail**: Myogawork@aol.com

**Teacher Background**: William Prottengier is a certified Iyengar instructor with more than 20 years of teaching experience. He is the director of the Minneapolis Yoga Workshop. In addition to Iyengar yoga, William also practices vispassana (insight) meditation, seeking to blend and balance concentration and precision in asana practice with mindfulness and compassion in daily living. His teaching is dynamic, precise, and joyful.

Gabriel Halpern holds an M.A. in health psychology. He is a full-time certified instructor trained at the Iyengar Yoga Institute in San Francisco and

Pune, India. An accomplished vegetarian chef and practitioner of "kitchen sink mysticism," Gabriel has practiced since 1970 and gives workshops nationally.

**Style of Yoga:** Iyengar method of yoga and vipassana meditation technique.

**Philosophy of Teachers:** "Yoga practice makes life workable, not forgettable. Practice is the key to success."

**Student Criteria:** This program is not appropriate for people with disabilities.

**Number Of Participants Possible:** 24

**Meals:** A vegetarian brunch is provided for all participants every day.

**Fee:** $1,000 per person per week includes instruction, accommodations at Villas Shanti, and daily brunch.

**Credit Cards:** Not accepted.

**Sample Daily Schedule:**

| | |
|---|---|
| 7:00–8:00 a.m. | Guided vispassana (insight) meditation |
| 8:15–10:00 | Asana class |
| 10:00 | Brunch |
| Free time | |
| 4:30–6:00 p.m. | Restorative/Pranayama class |

**Guest Comment:** *"Villas Shanti is a charming and well-kept haven in a relaxing, off-the-beaten-tourist-track village. It has the best yoga room of any resort I've visited, complete with props. It is an ideal setting for a week of Gabriel and William's challenging morning and restorative afternoon yoga classes. I also enjoyed the day-trip opportunities, such as snorkeling at the barrier reef and visiting Mayan ruins. Gabriel and William are excellent teachers, each with their own unique approach to Iyengar yoga and life. I have been on five of their vacations and look forward to another one."*

Sally Swanson—Chicago, Illinois

# FEBRUARY
## ONE-WEEK YOGA RETREAT
### and
# APRIL
## ONE-WEEK MAYA YOGA INTENSIVE

**Yoga Teacher:** Gayle Dielman
**Address:** P.O. Box 26133
116 Sherbrook St.
Winnipeg, MB
R3O 4K9
Canada
**Phone:** 204/783-0029
**Fax:** 204/783-8313
**E-mail:** 2nirvana@escape.ca

**Teacher Background:** Gayle Asha Deilman is a certified trainer of Kripalu Yoga Teachers. She has been a fitness professional for more than 15 years and has a background in music and dance. She is the founder of the Westminster Yoga Center in Winnipeg, Manitoba, Canada. For the last three years she has been studying Maya Yoga under the tutelage of Elder Hunbatz Men.

**Style of Yoga:** Gayle teaches a combination of Kripalu, Chakra, Maya, and Power yoga. Maya yoga, or "yok'ha," practices utilize the sun's energy to enliven the seven sacred centers within the body, thereby making cosmic consciousness possible.

**Philosophy of Teacher:** "Yoga is about transformation of self in body, mind, and spirit. My approach is geared toward self-knowledge and self-empowerment."

**Student Criteria:** Students should have at least six months experience studying yoga. The Maya Yoga Intensive is designed for yoga teachers and experienced practitioners of yoga.

**Number of Participants Possible:** 30

**Meals:** Meals are at your own expense.

**Fee:** The yoga retreat costs $680 per person and includes accommodations for one week at Villas Shanti (double occupancy) and all yoga classes. The Maya Yoga Intensive costs $1,200 per person and includes seven nights' lodging (double occupancy) at Villas Shanti, daily breakfast and lunch, a midweek tour to Mayan ceremonial sites, all meals on the tour, transportation on a private air-conditioned bus, entrance fees to archeological sites, and program/yoga instruction.

**Credit Cards**: Not accepted

**Sample Daily Schedule**:
| | |
|---|---|
| 7:00–9:00 a.m. | Moderate yoga |
| Free time | |
| 4:30–6:00 p.m. | Gentle yoga and meditation |

**Maya Yoga Intensive led by Gayle Deilman and Elder Hunbatz Men**:
| | |
|---|---|
| 7:00–8:00 a.m. | Salute the sun and solar meditation |
| 8:00–9:00 | Breakfast |
| 9:00–noon | Maya yoga (Mayan chakra system, mantras and sacred language, kundalini energy, and the Mayan calendar) |
| noon | Lunch |
| Free time | |
| 5:30–7:00 p.m. | Hatha yoga |

**Guest Comment**: *"The yoga retreat in Mexico was one of the best things I've ever done for myself. Gayle and our hosts at Villas Shanti provided a safe and nurturing environment in which all participants could fulfill their own expectations. I would recommend this vacation to anyone. It provided me with a stress-management tool that I can take anywhere, any time."*
Catherine Nickerson —
Victoria, British Columbia

# MARCH
## ONE WEEK

**Yoga Teacher**: Paula Kout
**Address**: White Iris Yoga

1822 N. Ridge Ave.
Evanston, IL 60201
**Phone**: 847/864-9987
**Fax**: 847/328-3394
**E-mail**: info@whiteirisyoga.com
**Web site**: www.whiteirisyoga.com

**Teacher Background**: Paula Kout has been teaching and studying yoga since 1975. Her approach is eclectic. Paula is the official yoga instructor of the Chicago Bulls professional basketball team.

**Style of Yoga**: Paula's approach is eclectic, a synthesis of dance, early study within the Iyengar and Sivananda traditions, as well as recent work with contemporary teachers. She encourages a fluid, breath-initiated Hatha yoga practice.

**Philosophy of Teacher**: "Don't force anything; use the breath."

**Student Criteria**: Students of all levels and nonparticipating spouses and partners are welcome.

**Number of Participants Possible**: 24

**Meals**: Two vegetarian dinners are catered for the group: one the night the group arrives, the other the night before departure. All other meals are at your own expense.

**Fee**: $1,115 per person includes accommodations for one week at Villas Shanti (double occupancy), ground transportation to and from Cancun/Puerto Morelos, all yoga classes, arrival dinner, departure dinner, and round trip airfare from O'Hare Airport in Chicago.

**Credit Cards**: Not accepted

**Sample Daily Schedule**:
| | |
|---|---|
| 8:00–10:00 a.m. | Yoga class |
| 4:00–5:30 p.m. | Restorative poses, chanting, and meditation |

The rest of the day is free.

**Guest Comment:** *"I found Villas Shanti to be the ideal place for practicing yoga. The accommodations are spotlessly clean and comfortable, and the staff are very attentive and service oriented. The actual yoga room is spacious, with gentle ocean breezes flowing through, and I loved practicing while listening to the singing sonnets of Mexican birds. The gloriously cool, thatch-covered hammock hut was converted into a 'meditation sanctuary' for the evening meditation class led by Paula."*

Elizabeth Walsh — Chicago, Illinois

## MARCH
### One Week

**Yoga Teacher:** Betsy Downing
**Address:** The Health Advantage Yoga Center
1041 Sterling Rd., Suite 202
Herndon, VA 20270
**Phone:** 703/435-1572
**Fax:** 703/435-1572
**Web site:** www.healthadvantageyoga.com

**Teacher Background:** Betsy Downing, Ph.D., has studied yoga since 1972 and has been teaching since 1973. Her major teacher is John Friend. She has also studied with Rodney Yee and Patricia Walden. She is the director of the Health Advantage Center in Herndon, Virginia. A guest instructor is invited each year to lead the retreat with Betsy.

**Style of Yoga:** Ansura Hatha yoga

**Philosophy of Teacher:** *"In my teaching I honor the dignity of each individual, while at the same time I challenge students to expand their limits."*

**Student Criteria:** Students should have at least six months of yoga experience.

**Number of Participants Possible:** 25

**Meals:** Brunch is provided daily for the group, as are a catered welcome dinner and a catered farewell dinner. All other meals are at your own expense and choice.

**Fee:** $775 per person includes accommodations for one week at Villas Shanti, daily brunch, two catered dinners, and all yoga classes with Betsy.

**Credit Cards:** Mastercard and Visa

**Sample Daily Schedule:**
7:30–9:30 a.m.   Morning yoga class
10:00   Brunch
Free time
4:00–5:30 p.m.   Afternoon yoga class

**Guest Comment:** *"An outstanding week in a great location. This has been a wonderful and uplifting week. I really appreciated the combination of serious yoga and carefree vacationing. The instructors were attentive, knowledgeable, and fun."*

Ed Abbott — Reston, Virginia

## APRIL
### One Week

**Yoga Teachers:** Vickie Labbe and Michael Doyle
**Address:** The Yoga Center
P.O. Box 1243
Portland, ME 04104
**Phone:** 207/775-0975

**Teacher Background:** Vickie Labbe began her yoga studies in 1975 and has been teaching for almost 20 years. She is codirector of the Yoga Center in Portland, Maine. Vickie has studied with nationally recognized yoga teachers, such as Patricia Walden and Judith Laster. Her special interest is utilizing yoga for the healing of the body, mind, and spirit.

Michael Doyle has been a student of Vickie's since 1980 and teaches at the Yoga Center in Portland, Maine. He has also studied with Patricia Walden and continues to attend workshops on a regular basis. Michael's ability to challenge and inspire combines with his gentle nature and sense of humor.

**Style of Yoga**: Iyengar-based Hatha yoga

**Philosophy of Teachers**: "We like to offer a balance between active and restorative yoga, between challenging and therapeutic classes."

**Student Criteria**: All levels are welcome.

**Number of Participants Possible**: 20

**Meals**: Two catered group dinners and an arrival snack are included. All other meals are at your own expense.

**Fee**: $1,299 per person includes round-trip airfare from Portland, Maine, to Cancun, Mexico; a 20-minute airport transfer to and from Villas Shanti, all yoga classes

and programs, accommodations for one week at Villas Shanti (double occupancy), all taxes and gratuities, an arrival snack, and two group dinners. The retreat costs $799 per person without airfare.

**Credit Cards**: Not accepted

**Sample Daily Schedule**:
8:30–10:30 a.m.   Morning active yoga
5:00–7:00 p.m.    Restorative yoga
One philosophy lecture is given during the week. Wednesday is a free day for sightseeing or relaxation.

**Guest Comment**: *"My yoga vacation at the lovely and serene Villas Shanti was healing, transformative, and fun! Vickie and Michael are caring, dedicated teachers who create a safe, loving, respectful environment in which their students are invited to explore the wonders and gifts of yoga. I loved having two yoga classes daily—I never felt better!"*

Susan Blanchard
—South Portland, Maine

# MAYA TULUM
# TULUM, QUINTANA ROO, MEXICO

### *Seasonal Yoga Retreats*

Maya Tulum is situated on an isolated stretch of beach adjacent to jungles and the turquoise Caribbean waters. Set up with a round palapa yoga room that faces the ocean, this retreat center hosts several yoga teachers each year. It is located at the entrance of Sian Ka'an (Mayan for "where the sky is born") Biosphere Preserve, a protected area with miles of empty beaches, rain forest, mangroves, and vast lagoons. It is home to all sorts of creatures, including birds, peccaries, tapir, alligators, manatees, iguanas, and sea turtles. Guests sleep in simple cabanas built in traditional Mayan style that blend into the gardens and have beautiful views of the sea and jungle.

**Address:** Maya Tulum
P.O. Box 3029
San Rafael, CA 94912
**Phone:** 888/515-4580
**Fax:** 415/457-3535
**E-mail:** maya@mayantulum.com
**Web site:** www.mayantulum.com

**Airport Information:** Fly into Cancun International Airport. Tulum is one and one-half to two hours south of the airport.

**How to Get There:** Tulum is on the Yucatán Peninsula only five kilometers south of the Tulum Mayan ruins.

**Disability Access:** No access

**What to Bring:** Comfortable, casual clothes, swimsuit, beach towel, sunscreen, sun hat, sunglasses, clothes for possible cool nights, rain jacket, flashlight, and alarm clock.

**Yoga Room Size and Description:** The yoga facility is a large palapa with windows that look out to the ocean. The room is equipped with a sound and video system as well as a range of cushions and meditation chairs.

**Accommodations:** Guests at Maya Tulum stay in cabanas that are built in the traditional Mayan style. Each cabana has views of the sea and jungle. Three styles of cabanas are available: standard, deluxe, and super deluxe. The standard cabanas are available in single or double occupancy and share a communal bath house. The deluxe cabanas are available in single or double occupancy and have private baths. The super deluxe cabanas are available in double occupancy only, are much larger, and have a private bath.

**Meals:** Meals are served in a round palapa overlooking the long line of the coast. The vegetarian restaurant provides three meals a day along with fresh seafood, and lobster served a la carte. Meals are served buffet style, and there is a wide range of choices. Particular dietary needs are accommodated if possible. Special care is taken in the preparation and cleaning of all fruits and vegetables to ensure the good health of guests.

**Other Activities**: Maya Tulum is situated close to many archaeological sites. The Tulum ruin is the largest Mayan structure on the coast. The Pyramids of Coba are isolated in the jungle, a 45-minute drive from Maya Tulum. The famous sites of Chichen Itza and Uxmal are a few hours' drive away. Less developed and newly discovered sites abound in the immediate area. At the resort itself there is a wonderful stretch of white-sand beach. Guests enjoy swimming, snorkeling, diving, turtle watching, and boat trips. May, June, and July find the Caguama turtles making their arduous trek up the deserted beaches to lay their eggs in the sand.

**Summary**: The Maya Tulum retreat offers miles of white-sand beaches next to the warm waters of the Caribbean. This secluded retreat is situated in a junglelike setting with a beautiful yoga room that looks out on the ocean. The Mayan ruins of Tulum and some unique freshwater swimming pools (*cenotes*) are close by.

SEE PHOTOS, PAGE 157.

## CALENDAR OF YOGA RETREATS AT MAYA TULUM:

### JANUARY
### ONE WEEK
*Stretch to Heaven Family Yoga Retreat*

**Yoga Teachers**: Marsha and Don Wenig
**Address**: Dancing Feet Yoga Center
2501 Oriole Tr.
Long Beach, IN 46360
**Phone**: 219/872-9611
**Fax**: 219/873-7612
**E-mail**: innerwrk@niia.net
**Web site**: www.yogakids.com

**Teacher Background**: Don Wenig was certified through the White Lotus Foundation in 1980 and taught at the Center for Yoga in Los Angeles, California, before moving to Indiana. He is the cofounder and owner of Dancing Feet Yoga in Long Beach, Indiana. Don is also a Phoenix Rising Yoga therapist.

Marsha Wenig's teaching style is influenced by Iyengar, White Lotus, Kundalini, and Kripalu yoga and teaching creative arts to children for more than 13 years. She is a pioneer in teaching yoga to children and was honored with the 1997 Parents Choice Award for her critically acclaimed video, *YogaKids*™.

**Style of Yoga**: Gentle flowing Hatha yoga integrated with creative movement, self-expression, creativity, keeping a journal, drumming, quiet and dynamic meditations, and pranayama breathwork.

**Philosophy of Teachers**: "To empower our students with an invitation to surrender to the self, open their hearts, breathe life into their practice at whatever level, discover their innate sense of joy, and establish a daily vacation that will stay with them long after they cross the border."

**Student Criteria**: The course is appropriate for beginner to intermediate levels.

**Number of Participants Possible**: 30, including children

**Fee**: $850–$1000 per person, depending on accommodations; this includes lodging for one week, three meals daily, and all classes. The rate for kids under 12 is $175 each for the week, including all meals and YogaKids classes.

**Credit Cards**: Not accepted.

**Sample Daily Schedule**:

| | |
|---|---|
| 8:00–9:45 a.m. | Morning yoga, pranayama, and meditation |
| 10:00 | Breakfast |
| Free time | |
| 2:00 p.m. | Lunch |

| | |
|---|---|
| 4:00–5:00 | YogaKids classes (three times a week) |
| 6:00–7:30 | Yoga class |
| 7:45 | Dinner |
| 9:00 | Evening program (dancing, movement, drumming, music) |

**Guest Comment:** *"We thank Marsha and Don Wenig for choreographing a fantastic, fun-filled family yoga vacation. Our experience was creative and enriching and nurtured our bodies, minds, and souls. Yes!!"*
                              Marcia and Tim Taebel —
                              Hallandale, Florida

# FEBRUARY
## ONE WEEK
*Yoga NIA Adventure*

**Yoga Teachers:** Jennifer Fox and Paul Gold
**Address:** 328 Swanton Rd.
Davenport, CA 95017
**Phone:** 408/466-0313
**Fax:** 408/466-0313
**E-mail:** yogarus@pacbell.net
**Web site:** www.limage.net.mx/yogania

**Teacher Background:** Jennifer Fox is a certified Iyengar yoga teacher who has been teaching yoga for more than 16 years. She is the former owner of the Mill Valley Yoga Studio and is a graduate of the San Francisco Iyengar Institute. She has trained with the Iyengars in India and with senior teachers of many other yoga methods throughout the United States.

Paul Gold is a former commodity futures trader and land developer who traded in his business careers and became a personal trainer with a degree in fitness training. He is now an avid meditator and yoga teacher who specializes in back care.

Both Jennifer and Paul have studied Astanga, Viniyoga, and Integrative Yoga Therapy, and they are students of Zen Buddhist meditation and Engaged Mindfulness Training.

**Style of Yoga:** Iyengar-based yoga. Jennifer and Paul place an emphasis on the inward journey.

**Philosophy of Teachers:** "Our goal is to communicate yoga in a joyful, down-to-earth manner in order to help students of all levels experience its many benefits to body, mind, and spirit."

**Student Criteria:** Beginners to advanced students are all welcome. Students should have a spirit for self-discovery.

**Number of Participants Possible:** 20

**Fee:** $1,095 per person includes one week's lodging, three meals daily, and all yoga instruction.

**Credit Cards:** Not accepted

**Sample Daily Schedule:**

| | |
|---|---|
| 6:00 a.m. | Beach meditation |
| 7:00–9:00 | Morning yoga (dynamic) |
| 9:00 | Breakfast |
| 11:00–noon | NIA (Neuromuscular Integrative Action) movement combined with sound, breath, and an eclectic blend of world music |
| noon | Lunch |
| 4:00–6:00 p.m. | Restorative yoga class |
| 6:00–7:00 | Inward bound class (meditation and inner discovery) |
| 7:00 | Dinner |

**Guest Comment:** *"My heart is still full from Tulum. It was relaxing, renewing, regenerating, healing, clearing, and loving. We have been to Maya Tulum five times with Paul and Jenni, and each year brings us new experiences and enriches our spiritual lives. They are beautiful people and have a loving, motivating, and wholistic method of teaching."*
                              Bee Elmore — Carbondale, Colorado

# FEBRUARY
## ONE WEEK

**Yoga Teachers**: Bob and Shannon Smith
**Address**: Hatha Yoga Center
4550 11th Ave. NE
Seattle, WA 98105
**Phone**: 206/632-1706
**Fax**: 206/362-8517

**Teacher Background**: Bob and Shannon Smith have been teaching yoga and offering yoga vacations for more than 20 years. Bob is the author of *Yoga for a New Age*.

**Style of Yoga**: Eclectic, flowing Hatha yoga. Inner awareness is the key focus for all posture and pranayama work.

**Philosophy of Teachers**: "Connect deep within and move from the core. Breath work, energy work, and meditation are crucial elements to the asana practice."

**Student Criteria**: At least six months' experience with Hatha yoga.

**Number of Participants Possible**: 30

**Fee**: $700 to $850 per person ($700 for a basic bungalow with access to central bathroom facilities, $775 for a basic bungalow with a bathroom, $850 for a deluxe bungalow with a bathroom). This includes three vegetarian meals per day, double-occupancy lodging, and all yoga classes and instruction.

**Credit Cards**: Not accepted

**Sample Daily Schedule**:
| | |
|---|---|
| 7:00–9:30 a.m. | Yoga and meditation |
| 9:30–10:30 | Breakfast |
| 10:30–1:00 p.m. | Free time |
| 1:00–2:00 | Lunch |
| 2:00–5:00 | Free time |
| 5:00–7:00 | Yoga and meditation |

During the week there will be some group excursions to *cenotes* or pyramids.

**Guest Comment**: *"The workshop provides a focus that can't be achieved through tourist travel to the same spot. Fascinating conversations are built into the occasion, and the refreshing, restoring, joy-affirming nature of the week can hardly be overstated without getting completely maudlin. I guess you had to be there."*
Pete Wheeler — Belleview, Washington

# DECEMBER
## ONE WEEK

**Yoga Teacher**: Barbara Kaplan
**Address**: 1331 Linda Vista Dr.
El Cerrito, CA 94530
**Phone**: 510/232-9955

**Yoga Teacher**: Mark Horner
**Address**: 475 Chalda Way
Morago, CA 94556
**Phone**: 925/927-7279
**E-mail**: markyoga@best.com

**Teacher Background**: Barbara Kaplan has practiced yoga and meditation since 1978. She teaches ongoing classes at the Yoga Room in Berkeley and at her private studio in Oakland. Barbara studied with the Iyengars in India in 1992, and she is also a Certified Phoenix Rising Yoga therapist. Barbara enjoys leading partner yoga workshops.

Mark Horner is the codirector of the Yoga and Movement Center in Walnut Creek, California, where he teaches weekly yoga classes. Mark has been practicing yoga and meditation for more than 15 years. He has trained in both the Iyengar and Ashtanga Vinyasa styles of yoga. His background includes eight years experience as a certified rolfer and consultant. Mark is especially interested in exploring and sharing with others the purifying effects of yoga, which help to awaken our inherent ease, well-being, happiness, and freedom.

**Style of Yoga**: Eclectic: Iyengar, Ashtanga Vinyasa, and partner yoga.

**Philosophy of Teachers**: "We strive to create a gentle, supportive yoga environment with clear guidance, humor, and passion."

**Student Criteria:** All levels are welcome.

**Number of Participants Possible:** 40

**Fee:** For the standard cabana, $765 per person for double occupancy and $875 for single occupancy; for the deluxe cabana, $785 per person for double occupancy and $1,065 for single occupancy; and for the super deluxe cabana, $850 per person for double occupancy. This includes three meals daily and all yoga classes with Barbara and Mark. Nonparticpating friends or mates pay $475 per person for the standard cabana (double occupancy), $550 per person for the deluxe cabana (double occupancy), and $610 per person for the super deluxe (double occupancy).

**Credit Cards:** Not accepted

**Sample Daily Schedule:**

| | |
|---|---|
| 7:00–9:00 a.m. | Yoga class |
| 9:00 | Breakfast |
| Free time | |
| 5:00–7:00 p.m. | Yoga class |
| 7:00 | Dinner |
| 8:45 | Meditation |

**Guest Comment:** *"From the moment I stepped off the bus and felt the warm sea breeze on my skin, heard the sounds of gentle music, and saw the twinkling lights from the main palapa, I knew Maya Tulum was going to be a special experience. We were guided to our cabana, where we slept in hanging beds that were rocked by the ocean breeze. The side trips to the ruins of Tulum and Coba complemented the yoga classes taught by Mark and Barbara. The rhythm of the ocean and the tropical breeze permeated our yoga classes in the expansive and beautiful yoga palapa. Maya was a truly delightful experience."*

Rhona Ory
—Lafayette, California

# CASA RADHA
# MERIDA, YUCATÁN, MEXICO

## YEAR-ROUND

Casa Radha is a vacation guest house located outside of Merida on an acre of land in the countryside. The interior of this two-story Spanish colonial-style home is spacious and comfortably appointed with Mexican decor. The property offers an orchard of fruit trees, including mango, banana, and avocado, and a small swimming pool bordered by coconut palms. Named after Swami Radha, founder of the Yasodhara Ashram in Canada, guests receive opportunities to explore yoga and Mayan culture study.

**Address:** Casa Radha
Apartado Postal 44
Cordemex, Yucatán
97310 Mexico
**Phone:** 011-52-99-49-55-51
**E-mail:** casaradha@sureste.com
**Web site:** www.geocities.com
/The Tropics/8677

**Airport Information:** Merida is the closest airport. You may also fly to Merida via Cancun or Mexico City.

**How to Get There:** Bus service from Cancun to Merida takes about four hours. Someone from Casa Radha will pick you up at the airport or bus station in Merida. To phone Casa Radha from Merida, call 90-99-49-55-51. From Cancun or Mexico City, call 91-99-49-55-51.

**Teacher Background:** Teachers are all certified by Yasodhara Ashram in Canada and offer the teachings of Swami Radha.

**Style of Yoga:** Hidden Language, Kundalini yoga, Dream yoga, and the Divine Light Invocation.

**Philosophy of Teachers:** "Become independent through your own reflective

work. We offer the tools passed down to us by Swami Radha, all of which involve taking personal responsibility and building a strong character foundation, available and open to all religious and spiritual traditions."

**Student Criteria:** Openness.

**Disability Access:** Yes

**What to Bring:** Cool clothing for hot, sunny weather. A light jacket may be necessary in winter months. Also bring a sun hat, sunglasses, sunscreen, insect repellent, a swimsuit, a beach towel, binoculars, and a pair of shoes for walking and climbing pyramids.

**Yoga Room Size and Description:** Screened-in palapa with a thatch roof measuring about 16' x 30' and set among palm trees. The room is decorated with ceiling fans and a painted Mexican flower border along the walls.

**Number of Participants Possible:** 13

**Accommodations:** On the main floor there is one guest room that accommodates two to three persons and has a private bathroom and shower. On the second floor there are three guest rooms; the largest can sleep up to four persons and has a full private bath. A second room sleeps up to three persons, and a third bedroom is for two persons. The smaller bedrooms on the second floor share a bathroom and shower. All the rooms are air-conditioned and brightly decorated with embroidered bedspreads.

**Meals**: Three meals are served each day, and fresh juices and coconuts are available throughout the day. A Yucatecan chef serves local and regional dishes with both vegetarian and nonvegetarian options. Dietary preferences are accommodated as much as possible. The main meal is usually in the early afternoon; the evening meal is lighter. Breakfast includes fresh fruits. Packed lunches are available upon request for those who will be gone for the day.

**Fee**: Package "A"—$600 U.S. per person includes one week shared accommodations, three meals a day, four hours daily of personal yoga instruction, one full-day trip to a tour site of your choice (Uxmal, Chichen Itza, etc.), and three short trips to other local places of interest (Merida, Dzibilchaltun, the beach); for two weeks pay $1,000 U.S. per person. Package "B"—without excursions, $500 U.S. for one week or $800 U.S. for two weeks. Package "C"—without excursions or yoga instruction pay $400 U.S. per person for one week. There are discounts on packages "A" and "B" for married couples and groups.

**Credit Cards**: Visa and Mastercard; processed in Canadian dollars.

**Sample Daily Schedule**:

| | |
|---|---|
| 7:00–7:30 a.m. | Mantra yoga |
| 7:30–9:00 | Hidden Language Hatha yoga |
| 9:30 | Breakfast |
| 12:30 p.m. | Lunch |
| 2:00 | Dream yoga, Kundalini yoga or other reflective-type yoga practices |
| 6:00 | Light dinner |
| 7:30 | Evening chanting |

**Other Activities**: Visit the Mayan sites of Dzibilchaltun, Uxmal, Chichen Itza, Kaba, Labna, or the Temple of the Seven Dolls at a site that dates back to 900 B.C. See the Loltun caves or visit the flamingo bioreserve. If you want to just rest and relax, Casa Radha has a swimming pool with lounge chairs and a library with books and videos on the Mayan culture and Swami Radha's life and teachings. A visit to nearby Merida also offers many cultural and sightseeing opportunities.

**Guest Comment**: *"I enjoyed the breezes and the warmth, the flowers and the birds. I'll keep fond memories of our trips to Merida—for the music and the dance and for the relaxed bumbling through the shops. Our trip to the ruins inspired me with awe. My inner work with the yoga is some of the most valuable I've done."*
Margaret Mills—Manotick, Ontario

**Summary**: Casa Radha, located just outside Merida in the heart of Mexico's Mayan state of Yucatán, offers yoga vacations that combine exploring the ancient spirituality of the Maya with exploring your own inner world of symbolism. Guests receive yoga lessons based on the teachings of Swami Radha, who established Casa Radha after her books began to be translated into Spanish. Guided tours to local Mayan sites are included in package stays, as are trips to nearby Merida.

# TEAHOUSES IN THE HIMALAYAS
# KATHMANDU, NEPAL

*Yoga in Nepal with Devorah Thompson and Debbie Dippre*

## MARCH AND APRIL
### THREE WEEKS

Imagine doing sun salutations at the foot of the majestic Himalaya Mountains. This yoga vacation takes people to the country of Nepal, with its pristine mountains, fertile valleys, tropical jungles, and exotic cities. Nepal is truly a land of contrasts. This tiny mountain kingdom is the only country in the world with a Hindu monarch and both Hindu and Buddhist traditions existing peacefully side by side. Although they live in one of the poorest countries in the world, the people of Nepal have a spiritual wealth not seen in the Western world and a fierce loyalty to family, community, and country.

This 21-day package includes all accommodations, all meals with the group, transportation inside Nepal (including three domestic flights), an 11-day teahouse trek with porters, and all yoga instruction. Morning yoga and stretching will be offered daily.

**Address**: Cross-Cultural Encounters
c/o Devorah Thompson
2826 Prince St.
Berkeley, CA 94075
**Phone**: 510/655-0864
**E-mail**: devotreks@aol.com
**Web site**: www.ccultural-encounters.com

**Airport Information**: Fly Thai Airlines to Kathmandu.

**How to Get There**: You will be picked up from the airport and taken to your hotel.

**Teacher Background**: Debbie Dippre is trained in many styles of yoga, including Iyengar, Ashtanga, Kundalini, and Hidden Language and is certified in Phoenix Rising Yoga Therapy. She has been studying yoga since 1978 and is the founder of Follow Your Heart Yoga and Massage.

Travel guide Devorah Thompson, who is also a registered nurse, is the owner of Cross-Cultural Encounters and has traveled extensively throughout the U.S., Europe, Thailand, Vietnam, and Nepal.

**Style of Yoga**: Hatha, Iyengar. Debbie teaches interdisciplinary-style yoga to mixed levels of students.

**Philosophy of Teachers**: "I combine the study of yoga with massage and the healing arts to offer a warm, direct approach to each student's individual needs."

**Student Criteria**: Participants need to be moderately physically fit for trekking. Be prepared for the unexpected. All levels of yoga are welcome.

**Disability Access**: No access

**What to Bring**: Participants are given a three-page list of what to bring and how to prepare for this three-week adventure.

**Yoga Room Size and Description**: In Kathmandu and Pokara, yoga is practiced in the hotel rooftop garden, which has views of the Himalayan peaks. On the trek, yoga is practiced outside or in the teahouse dining room.

**Number of Participants Possible**: 20

**Accommodations**: While in Kathmandu and Pokora, participants stay in modest, family-run guest houses. Rooms are double occupancy, with twin beds and bathrooms in each room. During the trek participants stay in modest guest quarters called "teahouses." Here you will use your own sleeping bag on a teahouse bed.

**Meals**: Three meals a day are included, and you can choose Nepalese, Indian, or international cuisine. Vegetarian options are available. The group will eat in restaurants while in Kathmandu and Pokara. During the trek a chef prepares vegetarian Nepalese food, which is served in the teahouses. Boiled water is provided. All other beverages are at your own expense.

**Fee**: $1,850 per person includes all lodging, meals with the group, transportation inside Nepal, an 11-day teahouse trek with porters, and all yoga instruction. Roundtrip airfare to Kathmandu is at your own expense.

**Credit Cards**: Not accepted

**Sample Daily Schedule**:
In Katmandu and Pokora:

| | |
|---|---|
| 7:30–8:30 a.m. | Yoga on rooftop |
| 9:00 | Breakfast |
| 10:00 | Sightseeing |
| 4:30–6:00 p.m. | Yoga |
| 6:30 | Dinner |

On Teahouse Trek:

| | |
|---|---|
| 7:00–7:30 a.m. | Yoga stretches |
| 8:00 | Break camp |
| 8:30 | Trekking begins |
| noon | Lunch |
| 1:00 p.m. | Trekking continues |
| 3:00 | Arrive at teahouse |
| 4:00 | Tea and cookie break |
| 6:30 | Dinner |
| 8:00 | Traditional dancing and singing |

**Other Activities**: Sightseeing; visiting temples, shrines, and monasteries; shopping; bicycling; swimming; kayaking; canoeing; and, of course, trekking.

**Services**: Massage is available.

**Guest Comment**: *"Nepal is fabulous! It's full of children, colors, earrings, and marketplaces. To me the Tibetan Plateau was the most beautiful. Very stark and eerie, and very cut-off from the rest of the world. No TV, no cars, just the wind and the sky. The Tibetan people who live up there have an otherworldliness about them. They seem so calm and satisfied, and they have so few material goods and work so hard. We were very grateful for the porters who carried our stuff. I would love to do the trek again and spend more time doing it. The scenery was everything from glaciers to tropical hot springs. The yoga included poses we needed to strengthen ourselves for the trek. The beauty of stretching into poses at 6:00 a.m. with birds singing and a view of the Himalayas cannot be described."*

Donna Ryan — Oakland, California

**Summary**: This active and unique vacation takes you to exotic Nepal and includes an 11-day mountain trek (with the assistance of porters who carry your gear). The group spends four days in Kathmandu upon arrival, three days in Pokora for a yoga intensive, and 11 days trekking in the Himalayas before returning to the bustling city of Kathmandu. Yoga stretching is included throughout the adventure.

# HATHA YOGA SCHOOL OF SUMNER
# CHRISTCHURCH, NEW ZEALAND

*Yoga Intensive with Donna Farhi and Mark Boukoms*

## FEBRUARY
### ONE WEEK

Five minutes from the beach in Christchurch, New Zealand, is the Hatha Yoga School of Sumner, directed by yoga teachers Donna Farhi and Mark Boukoms. In addition to holding daily yoga classes and ongoing workshops, the school offers a weeklong intensive every February that includes accommodations for those who need them. Visitors are booked in the Sister Eveleen Retreat House, which sits on a hill overlooking the ocean and has magnificent, panoramic views. This old Victorian house has a big kitchen, a dining room, and a lounge that creates a "family style" retreat setting. Students walk 20 minutes along the waterfront to yoga classes.

**Address**: The Hatha Yoga School of Sumner
c/o Donna Farhi and Mark Boukoms
42 Nayland St. Sumner
Christchurch 8, New Zealand
**Phone**: 011-64-03-326-5255
**Fax**: 011-64-03-326-5257

**Airport Information**: Fly into Christchurch Airport. A door-to-door shuttle from the airport to the retreat house in Sumner is available ($25 N.Z. funds). From the airport Sumner is a 40-minute drive.

**How to Get There**: Christchurch is a city on the east coast of the South Island of New Zealand. Sumner is a suburb south of Christchurch on the coast.

**Teacher Background**: Donna Farhi is a yoga teacher and Registered Movement Therapist who has been practicing yoga for more than 22 years and teaching for more than a decade. She is a regular writer for *Yoga Journal* magazine and author of *The Breathing Book*. She co-directs the Hatha Yoga School of Sumner and leads intensives and teacher training programs in the U.S., Mexico, and Australia.

Mark Bouckoms has practiced yoga for more than 14 years. His studies include two years of teacher training at the Himalayan Institute as well as intensive training with B. K. S. Iyengar and Shandor Remete. Mark currently directs the Hatha Yoga School of Sumner and teaches yoga workshops internationally.

**Style of Yoga**: Donna and Mark both have extensive training in the Iyengar method as well as other systems and now teach eclectic yoga using their knowledge and experience.

**Philosophy of Teachers**: "We are interested in helping others find a way of practicing yoga that suits their own constitution, personal goals, and values rather then enforcing a dogmatic formula or system that students must adapt to."

**Student Criteria**: Open-mindedness.

**Disability Access**: No access

**What to Bring**: Comfortable clothes for yoga, layered clothing for warm and cooler weather, swimsuit, sun hat, sunglasses, sunscreen, and waterproof jacket or windbreaker. A good pair of walking shoes is a must.

**Yoga Room Size and Description**: The Hatha Yoga School is housed in a beautifully renovated Salvation Army Hall. The hall has timber walls, wood floors, and skylights.

**Number of Participants Possible**: 20

**Accommodations**: Visitors stay in an old Victorian retreat house that sits on a hill and offers magnificent views of the ocean. The house, known as Sister Eveleen Retreat House, was bequeathed to the Anglican church as a site for inward meditation. To get to the house you walk up a steep, winding path covered with flowers and native brush. From wherever you look, there are panoramic views of the ocean and the Kaikoura Mountains. Guests sleep in simple double, twin, or single rooms. Two bathrooms are shared. The house has a large kitchen, dining room, and lounge, and is a 20-minute walk along the beach to the yoga school. Twelve students stay at the retreat house on a first-come, first-served basis. Other local housing is available for those unable to stay at the house.

**Meals:** Students make their own meals at the retreat house or eat out at local cafés and restaurants. The guest house is within walking distance (20 minutes) of the health-food store, supermarket, cafés, and restaurants of Sumner. Prior to participants' arrival, Donna buys a selection of fresh organic vegetables and fruit for the week from a local organic farm. Participants reimburse her for their share (usually amounts to about $5 N.Z. per person).

**Fee**: $575 per person includes accommodations and seven days of yoga instruction.

**Credit Cards**: Not accepted

**Sample Daily Schedule**:
9:30 a.m.–12:30 p.m    Morning yoga session
2:30–4:30    Afternoon yoga session

**Other Activities**: Christchurch is known as the garden city of the world. The city offers fantastic coastal walks and lots of beauty. There is a hot spring and extensive hiking tracks both north and south of Christchurch. Whale watching, sea kayaking, and trekking opportunities are within a few hours' drive.

**Guest Comment**: *"The course was wonderful. The class was divided almost in half between locals and visitors from Australia and the U.S. The visitors stayed at a fine hostel, shared a room, and cooked our own meals. Meals were shared at the dining room that overlooked the bay. It was an easy and pleasant walk by the beach and through town to get to and from the studio. I learned so much in that week. I was very challenged by the course but felt free to relax as well. If you are looking for a place to breathe deep and work hard on your yoga then check out the Sumner School."*
Rebecca Lynch — Kenwood, California

**Summary**: This weeklong yoga intensive offered on the South Island of New Zealand allows participants to settle into an in-depth yoga study with teachers Donna Farhi and Mark Boukoms. Accommodations are simple and affordable; participants walk along the beach to and from the yoga school. For those who want to stay longer than a week for deeper study, Donna and Mark will help you find economical housing with local students, but this must be arranged well in advance.

# WILKA T'IKA GARDEN GUEST HOUSE
# URUBAMBA, PERU

*Seasonal Yoga Retreats*

## YEAR-ROUND

Wilka T'ika, which means "sacred flower" in the Quechua language, is a retreat center in the heart of the Sacred Valley of the Incas. Situated between Cusco and Machu Picchu, this garden guest house is a base for those who wish to experience specialized tours and journeys into Machu Picchu, the Andes, and the Amazon in a noncommercial way. The center was built in 1995 by Carol Cumes, author of *Journey to Machu Picchu: Spiritual Wisdom of the Andes*, and founder of Magical Journey Sacred Tours, which has been bringing groups to Peru for more than 15 years. Wilka T'ika was designed to cater to special interest groups, especially yoga groups.

The gardens at Wilka T'ika are breathtaking, lavishly filled with flowers, shrubs, and flowering plants along with Andean medicinal herbs and indigenous grains and vegetables. There are green lawn areas and special sites used for traditional ceremonies such as offerings to Pachamama, the Mother Earth. All around is the pure energy of the mountains and rivers of Peru's Sacred Valley.

**Address**: Wilka T'ika/Magical Journey c/o Terry Cumes
915 Cole St., Suite 236
San Francisco, CA 94117
**Phone**: 888/PERU-070
**Fax**: 415/665-4645
**E-mail**: info@travelperu.com
**Web site**: www.travelperu.com

**Airport Information**: The nearest airport is in Cusco, an hour and 15 minutes from Wilka T'ika.

**How to Get There**: Wilka T'ika is in the Sacred Valley between Cusco and Machu Picchu, about three kilometers from the Andean community of Urubamba.

**Disability Access**: No access

**What to Bring**: Walking or hiking shoes with good tread, sunscreen, insect repellent, sun hat or visor, swimsuit, towel, warm clothes, waterproof jacket, camera, and lots of film.

**Yoga Room Size and Description**: The yoga room is approximately 20' x 40', with high ceilings and hardwood floors. Outdoor classes are held in designated lawn areas.

**Accommodations**: Bedrooms have deluxe mattresses and modern bathrooms. There are four single rooms, eight doubles, and two triples. All the bedrooms have garden views.

**Meals**: Only vegetarian meals are served at Wilka T'ika, and vegetables are grown organically in Wilka T'ika's gardens. Typically a buffet brunch is served after morning yoga and a dinner is served after the afternoon program or sightseeing excursion. Local herbal teas and coffee are readily available, and the water is filtered.

**Other Activities**: Participants can take an excursion to magnificent Inca ruins and colorful Andean markets or take day hikes to salt mines and mysterious stone circles in the Sacred Valley. Ceremonies with local Andean healers can be arranged, as can slide shows on Quechua culture and Andean cosmology. Guided tours of Wilka T'ika's indigenous plants and medicinal herbs are also available. Using Wilka T'ika as a base, Magical Journey also organizes a host of activites, including overnight camping, trekking, horseback riding, mountain biking, and river rafting on the Urubamba River.

**Summary**: Wilka T'ika is an idyllic setting for an exotic yoga vacation. Situated between the quaint historic town of Cusco and the towering Andes surrounding Machu Picchu, this guest lodge is minutes away from spectacular Inca ruins, Andean marketplaces, and the Urubamba River; it's also the perfect home base for many day hikes. The tranquil retreat center is comprised of secluded cottages surrounded by gardens and lawns, the main house (dining room, yoga room, and massage room), and a garden meditation spiral.

SEE PHOTOS, PAGE 158.

## CALENDAR OF YOGA RETREATS AT WILKA T'IKA:

### SEPTEMBER AND OCTOBER
### TWELVE DAYS

**Yoga Teacher**: Susan Winter Ward
**Address**: Yoga for the Young at Heart
P.O. Box 2228
Pagosa Springs, CO 81147
**Phone**: 970/731-9500; 800/558-YOGA
**Fax**: 970/731-9510
**E-mail**: info@yogaheart.com
**Web site**: www.yogaheart.com

**Teacher Background**: Susan Winter Ward, creator of Yoga for the Young at Heart, is a certified yoga instructor, author, and columnist based in Southern Colorado. Her programs are created and designed especially for seniors and beginners. Susan has been chosen as a cover model for *Yoga Journal* and has appeared in articles in numerous publications and on television programs.

**Style of Yoga**: Yoga for the Young at Heart is a gentle vinyasa, or flow, style of practice. It is a gentle adaptation of the Hatha yoga "Flow Series" as taught at White Lotus Foundation in Santa Barbara, California.

**Philosophy of Teacher**: "I believe in creating a loving atmosphere of self-acceptance, which makes the practice of yoga a personal pleasure and fun to do. I support each student in finding a pathway into their deeper self through Hatha yoga. I believe that the purpose of life is to recognize our own perfection and divinity, to create a foundation of peace within that we extend to the world. Yoga is that doorway to peace."

**Student Criteria**: All are welcome.

**Number of Participants Possible**: 20

**Fee**: $2,995 per person includes full nine-day program in Cusco and the Sacred Valley and three days in the Amazon jungle. It includes lodging and most meals, all land transportation, excursions, evening events, and surprises! Participants will need to arrange their own air travel to Cusco. Call

Susan for travel agent recommendations.

**Credit Cards**: Visa and Mastercard

**Sample Daily Schedule**:
Morning: Yoga, meditation, and pranayama session followed by a buffet brunch
Afternoon: Excursions to Inca ruins, such as the mystical Machu Picchu, the impregnable ruins of Ollantaytambu, the salt mine of Moras, and the enigmatic stone circles of Moray; exotic shopping at P'isaq Market; day hikes; and other adventures in Cusco and the Amazon Jungle
Evening: Programs may include visits with Andean healers, discussions on Peruvian history, time for individual reflection, gentle yoga, or pranayama class.

**Guest Comment**: *"What a pleasure it is taking yoga instruction with Susan Winter Ward. Her gentle style and thorough knowledge have helped us progress well in our practices while having a great time!"*
June and Derry Curran—
Pagosa Springs, Colorado

# OCTOBER
## Two Weeks

**Yoga Teacher**: Larry Schultz
**Address**: It's Yoga
848 Folsom St.
San Francisco, CA 94107
**Phone**: 415/543-1970
**Web site**: www.itsyoga.com

**Teacher Background**: Larry Schultz is the founder of the San Francisco Ashtanga yoga school It's Yoga and author of *Ashtanga Yoga as Taught by Shri K. Pattabhi Jois*. He has been teaching Ashtanga yoga for 20 years.

**Style of Yoga**: Ashtanga yoga through daily practice and modified postures.

**Philosophy of Teacher**: "It's Yoga is a way to make Ashtanga yoga accessible to as many people as possible. The practice is about being awake in the present moment and letting the pose arise from the breath. This gives us freedom."

**Student Criteria**: All levels are welcome.

**Number of Participants Possible**: 15

**Fee**: $2,500 per person includes lodging, entrance fees, round-trip flight to the Amazon, ground transportation, professional guides, ceremonies with jungle shaman and Andean healers, yoga workshop, and all meals at Wilka T'ika and the Jungle Lodge. Airfare to Cusco is not included, although discounted round-trip group fares can be arranged for those who would like help booking their fares.

**Credit Cards**: Not accepted

**Sample Daily Schedule**:
7:00–9:00 a.m. Ashtanga yoga class
9:00 Buffet brunch
Daily excursions to the Sacred Valley, Inca ruins, salt mines of Moras, markets of P'isaq, canyons, hot springs, and villages.
5:00 p.m. Dinner
7:00 Chanting, meditation, and storytelling
A full week will be spent at the Wilka Ti'ka Garden guest house. The journey will culminate at Machu Picchu, with three days to explore the mysteries of this lost city of the Incas. Included in this program is a four-day expedition to the Amazon jungle, where participants stay at the Cusco Amazonica Lodge.

**Guest Comment**: *"What could be a better place to practice sun salutations than the Incan Temple to the Sun—Machu Picchu!"*
Katie Cariffe—
San Francisco, California

# HOTEL CHESA QUADRATSCHA
# SAMEDAN, SWITZERLAND

*Hiking and Yoga in Switzerland*
*with Sandra Uyterhoeven*

## AUGUST
### EIGHT NIGHTS

Samedan, Switzerland, is located in the upper Engadine Valley and, at 5,610 feet, is the starting point for many good hikes. The views of the snow-covered mountains in this area are spectacular. The hiking is glorious, and the air that you breathe is so pure you will never forget the experience. Hiking guides Romy and Juerg Boss lead moderate and challenging day hikes each day and offer maps and suggestions for those who wish to hike alone. The yoga, taught by Sandra Uyterhoeven, is geared to the needs of hikers, with emphasis on stretching and loosening up the neck and shoulders (after carrying a knapsack on your back all day), knees (which can take a strain on the steep descents), and on the lower back. Yoga is practiced both before and after hiking. Participants stay in a four-star hotel called Hotel Chesa Quadratscha, which has a large indoor pool with an adjacent sauna.

**Address**: Yoga for Mainstream People
c/o Sandra Uyterhoeven
975 Memorial Dr., Suite 401
Cambridge, MA 02138
**Phone**: 617/354-0570
**Fax**: 617/547-0934
**E-mail**: sbu@world.std.com

**Airport Information**: Fly into Zürich. Samedan is easily accessible by train from Zürich Airport.

**How to Get There**: Samedan is in the upper Engadine Valley and is only 10 minutes by bus to fashionable St. Moritz and Pontresina.

**Teacher Background**: Sandra Uyterhoeven is a certified Kripalu yoga teacher. She has studied extensively with Tom Stiles and Arthur Kilmurray and has taken the Integrative Yoga Therapy training. She also studies Sanskrit and has been teaching yoga for more than six years.

Guides Romy and Juerg Boss have been hiking in the Alps all of their lives. They are very familiar with the hiking trails.

**Style of Yoga**: Sandy teaches a gentle, flowing (vinyasa) style of yoga. Her classes emphasize breathing, meditation, and relaxation.

**Philosophy of Teachers**: "I believe that yoga and hiking are inherently complementary; each can be thought of as a counter pose to the other. I use Pantanjali's eight-fold path as a model for my teaching philosophy."

**Student Criteria**: All levels welcome. Participants need to be fit enough for moderate daily hiking.

Yoga for Mainstream People

*Yoga and hiking in Switzerland with yoga instructor Sandra Uyterhoeven*

**Disability Access:** No access

**What to Bring:** Comfortable clothes for yoga, a light day backpack, hiking shorts, one pair of long pants, two T-shirts, a long-sleeved shirt, a wool sweater or jacket, wind jacket, rain gear, hiking socks, hiking boots, gloves, wool hat, visor for sun protection, water bottle, sunglasses, sunscreen, lip balm, and a simple dress or shirt and pants for the hotel.

**Yoga Room Size and Description:** Classes are held in a large, carpeted lounge in the hotel. One wall of the room consists of windows with a spectacular mountain view. Weather permitting, classes are also held on the hotel's spacious grassy terrace overlooking the valley and the mountains.

**Number of Participants Possible:** 15

**Accommodations:** Participants stay in Hotel Chesa Quadratscha, a four-star hotel. Rooms are modern and have private bathrooms, a radio, a television, a telephone, a minibar, and a balcony with spectacular views of the mountains.

**Meals:** Breakfasts and dinners are served in the hotel's pine-paneled dining room. Breakfasts include a variety of nutritious breads, honey, fruit preserves, cheeses, cold cuts, cereals, fresh fruits, and eggs. Evening meals are typically Swiss, emphasizing local specialties, such as fondue, *rösti* (shoestring potatoes), *bunderfleish* (dried ham), fresh local salad greens, and celery-root salad. Vegetarian and lactose-free meals are available.

**Fee:** $1,300 per person includes eight nights at Hotel Chesa Quadratscha (double occupancy), all hotel taxes and gratuities, daily breakfast and dinner, guided daily hikes, and two yoga classes each day. Discounts are given for nonparticipating spouses or friends.

**Credit Cards:** Not accepted

**Sample Daily Schedule**:

| | |
|---|---|
| 7:00–8:00 a.m. | Yoga |
| 8:15 | Breakfast |
| 9:30 | Depart on foot, bus, or train for the day's hike. |
| 4:30 p.m. | Return from hike |
| 5:00–6:00 | Yoga |
| 7:00 | Dinner |

**Other Activities**: The hotel has an indoor pool and sauna with views of the mountains. There is also a fitness room and solarium for guest enjoyment. An 18-hole golf course is within walking distance from the hotel.

**Services**: Massage is available.

**Guest Comment**: *"Each morning, before embarking on a hiking excursion, I would eagerly look forward to our early morning yoga session. Yoga helped prepare our bodies and our minds for whatever lay ahead for the day. For some it was the challenge of traversing, somewhat precariously, across glaciers. For others, more sedate walks exploring the beautiful mountain vistas of the Alps seemed the wiser choice. On occasion, yoga sessions were held outdoors in the early morning mountain air. The wonderfully stimulating yet relaxing postures of yoga took on a new, almost spiritual, meaning during those times."*

Ann-Elizabeth Snider —
Belmont, Massachusetts

**Summary**: Enjoy hiking in the beautiful Swiss Alps combined with yoga classes before and after each day's journey. Participants stay in a lovely Swiss hotel with a pool and a sauna, which becomes a nurturing base to return to after a day of spectacular hiking through the mountains. Yoga teacher Sandra Uyterhoeven lived in Switzerland for two years and enjoys returning to the area with groups to this land where the air is fresh and you feel alive. Hikes are led by Swiss residents Romy and Juerg Boss, who have more than 40 years of experience hiking in Switzerland.

# APPENDIX

## YOGA PROPS RESOURCE LIST

BHEKA Yoga Suplies
P.O. Box 3205
Grass Valley, CA 95945
800/366-4541

Hugger-Mugger Yoga Products
31 W. Gregson Ave.
Salt Lake City, UT 84115
800/473-4888

Living Arts
2334 Main St., 2nd Floor
Santa Monica, CA 90405
800/254-8464

Yoga Zone
3342 Melrose Ave. NW
Roanoke, VA 24017
888/264-9642

Fish Crane
P.O. Box 791029
New Orleans, LA 70179
800/959-6116

Tools For Yoga
P.O. Box 99
Chatham, NJ 07928
888/678-9642

YogaMats
P.O. Box 885044
San Francisco, CA 94188
800/720-9642

## SUGGESTED READING

### *Yoga magazines*

*Yoga International*
RR1, Box 407
Honesdale, PA 18431
800/253-6243

*Yoga Journal*
2054 University Ave., Suite 600
Berkeley, CA 94704
800/600-9642

### *Books on yoga*

*Awakening the Spine*
Vanda Scaravelli
Harper San Francisco,
San Francisco, CA

*Back Care Basics*
Mary Pullig Schatz, M.D.
Rodmell Press, Berkeley, CA

*Hatha Yoga: The Hidden Language*
Swami Sivananda Radha
Shambala Publications, Boston, MA

*Light on Pranayama*
B. K. S. Iyengar
Crossroad, New York, NY

*Light on Yoga*
B. K .S. Iyengar
Schocken Books, New York,
NY

*Preparing for Birth with Yoga*
Janet Balaskas
Element Books, Rockport,
MA

*Power Yoga*
Beryl Bender Birch
Simon & Schuster, New York,
NY

*Relax & Renew*
Judith Lasater
Rodmell Press, Berkeley, CA

*Stretch and Surrender*
Annalisa Cunningham
Sterling Publications, New York, NY

*Yoga Over 50*
Mary Stewart
Simon & Schuster, New York, NY

*The Breathing Book*
Donna Farhi
Henry Holt and Company,
New York, NY

*The Fitness Option — Five Weeks
to Healing Stress*
Valarie O'Hara
La Jolla Institute for Stress
Management, Nevada City, CA

*The Heart of Yoga — Developing a Personal
Practice*
T. K. V. Desikachar
Inner Traditions International,
Rochester, VT

*The Sivananda Companion to Yoga*
Sivananda Yoga Center
Simon & Schuster, New York, NY

*Yoga: A Gem for Women*
Geeta S. Iyengar
Timeless Books, Spokane, WA

*Yoga and You*
Esther Myers
Shambala Publications,
Boston, MA

*Yoga Basics*
Mara Carrico
Henry Holt & Company,
New York, NY

*Yoga for the Young at Heart*
Susan Winter Ward
Copra Press, Santa Barbara, CA

*Yoga for Your Spiritual Muscles*
Rachel Schaeffer
Quest Books, Wheaton, IL

*Yoga Mind & Body*
The Sivananda Yoga Vandanta Center
D.K. Publishing, New York, NY

*Yoga the Iyengar Way*
Silva, Mira, and Shyam Mehta
Alfred A. Knopf, New York, NY

# INDEX

## INDEX OF YOGA INSTRUCTORS

# ABOUT THE AUTHOR

AUTHOR ANNALISA CUNNINGHAM has been a certified Hatha Yoga instructor for more than 15 years and a certified massage therapist for more than 20 years. She has an M.A. in counseling and organizes yoga vacations and retreats in the U.S. and Mexico. Her first book, *Stretch and Surrender*, is a guide to yoga for people in recovery.

---

# I WANT TO HEAR FROM YOU!

This book will be updated, and your thoughts and ideas are important to me. Tell me about your favorite yoga vacation and any additional information you would like to see in future editions. Or if you offer a retreat or vacation and would like to be considered for this book, please write to me. You can reach me at:

Annalisa Cunningham
P.O. Box 3363
Chico, California 95927
RioAnalisa@aol.com

Thank you.